ANALYSIS OF NUCLEAR LEGISLATION

This study is part of a series of analytical studies of the major aspects of nuclear legislation, originally in OECD Member countries only. It brings up to date the previous study on the same subject published in 1976 and this time expands it to cover non-OECD countries with legislation dealing with nuclear third party liability.

The analytical studies published to date are:

- Regulations governing Nuclear Installations and Radiation Protection, 1972;
- Nuclear Third Party Liability, 1976;
- Regulations governing the Transport of Radioactive Materials, 1980;
- Regulatory and Institutional Framework for Nuclear Activities, Volume I, 1983, Volume II, 1984;
- The Regulation of Nuclear Trade, Volume I, International Aspects, Volume II, National Regulations, 1988.

In addition, a Description of Licensing Systems and Inspection of Nuclear Installations in OECD countries was published in 1986 and will be updated and expanded in 1991.

*

* *

The study has been prepared by the Secretariat with the assistance of the national experts in the countries concerned. The Secretariat thanks them for the help so kindly provided.

This study is based on information available to the Secretariat in July 1990 and neither the Secretariat nor the national authorities assume any liability therefor.

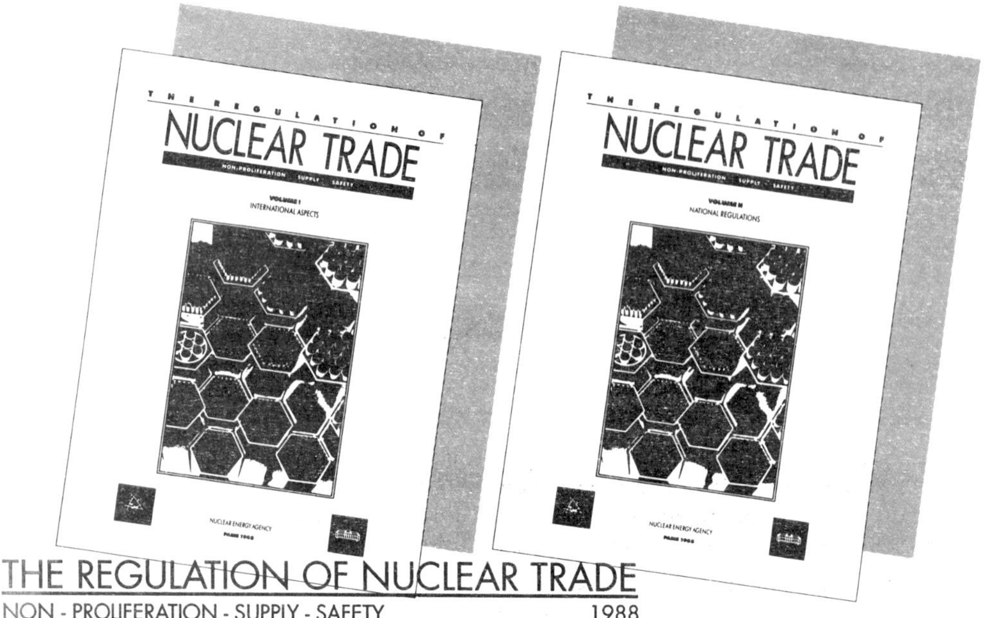

THE REGULATION OF NUCLEAR TRADE

NON - PROLIFERATION - SUPPLY - SAFETY 1988

This two-volume set provides an in-depth analysis of the regulation of trade in nuclear material, equipment and technologies and was prepared in the framework of the OECD Nuclear Energy Agency's analytical studies on the different facets of nuclear law.

Volume I on the international aspects of the regulation of nuclear trade reviews the various sources of international law in this field and reproduces the major relevant texts. This analysis is completed by basic data on technical and economic factors. ISBN 92-64-23121-8

Volume II covers the national legislation on import and export controls and safety of the 16 OECD countries with significant nuclear trading activities: Australia, Austria, Belgium, Canada, Finland, France, the Federal Republic of Germany, Italy, Japan, the Netherlands, Norway, Spain, Sweden, Switzerland, the United Kingdom and the United States. ISBN 92-64-13121-3

Each volume: £ 32.00 US$ 60.00 FF270.00 DM 117.00 Y 10260 The two volumes: £ 57.50 US$ 108.00 FF 490.00 DM 211.00 Y 18620

THE NUCLEAR LAW BULLETIN

The Bulletin is the only international legal publication of its type. It informs on national legislative and regulatory work, jurisprudence, international agreements and also reports on the regulatory work of the competent international organisations in the nuclear sector. It contains articles or studies, prepared by acknowledged legal specialists and includes bibliographies of recent publications. It also provides in the form of free supplements, the full texts of many important laws, regulations and agreements. In addition, an analytical Index is sent to subscribers after every five issues.

Published also in French, the Bulletin is the standard reference work for professionals and academics due to its world-wide consistent coverage of nuclear law.

ISSN 1016-4995 (Biannual)

Subscription: £ 20.00 US$ 36.00 FF 170.00 DM 67.00 Y 6000

FOREWORD

This study reviews national legislation in the field of third party liability for nuclear damage, revising the 1976 study to include countries worldwide with specific legislation in this respect or other provisions applicable to the liability of nuclear operators and on which the Secretariat has received authoritative information. Most laws on the subject have been revised since 1976, in general raising the nuclear operator's limit of liability and in some cases doing away altogether with that limitation. Furthermore, the Paris Convention on Third Party Liability in the Field of Nuclear Energy and the Brussels Supplementary Convention have been amended, the latter, in particular, to increase the amount of compensation to be paid at State level, which has also led to a consequent revision of the national implementing laws. In addition, a Joint Protocol now links the Vienna Convention on Civil Liability for Nuclear Damage and the Paris Convention, increasing the geographical scope of the Conventions for the greater protection of victims of a nuclear incident.

The study is divided into three parts. The first part covers the international Conventions on nuclear third party liability, explaining their principles and provisions and giving their status of signatures and ratifications. The second and most important part deals with national legislation on the liability of operators of nuclear installations according to a plan, standardised to the extent possible, to facilitate research and comparison. The last part contains a brief analysis of laws governing the liability of operators of nuclear-powered ships.

TABLE OF CONTENTS

Part I

INTERNATIONAL AGREEMENTS ON THIRD PARTY LIABILITY IN THE FIELD OF NUCLEAR ENERGY

INTERNATIONAL AGREEMENTS ON THIRD PARTY LIABILITY IN THE FIELD OF NUCLEAR ENERGY

From the early days of the development of the nuclear power industry, it was recognised that nuclear power raised particular issues in relation to third party liability which could best be addressed by the development of a special nuclear third party liability regime. While the high safety standards of the industry meant that the risk of a nuclear incident was very low, the possible magnitude of damage should such an incident occur seemed very high. Indeed, it was almost impossible at that time to make any real assessment of the potential extent of damage and thus of any resulting claims for compensation. If nuclear damage had been left to be covered by general third party liability law these considerations would have raised difficulties in relation to obtaining insurance coverage.

In addition, as has since been illustrated by the Chernobyl catastrophe, the consequences of a serious nuclear incident overlook national boundaries. Any special system of nuclear third party liability had therefore to be international. The hazards generated by the transport of nuclear materials provided a further reason for the issue to be dealt with at the international rather than the national level.

Consequently, in 1960, the Paris Convention was established under the auspices of the then OEEC European Nuclear Energy Agency, now the OECD Nuclear Energy Agency (OECD/NEA), with the aim of providing a special uniform nuclear third party liability regime for Western Europe. This Convention was supplemented shortly after, in 1963, by the Brussels Supplementary Convention which provided for further compensation to be made available to the victims of a nuclear incident from public funds supplied by the Contracting Parties. Also in 1963, the Vienna Convention, which aimed to establish a world-wide system based on the same principles as the Paris Convention, was adopted under the auspices of the International Atomic Energy Agency (IAEA). In addition, a Convention on the Liability of Operators of Nuclear Ships with provisions similar to those of the Paris and Vienna Conventions to cover reactors installed as a means of power for ships was adopted in 1962. As cover for liability for the transport of nuclear materials had given rise to certain difficulties, a further Convention aimed at ensuring that nuclear third party liability law and not maritime law would apply to carriage of nuclear materials was adopted in 1971. More recently, in 1988, the Paris and Vienna Conventions have been linked by the adoption, under the auspices of the OECD/NEA and the IAEA, of a Joint Protocol, constituting a further step towards a greater integration of the nuclear third party liability regimes.

I. CONVENTION ON THIRD PARTY LIABILITY IN THE FIELD OF NUCLEAR ENERGY (PARIS CONVENTION)

The OECD/NEA Paris Convention, adopted on 29th July 1960, aims, as stated in its Preamble, to ensure *adequate and equitable compensation for persons who suffer damage caused by nuclear incidents whilst taking the necessary steps to ensure that the development of the production and uses of nuclear energy for peaceful purposes is not thereby hindered.* It was amended by a Protocol of 28th January 1964 to bring it closer to the then new Vienna Convention and by a Protocol of 16th November 1982 to bring the Convention up-to-date, particularly by replacing the European Monetary Agreement unit of account with the Special Drawing Right (SDR) of the International Monetary Fund as the unit of account for the Convention.*

The Paris Convention established, for the first time, the main principles upon which all international agreements on nuclear liability and most national legislation in this field are now based. These principles are briefly stated below.

A. ABSOLUTE AND EXCLUSIVE LIABILITY

The objective of protecting victims of nuclear incidents has led to the adoption of the basic principle that the operator of a nuclear installation is absolutely liable, that is regardless of fault, for all damage caused by a nuclear incident in his installation or involving nuclear material being transported to or from his installation. This principle was drawn from the general practice in most Western European countries favouring liability irrespective of fault for damage caused by a dangerous activity. In addition, the operator is exclusively liable: no person other than the operator can be held liable for nuclear damage. Liability is therefore *channelled* by law to the operator, and he has a right of recourse only in a limited number of precisely defined cases. This system of liability avoids the difficulty for the victim of having to prove that the incident was due to fault and to identify the person responsible for such fault. Given both the complex techniques of atomic energy and the likelihood of certain types of nuclear damage being delayed, to prove fault on the part of a particular person would in many circumstances be very difficult, if not impossible. Channelling of liability also relieves the various persons who contribute to the operation of a nuclear installation, such as suppliers and carriers, from the need to have insurance coverage additional to that held by the operator.

B. LIMITATION OF LIABILITY

The objective of not hindering the growth of the peaceful nuclear industry has been achieved, in particular, by limiting the operator's liability, both as regards the amount of financial compensation and the period of time within which claims may be brought against him. This can be regarded as a counterpart to absolute liability. Under the Paris Convention the maximum amount of liability is 15 million SDRs. However, in relation to its own

* A Special Drawing Right amounts to approximately $1.

operators a Contracting State may, taking into account the availability of financial security, fix a higher or lower amount, to a lower limit of five million SDRs, by national legislation.

As regards the limitation in time, the Paris Convention provides the general rule that rights to compensation are extinguished if an action is not brought within ten years from the date of the nuclear incident. Subject to the availability of financial security, this period may be extended by a Contracting State in relation to its own operators. A Contracting State may also fix a shorter period of not less than two years in relation to its own operators, running from the date at which the victim knew (or ought reasonably to have known) of the damage and the identity of the operator liable.

C. COMPULSORY FINANCIAL SECURITY

To ensure that the operator's obligation under the Convention to compensate victims will be met, the Convention provides that each operator shall be required to have and maintain insurance or other financial security covering the amount of his liability.

D. UNITY OF JURISDICTION

A single jurisdictional organ ensures that the limitation of liability is not exceeded and compensation is equitably distributed. The general rule is that, when the incident occurs in the territory of a Contracting State, the courts of that State are exclusively competent. There are precise provisions determining jurisdictional competence when the incident occurs wholly or partly in the territory of another State or when there is uncertainty as to the place where the incident occurred.

As a corollary to the principle of jurisdictional unity, the Convention guarantees enforcement in all Contracting States of the final judgments entered by the competent court after completion of the formalities required by law and excludes all further proceedings on the merits of the claim.

E. NON-DISCRIMINATION

The Convention expressly states that it shall be applied without any discrimination based upon nationality, domicile or residence. The same principle applies to the law of the State whose courts have jurisdiction over claims arising out of a nuclear incident. This means in particular that nationality, domicile or residence is not to affect the access of victims to administrative institutions and procedures set up for the examination and satisfaction of claims and for the distribution of available funds, as well as to the competent court.

The Convention, as amended by the 1964 Protocol came into force on 1st April 1968. The 1982 Protocol came into force on 7th October 1988. The Signatories and Parties are set out in the following table.

PARIS CONVENTION

Signatories	Date of ratification or accession		
	Convention	1964 Additional Protocol	1982 Protocol
Austria	...	...	...
Belgium	3rd Aug. 1966	3rd Aug. 1966	19th Sept. 1985
Denmark	4th Sept. 1974	4th Sept. 1974	16th May 1989
Finland (acc.)	16th June 1972	16th June 1972	22nd Dec. 1989
France	9th Mar. 1966	9th Mar. 1966	6th July 1990
Germany, F.R.	30th Sept. 1975	30th Sept. 1975	25th Sept. 1985
Greece	12th May 1970	12th May 1970	30th May 1988
Italy	17th Sept. 1975	17th Sept. 1975	28th June 1985
Luxembourg	...	...	...
Norway	2nd July 1973	2nd July 1973	3rd June 1986
Netherlands	28th Dec. 1979	28th Dec. 1979	...
Portugal	29th Sept. 1977	29th Sept. 1977	28th May 1984
Spain	31st Oct. 1961	30th Apr. 1965	7th Oct. 1988
Sweden	1st Apr. 1968	1st Apr. 1968	8th Mar. 1983
Switzerland	...	...	...
Turkey	10th Oct. 1961	5th Apr. 1968	21st Jan. 1986
United Kingdom	23rd Feb. 1966	23rd Feb. 1966	19th Aug. 1985

II. CONVENTION SUPPLEMENTARY TO THE PARIS CONVENTION OF 29TH JULY 1960 ON THIRD PARTY LIABILITY IN THE FIELD OF NUCLEAR ENERGY (BRUSSELS SUPPLEMENTARY CONVENTION)

On 31st January 1963, not long after the adoption of the Paris Convention, most of its Signatories adopted a supplementary Convention providing for additional compensation from public funds to be made available should the compensation under the Paris Convention prove insufficient to cover the damage caused by a nuclear incident. Like the Paris Convention, the Brussels Supplementary Convention was amended by Protocols of 28th January 1964 and 16th November 1982. The former Protocol made amendments consequential upon those made at the same time to the Paris Convention. The latter Protocol, as in the case of the 1982 Protocol to the Paris Convention, introduced the SDR as the unit of account for the Convention, but also substantially increased the amount of compensation to be made available under the Convention.

The Brussels Supplementary Convention, together with the Paris Convention, provides for compensation of up to 120/300* million SDRs. This compensation is comprised of three tiers. The first tier is covered by the operator's insurance or other financial security according to the Paris Convention and must amount to at least five million SDRs. The second tier is to be provided by the Government of the Contracting State in whose territory the installation of the nuclear operator liable is situated. This tier provides for compensation beyond that provided by the first tier up to an aggregate of 70/175 million SDRs. The third tier is covered jointly by the Contracting States according to a formula based 50 per cent on the gross national product and 50 per cent on the thermal power of the reactors situated in the territory of each Contracting State. This third tier provides for additional compensation of 50/125 million SDRs.

The Brussels Supplementary Convention came into force, as amended by the 1964 Protocol, on 4th December 1974. The 1982 Protocol is not yet in force. To enter into force it requires the ratification of all Parties to the Brussels Supplementary Convention. The Signatories and Parties are set out in the table below.

BRUSSELS SUPPLEMENTARY CONVENTION

Signatories	Date of ratification or accession	
	Convention and 1964 Additional Protocol	1982 Protocol
Austria	...	...
Belgium	20th Aug. 1985	20th Aug. 1985
Denmark	4th Sept. 1974	10th May 1989
Finland (acc.)	14th Jan. 1977	15th Jan. 1990
France	30th Mar. 1966	11th July 1990
Germany, F.R.	1st Oct. 1975	25th Sept. 1985
Italy	3rd Feb. 1976	14th June 1985
Luxembourg	...	...
Norway	7th July 1973	13th May 1986
Netherlands	28th Sept. 1979	...
Spain	27th July 1966	29th Sept. 1988
Sweden	3rd Apr. 1968	22nd Mar. 1983
Switzerland	...	...
United Kingdom	24th Mar. 1966	8th Aug. 1985

* Although the 1982 Protocol to the Brussels Supplementary Convention is not yet in force, the relevant figures are given for before and after the entry into force of this Protocol.

III. CONVENTION ON CIVIL LIABILITY FOR NUCLEAR DAMAGE (VIENNA CONVENTION)

The IAEA Vienna Convention, adopted on 21st May 1963, is based on the same principles as the Paris Convention.

The Signatories and Parties are set out in the table below.

VIENNA CONVENTION

Signatories	Date of ratification or accession
Argentina	25th Apr. 1967
Bolivia (acc.)	10th Apr. 1968
Cameroon (acc.)	6th Mar. 1964
Chile	23rd Nov. 1989
Colombia	...
Cuba	25th Oct. 1965
Egypt	5th Nov. 1965
Hungary (acc.)	28th July 1989
Mexico (acc.)	25th Apr. 1989
Morocco	...
Niger (acc.)	24th July 1979
Peru (acc.)	26th Aug. 1980
Philippines	15th Nov. 1965
Poland (acc.)	23rd Jan. 1990
Spain	...
Trinidad & Tobago (acc.)	31st Jan. 1966
United Kingdom	...
Yugoslavia	12th Aug. 1977

IV. JOINT PROTOCOL RELATING TO THE APPLICATION OF THE VIENNA CONVENTION AND THE PARIS CONVENTION (JOINT PROTOCOL)

On 21st September 1988, a Joint Protocol to link the Paris and Vienna Conventions was adopted by an international conference convened jointly by the OECD and the IAEA. Previously, victims in the territory of Parties to one Convention were left without protection if an incident occurred at an installation in the territory of a Party to the other Convention. The Joint Protocol extends the application of both Conventions to cover victims in the territory of Parties to either Convention. It also resolves potential conflicts between the two Conventions, particularly in the case of transport, by ensuring that only one Convention applies to any one incident. The Joint Protocol is not yet in force. It will enter into force once it has been ratified or acceded to by at least five Parties to the Paris Convention and five Parties to the Vienna Convention. The following table shows the status of signatures, ratifications and accessions to the Joint Protocol.

JOINT PROTOCOL

Signatories	Date of ratification or accession
Argentina (VC)	...
Belgium (PC)	...
Cameroon (VC)	...
Chile (VC)	23rd Nov. 1989
Denmark (PC)	26th May 1989
Egypt (VC)	10th Aug. 1989
Finland (PC)	...
France (PC)	...
Germany, F.R. (PC)	...
Greece (PC)	...
Hungary (VC)	26th Mar. 1990
Italy (PC)	...
Morocco (VC)*	...
Netherlands (PC)	...
Norway (PC)	...
Philippines (VC)	...
Poland (VC) (acc.)	23rd Jan. 1990
Portugal (PC)	...
Spain (PC)	...
Sweden (PC)	...
Switzerland (PC)*	...
Turkey (PC)	...
United Kingdom (PC)	...

(PC) Paris Convention
(VC) Vienna Convention
* Signatory only of the Convention.

V. CONVENTION RELATING TO CIVIL LIABILITY IN THE FIELD OF MARITIME CARRIAGE OF NUCLEAR MATERIAL

This Convention was adopted in Brussels under the auspices of the OECD, the IAEA and the International Maritime Organization (IMO) on 17th December 1971. Its purpose is to establish the primacy of the application of nuclear law over maritime law by ensuring that the operator of a nuclear installation will be exclusively liable for damage caused by a nuclear incident occurring in the course of maritime carriage of nuclear material, thus exonerating shipowners from liability under maritime law for such nuclear damage. As the Paris and Vienna Conventions do not affect the application of existing international conventions in the field of transport, a dual liability could arise under both nuclear and maritime transport conventions. It is the aim of the 1971 Brussels Convention to preserve the principle of channelling all liability onto the nuclear operator. The Convention came into force on 15th July 1975. The Signatories and Parties are set out in the following table.

CONVENTION RELATING TO CIVIL LIABILITY IN THE FIELD OF MARITIME CARRIAGE OF NUCLEAR MATERIAL

Signatories	Date of ratification or accession
Argentina (acc.)	18th May 1981
Belgium	15th June 1989
Brazil	...
Denmark	4th Sept. 1974
Finland	...
France	2nd Feb. 1973
Gabon (acc.)	21st Jan. 1982
Germany, F.R.	1st Oct. 1975
Italy	21st July 1980
Liberia (acc.)	17th Feb. 1981
Norway	16th Apr. 1975
Portugal	...
Spain (acc.)	21st May 1974
Sweden	22nd Nov. 1974
United Kingdom	...
Yemen (acc.)	6th Mar. 1979
Yugoslavia	...

VI. CONVENTION ON THE LIABILITY OF OPERATORS OF NUCLEAR SHIPS

This Convention was adopted in Brussels on 25th May 1962 for the purpose of setting up for nuclear ships a system of rules founded on the same principles as those of the Paris and Vienna Conventions for land-based nuclear installations.

The Convention has not entered into force. It will come into force three months after the deposit of an instrument of ratification by at least one State which operates or which has authorised the operation of a nuclear ship under its flag, and one other State. The status of signatures, ratifications and accessions is given in the table below.

CONVENTION OF THE LIABILITY OF OPERATORS OF NUCLEAR SHIPS

Signatories	Date of ratification or accession
Belgium	...
China, People's Rep. of	...
Egypt	...
Germany, F.R.	...
India	...
Indonesia	...
Ireland	...
Korea, Rep. of	...
Lebanon	3rd June 1975
Liberia	...
Madagascar (acc.)	13th July 1965
Malaysia	...
Monaco	...
Netherlands	20th Mar. 1974
Panama	...
Philippines	...
Portugal	31st July 1968
Suriname	20th Mar. 1974
Syria (acc.)	1st Aug. 1974
Yugoslavia	...
Zaire (acc.)	17th July 1967

Part II

LIABILITY REGIME OF OPERATORS OF NUCLEAR INSTALLATIONS

GENERAL PLAN OF STUDY BY COUNTRY

INTRODUCTION

I. THIRD PARTY LIABILITY

A. SCOPE AND DEFINITIONS
B. NATURE AND ASSIGNMENT OF LIABILITY

- **a) General – Nuclear Installations**
- **b) Transport**
- **c) Rights of Recourse**
- **d) Exoneration from Liability**

C. AMOUNT OF LIABILITY
D. NUCLEAR DAMAGE

- **a) Damage Covered**
- **b) Damage Excluded**

II. COVER AND COMPENSATION

A. INSURANCE OR OTHER FINANCIAL SECURITY
B. STATE INTERVENTION
C. COMPENSATION
D. TIME LIMITS FOR BRINGING CLAIMS
E. COMPETENT COURTS AND PROCEDURE

ARGENTINA

INTRODUCTION

Argentina has a diversified nuclear programme including several nuclear power plants and installations covering various stages of the nuclear fuel cycle. Two nuclear power reactors are in operation (Atucha I and Embalse – some 900 MWe), while a third is being constructed (Atucha II). Argentina also exports nuclear equipment and services.

The operator of these various installations is the National Atomic Energy Commission (NAEC). Under the Electricity Act No. 15.336 of 20th September 1960 (published in the Official Gazette, *Boletin Oficial* or *B.O.*, of 22nd September 1960), the Federal Government gave itself the exclusive right to produce electricity from nuclear power.

For the moment, there is no special legislation on nuclear third party liability; a Bill was drafted some years ago but has not yet been submitted to Parliament. However, on 25th April 1967, Argentina ratified the Vienna Convention, the text sanctioning this ratification being Act No. 17.048, published in the Official Gazette of 16th December 1966.

I. GENERAL PROVISIONS

In the absence of special legislation, the general provisions of the Vienna Convention are made applicable in Argentina under contracts concluded by the Argentine Government, represented by the NAEC in its capacity as operator. The Vienna Convention is thus considered as a reference standard in these contracts. In addition, Article 31 of the Constitution provides that the international treaties to which Argentina is Party, make up (along with the Constitution and the ordinary legislation promulgated by the National Parliament) the supreme law of the land; Federal and Provincial authorities are therefore obliged to comply with them.

II. PRINCIPLE OF CHANNELLING LIABILITY – RELATIONS WITH FOREIGN SUPPLIERS

The principle that liability should be channelled to the nuclear operator has been included in agreements concluded with foreign suppliers of Argentine nuclear power plants.

This has taken the form either of an undertaking by the NAEC to assume absolute liability for nuclear damage in accordance with the provisions of the Vienna Convention, or of a clause (Hold Harmless Clause) exonerating the builder and his contractors from all liability for nuclear damage, again in accordance with the Vienna Convention.

These contractual arrangements have been completed by a statement by the Argentine Government undertaking to pay compensation for any nuclear damage claimed from contracting enterprises and their sub-contractors.

On the basis of this undertaking and in accordance with Act No. 22.179 of 4th March 1980 (published in the *B.O.* of 7th March 1980), the Executive authorised the Treasury, by Decree No. 1337 of 1980, to give the following guarantee:

1. *The **guarantor** irrevocably guarantees that the Argentine Republic will settle all claims and compensation with which (the supplier), his contractors or employees, past or present, have to deal in respect of nuclear damage caused by nuclear power plants which are the subject of contracts (concluded with the NAEC) or by their operator.*
2. *This guarantee will remain valid throughout the period of operation of the (above-mentioned) nuclear power plants and will be valid in all countries and before all courts in which (the supplier), his contractors or employees, past or present, are convicted.*
3. *In no case and under no circumstances will (the supplier) be considered as the operator of the said nuclear power plant.*
4. *This statement is issued in compliance with the Vienna Convention on Civil Liability for Nuclear Damage, ratified by Act No. 17.048.* (Unofficial translation.)

III. THE RULES GOVERNING LIABILITY FOR NUCLEAR DAMAGE

A. TERRITORIAL SCOPE

In the absence of any special legislative provision, there is no reason to assume any territorial limit for damage caused by a nuclear installation situated in Argentina or placed under its jurisdiction.

B. THE OPERATOR LIABLE

The operator liable in the event of a nuclear incident is, in fact and in law, the Argentine Government, through the NAEC. For the Commission does not have the status of a private law company or a State corporation and is considered as forming part of the government. In accordance with the Vienna Convention, this liability is absolute and exclusive.

C. AMOUNT OF LIABILITY

In view of the ordinary law on tort liability and of case law, liability for nuclear damage should be considered as unlimited.

D. FINANCIAL SECURITY

Given that Argentina's nuclear power plants are operated by the State (represented by the NAEC), no insurance or financial guarantee has yet been established (apart from statements on security given to foreign constructors).

E. COMPENSATION

Claims for compensation must be submitted in accordance with the rules of the national Civil and Commercial Code of Procedure.

F. TIME LIMITS FOR BRINGING CLAIMS

The ten-year time limit provided for under the Vienna Convention for bringing actions for compensation is the same as the ten-year period also laid down by the Argentine Civil Code (Article 4023) for bringing actions of this type.

G. COMPETENT COURTS AND PROCEDURE

Given that the Argentine Government (through the NAEC) bears sole liability for nuclear damage, only the Federal courts are competent to decide claims for compensation. However, there is nothing to prevent victims from submitting claims directly to the Government through administrative channels.

AUSTRIA

INTRODUCTION

Austria has no nuclear power programme and in 1978, a Federal Act was passed in Austria prohibiting the use of nuclear fission for energy purposes (Federal Act of 15th December 1978, Federal Gazette No. 676/1978 – *Bundesgesetzblatt* – BGBl). However, there are three research reactors in the country respectively operated by the Seibersdorf Research Centre (*Oesterreichisches Forschungszentrum Seibersdorf GmbH*), the Atomic Institute of the Austrian Universities (*Atominstitut der Oestereichischen Universitaten*) and the Reactor Institute of the Association for the Advancement of Nuclear Energy Applications (*Reaktorinstitut des Vereines zur Förderung der Anwendung der Kernenergie*).

Responsibility for nuclear matters is shared by the different Federal Ministries under the overall authority of the Federal Chancellor. In particular, the Federal Ministry of Justice (*Bundesministerium für Justiz*) is competent in the field of third party liability, while the Federal Ministry of Finance decides on questions related to the amount and nature of the nuclear operator's financial security.

Austria has signed but not ratified the Paris Convention and the Brussels Supplementary Convention as well as the 1982 Protocols amending them respectively.

The regime governing nuclear third party liability in Austria is contained in the Federal Act of 29th April 1964 on Liability for Nuclear Damage – Nuclear Liability Act – (Federal Gazette 1964 No. 117) which entered into force on 1st September 1964. The Act was amended by a Federal Act of 25th February 1976 amending amounts and limits of the civil law (*Wertgrenzennovelle* 1976, Federal Gazette 1976, No. 91), which entered into force on 1st April 1976. The 1964 Act is extensively based on the Paris Convention. All references below are to the Nuclear Liability Act, as amended by the Act of 25th February 1976.

I. THIRD PARTY LIABILITY

A. SCOPE AND DEFINITIONS

The Act applies to nuclear incidents occurring and damage suffered in Austria [Section 3]. Where a nuclear incident occurring in Austria causes damage abroad, the Act applies only if the claimant is an Austrian citizen or, in the case of death, if the deceased person was an Austrian citizen [Section 33].

The Act defines a *nuclear incident* as an occurrence causing damage through a process of nuclear transmutation:

- during construction or operation of a nuclear installation or during manufacture, carriage, possession or handling of nuclear substances;
- during extraction, manufacture, carriage, possession or handling of radioisotopes.

A nuclear incident is also that which occurs in conjunction with other chemical, physico-chemical or physical properties of the nuclear substances or radioisotopes [Section 1]. *Nuclear installations* mean reactors and factories for the manufacture, processing, use, storage or reprocessing of nuclear substances and for the separation of radioisotopes therefrom; particle accelerators and installations for nuclear fusion also come under that definition [Section 2(1)]. The term *nuclear substances* covers fissile nuclear fuels and radioactive products and waste [Section 2(2)].

B. NATURE AND ASSIGNMENT OF LIABILITY

a) General – Nuclear Installations

The operator of a nuclear installation is absolutely liable for damage caused by a nuclear incident involving nuclear substances or nuclear fuel in his installation or directly originating therefrom [Section 3(1)]. The operator's liability extends to all incidents occurring until such time as the nuclear substances or nuclear fuel have been taken in charge by another operator of a nuclear installation situated in Austria [Section 3(2)]. Any agreement excluding or limiting such liability in advance shall be null and void [Section 8].

If the same person is liable for a single nuclear incident involving several installations, nuclear substances or radioisotopes, which are located in the same geographical site, his liability is limited to the highest relevant maximum amount [Section 5 and Section 30(1)].

If damage caused by several nuclear incidents gives rise to the liability of several persons, they shall be jointly and severally liable, provided that each shall be liable in accordance with the provisions applicable to him and, insofar as his liability is limited up to the maximum amount established in his respect [Section 6(1)]. The same applies in the event of a single nuclear incident; however, the joint and several liability is limited to the highest applicable maximum amount with respect to any of the persons liable [Section 6(2)].

Where, in the light of the circumstances, several nuclear incidents originating from different nuclear installations, nuclear substances or radioisotopes are the probable cause of the same damage, such damage shall be presumed to have been caused jointly by such incidents. This presumption may be refuted upon proof that the damage was unlikely to have been caused by one or several of such incidents [Section 11(1)].

Where persons are jointly and severally liable in relation to each other, their liability to pay compensation and its extent, as well as the distribution between them, depends on the circumstances, in particular on the extent to which the damage was caused or was likely to have been caused by one or the other [Section 10(1)]. Each of them is liable in accordance with the provisions applicable to him and up to the maximum amount, if any, established in his respect [Section 10(2)].

The provisions on joint liability are equally applicable to transport and to radioisotopes [Sections 30(1) and 31].

Subject to international agreements in the field of transport, persons who have supplied a nuclear installation or any of its components or nuclear substances, or have provided supplies or services for the construction or modification of a nuclear installation or any of its components, or have contributed to its design and planning, shall not be liable under the provisions of civil law except under the conditions of recourse. The same applies with certain exceptions [Section 4(3)], mutatis mutandis, to the transport of nuclear substances [Section 37].

b) Transport

If a nuclear incident occurs during the carriage of nuclear substances, including storage incidental thereto, the operator of the nuclear installation situated in Austria from which the nuclear substances came is liable until the nuclear substances:

- are taken in charge by the operator of another nuclear installation situated in Austria;
- in the case of export, are unloaded from the means of transport by which they have arrived abroad [Section 4(1)].

In the case of import, the operator of the nuclear installation receiving the nuclear substances is liable from the time the substances have been loaded on the means of transport, provided that they are consigned with his written consent [Section 4(2)].

The carrier is liable, however, where nuclear substances are merely in transit through Austria, or when the nuclear substances are sent to Austria without the written consent of the operator of the nuclear installation situated in Austria, or when the nuclear substances are not consigned to a nuclear installation or such an installation cannot be identified, unless the carrier proves that he neither knew nor should have known that the substance in question was a nuclear substance; where he is bound by law to carry nuclear substances, his liability is transferred to the Government [Section 4(3)].

c) Radioisotopes

The person liable for damage caused by a radioisotope is the holder of the isotope at the time of the incident, unless he proves that he neither knew nor should have known that the substance in question was a radioisotope [Section 24].

If another person takes possession of a radioisotope, without the consent of the former holder, both are liable. In addition, the new holder is liable for any damage which would not have been suffered but for his action [Section 25(1)].

If another person handles a radioisotope without the holder's consent, he is liable jointly with the holder unless he can prove that he neither knew nor should have known that the substance in question was a radioisotope. If he is held liable he is also liable for any damage which would not have been suffered but for his action [Section 25(2)].

Where the holder of a radioisotope delivers a radioisotope to a person whom he knew or should have known to be unauthorised to take possession thereof, the holder remains liable besides such person [Section 26].

The holder remains liable, if the radioisotope is stolen, lost, jettisoned or otherwise abandoned [Section 27].

d) Rights of Recourse

The operator of a nuclear installation and the carrier of nuclear substances (if he is liable) have a right of recourse under Section 38:

- if the nuclear damage resulted from an act or omission done with intent to cause damage against the individual acting or omitting to act with such intent;
- if and to the extent that it is expressly so provided by contract.

The insurer or guarantor who has paid compensation for damage caused intentionally also has a right of recourse against the person having caused such damage [Section 40(1) and (2)].

Whoever has paid compensation for nuclear damage by virtue of an international agreement in the field of transport acquires the rights of the persons having suffered the damage against the operator or carrier, unless the latter have a right of recourse against the person having paid compensation [Section 39].

To the extent that the Government has intervened and paid compensation, it has a right of recourse against any person liable who has acted wilfully or by gross negligence, against the operator or carrier up to the amount of their financial security (whether or not it has been provided), and against the supplier or other contractors if they have caused the damage intentionally [Section 21(2)].

e) Liability under Other Laws and of Other Persons

The provisions of this Act do not affect the application of other laws (e.g. the Civil Code) under which the operator, carrier or holder of radioisotopes are liable to a larger extent, or under which other persons are liable, provided that the damage was caused intentionally or by gross negligence [Section 35].

f) Exoneration from Liability

The operator and carrier are exonerated from liability, if a nuclear incident is due to an act of war, hostilities, civil war, rebellion or insurrection [Section 9].

Subject to Sections 24 to 27 referred to above (radioisotopes), the holder of a radioisotope is exonerated from liability for a nuclear incident, if he proves that he or the persons acting on his behalf have taken every necessary precaution to avoid damage. Where the radioisotope is applied in medical treatment by or under the supervision of a physician, dentist or veterinarian, or the injured person has accepted the risk involved, the holder shall not be liable, unless the injured person proves that the holder or the persons acting on his behalf have failed to take every necessary precaution to avoid damage [Section 28].

It is recalled that in the event of a nuclear incident during transport, if the carrrier can prove that he neither knew nor should have known that the substances he was carrying were nuclear substances, he is exonerated from liability [Section 4(3)].

C. AMOUNT OF LIABILITY

With respect to operators of *nuclear installations and carriers*, the maximum amount of liability per nuclear incident is fixed at 500 million Austrian schillings (approximately 30 million Special Drawing Rights of the International Monetary Fund – SDRs), of which up to 375 million Sch. are to be used for death and personal injury and up to 125 million Sch. for damage to property [Sections 15 and 35].

The aggregate liability of all persons may not, however, exceed 500 million Sch. [Section 15].

The maximum amount of liability of a holder of *radioisotopes* depends on the radioactivity and radiotoxicity of the radioisotopes and on whether they are in sealed or unsealed form. With respect to death of or injury to one person the maximum amount of liability is 600 000 Sch. As regards death of or injury to more than one person, the Act makes a distinction between six groups of radioisotopes providing for maximum amounts ranging from 1.2 million to 18 million Sch. [Section 29(1)].

Such maximum amounts do not include the costs for investigation and settlement of claims, legal costs, fees and interest [Sections 15(3) and 30(2)].

D. NUCLEAR DAMAGE

a) Damage Covered

The Act covers any damage to persons or property resulting from a nuclear incident which is caused by nuclear installations, nuclear substances or radioisotopes [Sections 1, 2 and 24].

If the damage is caused jointly by a nuclear incident and another incident, that part of the damage which is caused by such other incident, to the extent that it is not reasonably separable from the damage caused by the nuclear incident, is deemed to be damage caused by the nuclear incident [Section 11(2)].

b) Damage Excluded

The liability of the operator of a nuclear installation under the Act does not extend to damage to the nuclear installation itself or to property on the site of such installation which is used or to be used in connection therewith [Section 3(3)].

II. COVER AND COMPENSATION

A. INSURANCE OR OTHER FINANCIAL SECURITY

The operator of a nuclear installation and the carrier of nuclear substances (except the Government) must provide adequate financial security to cover their liability. Such security must be maintained until ten years after the nuclear incident; if the incident was caused by nuclear substances which have been stolen, lost, jettisoned or abandoned, this period is twenty years after the theft, loss, jettison or abandonment [Section 17(1)].

The amount of financial security is fixed at 130 million Sch., of which 97.5 million cover damage to persons and 32.5 million damage to property. For installations for nuclear fusion and particle accelerators, the security is reduced to 3 million Sch. (2.4 million for personal injury and 600 000 for property damage) [Section 17(2)].

The Federal Ministry of Finance decides on the appropriateness of the financial security. Third party liability insurance constitutes an adequate security only if taken out with an insurer licensed in Austria in conformity with the general insurance conditions approved by the Ministry. Where the carrier is liable (e.g. in the case of transit) third party liability insurance taken out with a foreign insurer may be approved [Section 17(3)].

The Federal Minister of Finance is authorised to guarantee the operator's or the carrier's liability, if this is in the public interest and the person liable does not have the necessary means to provide security [Section 17(3)].

Any cancellation or suspension of financial security only becomes effective after the insurer or guarantor has given two months' notice in writing to the Federal Ministry of Finance. In the case of carriage of nuclear substances, a cancellation or suspension becomes effective only after the carriage is completed [Section 18(1)].

The insurer or guarantor must inform the Ministry of Finance as soon as he has knowledge of any incident involving or likely to involve payment of compensation exceeding 1/20 of the sum insured [Section 18(3)].

The holder of radioisotopes, with the exception of the Government, must provide financial security by third party liability insurance taken out with an insurer licensed in Austria and covering the holder's maximum liability. If the same holder is liable for several radioisotopes of different risks on the same geographical site, the radioisotope in the highest risk group determines the amount of security [Section 30(2)].

B. STATE INTERVENTION

The Government shall, up to a maximum amount of 500 million Sch., indemnify all persons liable under the Act and under other legal provisions against claims for compensation to the extent that their liability is not covered by or claims cannot be satisfied out of their financial security [Sections 21(1), 22(1) and 23(1)].

Any agreement by which the person liable waives his right to Government indemnification shall be null and void [Section 8].

The person liable must immediately notify the State Attorney for financial matters (*Finanzprokuratur*) in writing of any nuclear incident and any claims against him which may involve such State intervention. The person liable failing to do so will be liable to pay damages to the Government [Section 23(3)].

C. COMPENSATION

a) Extent of Compensation

In the event of death, compensation covers the pecuniary loss sustained by the deceased before his death, adequate damages for pain and suffering in case of protracted illness and appropriate funeral expenses. Where, at the time of the injury, the deceased was legally bound to support third persons, such persons, including those conceived and not yet born at the time of the incident, may claim compensation for loss of maintenance [Section 12].

In the case of personal injury, compensation may be claimed for medical expenses, temporary or permanent loss of earning capacity, expenses due to increased needs, adequate damages for pain and suffering in the event of protracted illness, and adequate damages for a permanent disfigurement or deformity [Section 13].

Compensation of a continuing character is to be paid in the form of an annuity; if justified, the victim may claim the payment of a capital sum [Section 14].

As already mentioned, the maximum liability for a nuclear incident under the Act is limited to 500 million Sch. apportioned at 375 million for death and personal injury and 125 million for property damage [Section 15]. If such death or personal injury is due to an incident caused by installations for nuclear fusion or particle accelerators, compensation is limited to 2.4 million Sch. [Section 15].

Liability is limited to 1.2 million Sch. for the death or personal injury of any single person [Sections 15(1) and 29(2)]. Any compensation exceeding this amount may be claimed under other legal provisions only if the person liable acted wilfully or with gross negligence [Section 35(1)](see under "Liability under Other Laws and of Other Persons" above).

Compensation for damage to property caused by a nuclear incident arising from a nuclear installation, nuclear substances or radioisotopes is limited to the ordinary value of the property plus decontamination costs, but may in no case exceed 900 000 Sch. [Sections 15(1) and 29(1)]. Compensation for such damage due to a nuclear incident arising from installations for nuclear fusion or particle accelerators is limited to 600 000 Sch. [Section 15(1)].

If the maximum amounts of compensation are not or only partly spent for one category of damage they may be used for the other category [Section 15(2)].

If the person suffering damage has contributed to the damage, his compensation may be reduced in accordance with the provisions of the Civil Code [Section 7].

Nothing in the Act shall affect the provisions relating to social security [Section 41].

b) Apportionment of Claims

Where it is not possible, within four months following the nuclear incident, to determine with certainty whether the maximum amounts of liability will be sufficient to satisfy all claims, such amounts are to be apportioned by category (damage to persons, damage to property) as follows [Section 16(1)]:

- 70 per cent for the compensation of damage known within four months following the nuclear incident;
- a further 14 per cent and the remainder, if any, of the abovementioned 70 per cent for damages claimed after such four months and within two years from the date of the nuclear incident;
- the remaining 16 per cent, together with any unused balance of the foregoing 84 per cent, to cover damages claimed after two years but within ten years from the date of the nuclear incident.

If the total compensation exceeds the respective percentages, the individual amounts of compensation are to be reduced proportionally [Section 16(2)].

Delayed damage claimed after ten years from the date of the nuclear incident is to be satisfied only to the extent that the maximum amounts of liability have not been used to compensate damage previously claimed. Such claims are to be satisfied in their order; claims brought in each period of two years have the same rank and are to be met proportionally if the remaining balance is insufficient to satisfy them in full [Section 16(3)].

D. TIME LIMITS FOR BRINGING CLAIMS

Claims for compensation for nuclear damage are barred by limitation after three years from the date at which the person entitled to compensation had knowledge of both the damage and the person liable, and irrespective thereof, thirty years from the date of the nuclear incident [Section 34(1)].

E. COMPETENT COURTS AND PROCEDURE

The court of the *Land* or county in whose venue the nuclear incident originated, has exclusive jurisdiction in all matters relating to nuclear damage. Where, in the case of a nuclear incident, a number of courts are involved, the court before which the claimant or one of the several claimants first brings proceedings shall have exclusive jurisdiction. Any change agreed to by the parties with respect to the jurisdiction of the courts is not admissible [Section 42(1)].

Section 44 of the Act on the Judiciary System shall apply as appropriate if a claim or application for quashing measures for provisional execution is made to a local court which does not have jurisdiction. If proceedings are transferred, those previously completed remain effective. Section 261, paragraph 6 of the Code of Civil Procedure otherwise applies as appropriate.

BELGIUM

INTRODUCTION

In 1990, Belgium's installed nuclear power capacity amounted to some 5 500 MWe (7 reactors). The main nuclear operators are electricity companies governed by private law (Ebes, Intercom, Unerg) or public law (SPE), the government-controlled corporations Synatom and Belgonucléaire, and the Nuclear Energy Research Centre at Mol. The main supervisory authority in the field of nuclear energy is the Minister of Economic Affairs, especially as concerns questions of insurance. The Ministers of Justice, of Employment and Labour and of the Interior, however, also have powers in this field.

Belgium is a Party to the Paris Convention and to the Brussels Supplementary Convention, as amended in 1982. It has also signed the Joint Protocol relating to the Application of the Vienna Convention and the Paris Convention.

The provisions regulating liability for nuclear damage are contained in the Act of 22nd July 1985 on Third Party Liability in the Field of Nuclear Energy, published in the *Moniteur Belge* (Belgian Official Gazette) on 31st August 1985 (the text of this Act is reproduced in the Supplement to Nuclear Law Bulletin No. 37). Mention should also be made of a Royal Order of 28th April 1986 (Moniteur Belge of 16th May 1986) determining the financial security certificate for the transport of nuclear substances.

I. THIRD PARTY LIABILITY

A. SCOPE AND DEFINITIONS

Section 2 of the Act, based on the Recommendation of 22nd April 1971 of the OECD Steering Committee for Nuclear Energy, provides that the Act applies to damage resulting from a nuclear incident for which the operator of a nuclear installation located in Belgian territory is liable, provided:

- the incident occurs in the territory of a Contracting State (to the Paris and Brussels Conventions) or a non-Contracting State, or on or over the high seas;
- and that the damage was suffered;
  - in the territory of a Contracting State, or

- on or over the high seas on board a ship or aircraft registered in the territory of a Contracting State, or
- on or over the high seas by a national of a Contracting State provided that, in the case of damage to a ship or an aircraft, the ship or aircraft is registered in the territory of a Contracting State.

Consequently, the determining factor is not the place of the incident but the place in which the damage is suffered. The King (the Executive) may however decide, by Order made in the Council of Ministers, to extend the scope of the Act to nuclear damage suffered by a national of a Contracting State in the territory of a non-Contracting State [Section 2(2)].

For the purposes of the Act, territorial waters are deemed to form part of national territory [Section 2(3)].

The definitions of the terms *nuclear incident, nuclear fuel, radioactive products or waste* and *nuclear substances* refer back to those in the Paris Convention. The same applies to *nuclear installation* which also includes any installation for the disposal of nuclear substances during the pre-closure phase. Furthermore, the *Minister* within the meaning of the Act, is the Minister responsible for nuclear insurance matters, namely the Minister of Economic Affairs [Section 1].

B. NATURE AND ASSIGNMENT OF LIABILITY

a) General – Nuclear Installations

The operator of a nuclear installation is liable for the damage caused by a nuclear incident in accordance with the provisions of the Paris Convention; his liability is therefore absolute, exclusive and limited [Section 5]. For the purposes of the Act, a nuclear operator is any person who has in his possession or uses, in a nuclear installation, nuclear fuel or radioactive products or waste, or who takes charge of nuclear substances intended for his installation and who has been officially recognised as a nuclear operator [Sections 3 and 9].

A nuclear operator is recognised as such by Order of the King, upon proof that, for the purpose of covering his liability, he has taken out insurance or other sufficient financial security [Section 10]. Recognition may be granted for a limited period and may be withdrawn. Recognition of the status of nuclear operator as well as the location and boundaries of each nuclear installation are published in the Moniteur Belge. They are also recorded in a register made available to the public by the Minister of Economic Affairs [Section 13 and Ministerial Order of 9th March 1987 on the Nuclear Installations Register]. An extract of the register including recognition of the status of nuclear operator is also made available to the public by the local authority concerned.

The operator's liability continues until final closure of his installation, as sanctioned by an Order made in the Council of Ministers [Section 3 of the Act].

For the purposes of the Act, two or more nuclear installations run by one operator and located on the same site may be treated as a single nuclear installation, but the amount of insurance to be taken out by the operator is, in such a case, the sum of the amounts required for each installation taken separately. Similarly, non-nuclear installations operated jointly with a nuclear installation located on the same site may be treated as a single nuclear installation [Section 4].

If damage gives rise to the liability of more than one operator, their liability is joint and several, but cannot exceed, for any given operator, the maximum liability amount established with respect to him [Section 18].

b) Transport

The operator of a nuclear installation is liable, in accordance with the provisions of Article 4 of the Paris Convention, for damage caused by a nuclear incident occurring during the transport of nuclear substances, including storage during transport [Section 14].

However, a carrier may, with the agreement of the operator concerned and the competent Minister, replace the operator for purposes of liability for damage caused by a nuclear incident occurring outside the installation, provided he has arranged adequate financial security. In this case, he will, for nuclear incidents occurring during the transport of nuclear substances, be regarded as the operator of a Belgian nuclear installation [Section 14].

In the event of the transit of nuclear substances through Belgium, including their storage, the carrier is held liable for any damage suffered on Belgian territory as a result of any nuclear incident involving such substances and in relation to which the Paris Convention makes no arrangements for compensation [Section 31].

c) Rights of Recourse

The insurer or person providing financial security is entitled, by subrogation, to recourse against any physical person who intentionally caused the damage and against any person who has given an express contractual right of recourse to the nuclear operator [Section 25].

The rights of recourse of the State are considered under the heading "State Intervention".

d) Exoneration from Liability

Nuclear operators are not liable for damage arising from a nuclear incident directly caused by acts of armed conflict, hostilities, civil war or insurrection. However, the exoneration provided for under the Paris Convention does not apply in the case of damage caused by a nuclear incident when such incident is directly due to a grave natural disaster of an exceptional nature [Section 5].

C. AMOUNT OF LIABILITY

The maximum liability of an operator amounts to BF 4 billion (approximately 90 million Special Drawing Rights of the International Monetary Fund – SDRs) for each nuclear incident [Sections 7 and 18].

By Order made in the Council of Ministers, the King may increase or reduce this figure (provided it complies with the minimum amount specified in the Paris Convention), so as to keep its value constant, or having regard to the nature of the installation or of the transport in question or of any other relevant circumstance [Section 7].

D. NUCLEAR DAMAGE

a) Damage Covered

The damage covered is that caused by a nuclear incident within the meaning of the Paris Convention, subject to the above-mentioned provisions regulating the territorial scope of the Act [Section 2].

Damage caused to the means of transport on which the nuclear substances were at the time of the nuclear incident is also covered when the operator is liable for damage caused during the transport in question in accordance with the Paris Convention. Compensation of this type of damage may not, however, reduce the liability of the operator for other damage so as to bring it below BF 4 billion [Section 6].

Damage caused in Belgium by sources of ionizing radiation in an installation designated as a nuclear installation by the King, is covered by the liability of the operator of the installation in question [Section 32].

b) Damage Excluded

The operator of a nuclear installation is not liable for damage caused to the nuclear installation itself or to any other nuclear installation located on the site, including those under construction, or for damage to any property on the site which is being or is to be used in connection with any such installation [Section 6].

II. COVER AND COMPENSATION

A. INSURANCE OR OTHER FINANCIAL SECURITY

The operator of a nuclear installation is required to take out and maintain insurance or other financial security deemed appropriate by the Minister, to cover his maximum liability under the Act. He is required to renew this cover within sixty days following an incident [Section 8]. The obligation to take out insurance does not apply to the State as operator [Section 12].

No insurer (or guarantor) may suspend or cancel the financial cover without giving notice in writing of at least two months to the Minister of Economic Affairs [Section 8].

The sums provided as insurance, reinsurance, or other financial security may be drawn upon only for compensation for damage caused by a nuclear incident [Section 8].

Carriers of nuclear substances must be in possession of a certificate issued by or on behalf of the insurer or other financial guarantor, stating that the statutory requirements in relation to cover for liability have been satisfied [Section 15]. A Royal Order of 28th April 1986 specifies the information to be given in the financial security certificate for the transport of nuclear substances.

The transit of nuclear substances through Belgian territory is subject to the condition that the foreign operator liable for the transport assumes at least the same financial obligations as those applying to the operator of a nuclear installation located in Belgium [Section 16 of the Act].

B. STATE INTERVENTION

The State intervenes in a subsidiary and complementary capacity in the compensation of damage.

In the first place, the State pays compensation for damage not covered by insurance, up to the maximum amount of the operator's liability. In this case, the State, up to the amount it has paid, acquires by subrogation all the rights and actions of the victims [Section 22].

Moreover, if the damage caused by a nuclear incident exceeds the maximum amount of the liability of the operator in question, the Act provides that compensation in excess of that amount shall, if the Brussels Supplementary Convention applies, be paid out of the public funds made available for the second and third tiers of compensation under the said Convention [Section 19].

If payments have been made by the Belgian State or by other Contracting Parties of the Brussels Supplementary Convention in compliance with the Convention, the Belgian State, within the limits of the sums paid, has a right of recourse against the operator in question for the recovery of the public funds allocated by it and by the other Contracting Parties, provided the damage was caused by a nuclear incident attributable to the gross negligence of the operator [Section 25(3)]. The cases of gross negligence which may give rise to an action against the operator are determined by the King.

Within the thirty-year prescriptive period, the State intervenes to compensate damage in respect of which the right of recourse against the operator liable has been extinguished (see under "Time Limits for Bringing Claims").

The King may, in accordance with rules to be determined, decide to pay compensation for damage suffered on Belgian territory and caused by a nuclear incident for which the operator liable is a national of a non-Contracting State, when the victim cannot obtain compensation in that State for the damage suffered [Section 34].

When damage is caused on Belgian territory by nuclear substances in transit or sources of ionizing radiation to which the Paris Convention does not apply, or when it is the Brussels Supplementary Convention which does not apply although the operator is liable under the Paris Convention and the Belgian Act, the King determines, for damage suffered in Belgium, the manner whereby the State will make payment of compensation exceeding the operator's liability ceiling, i.e. BF 4 billion [Section 33].

C. COMPENSATION

The victim of damage caused by a nuclear incident has a direct right of action against the insurer or other financial guarantor and, in the event of intervention by the State in a subsidiary capacity, against the State [Section 27]. For their part, the insurer or financial guarantor can join the operator in any proceedings brought against them by victims [Section 28].

The State may intervene in any proceedings for compensation based on the provisions of the Paris Convention, the Brussels Supplementary Convention or this Act [Section 28(1)]. The King is responsible for supervising the payment of compensation by the insurers and for determining the conditions under which those entitled to compensation may obtain information concerning the relevant insurance policies or contracts for financial security [Section 29]. He may also, with regard to compensation from public funds, set up an administrative or legal conciliation procedure which, in any event, must precede any hearing before the court [Section 30].

When the total amount of compensation for an incident does not exceed the maximum compensation amount of the operator or the limits provided for in the Brussels Supplementary Convention (2nd and 3rd tiers), compensation is awarded in accordance with the ordinary law. Where, on the other hand, total compensation exceeds – or is likely to exceed – the funds thus available, the King is responsible for determining criteria for the equitable apportionment of the compensation [Section 20].

The cases of beneficiaries under schemes for sickness and disability insurance or for compensation for industrial accidents and occupational diseases remain governed, even in the event of a nuclear incident, by the legislation regulating such schemes. It is only inasmuch as compensation for damage caused by a nuclear incident is not payable under such legislation, and provided such beneficiaries are entitled to institute proceedings against the operator liable, that they may claim compensation for damage in accordance with the Act [Section 21].

Any social security and industrial accident organisations which have paid out benefits to the victims of a nuclear incident are, subject to the limits referred to in the Act, entitled to a right of recourse against the operator or his insurer [Section 21].

Any person having suffered damage caused by a nuclear incident who has brought an action for compensation within the statutory time limits, may nevertheless amend his claim in the event of an aggravation of the damage after expiry of these time limits, provided no judgment has been entered definitively establishing the amount of compensation [Section 23(4)].

When the nuclear incident or the damage suffered was caused by the victim intentionally, he is not entitled to any compensation [Section 24].

D. TIME LIMITS FOR BRINGING CLAIMS

Actions for compensation must, on pain of forfeiture, be brought within ten years from the date of the incident. However, the right of action is in any event forfeited three years after the time when the injured party became aware (or ought reasonably to have become aware) of the damage and the identity of the operator concerned, should this occur before expiry of the above-mentioned time limit [Section 23(1) and (3)].

In the case of damage caused by a nuclear incident involving nuclear fuel or radioactive products or waste which, at the time of the incident, were stolen, lost, jettisoned or abandoned and had not been recovered, the right of action for compensation is forfeited ten years after the incident; this time limit may, however, in no case exceed twenty years after the date on which the nuclear fuel or radioactive products or waste were stolen, lost, jettisoned or abandoned [Section 23(1)].

When damage caused in Belgium by a nuclear incident is first noted after actions for compensation against the operator liable have been extinguished, but within a period of thirty years from the date of the nuclear incident, the State will compensate the damage in question [Section 23(2)].

E. COMPETENT COURTS AND PROCEDURE

The Act adopts a single jurisdiction approach by providing that legal proceedings based on the Paris and Brussels Conventions and on the Act itself, will first be brought before the Brussels Court of First Instance, sitting as a civil court [Section 26].

A judgment delivered in a case arising from damage caused by a nuclear incident cannot be enforced against the operator in question, the insurer or victims, unless these various parties appeared before the court or were summoned to do so. However, a judgment handed down in a case between a victim and the operator is enforceable against the insurer (or other financial guarantor) if it is established that the insurer or guarantor was, in fact, in control of the defence [Section 28].

BRAZIL

INTRODUCTION

There is one nuclear power plant supplying electricity at present in Brazil, ANGRA-I, a 626 MWe pressurized water reactor (PWR), operated by Furnas Centrais Elètricas SA, a mixed economy company with the Government a majority shareholder; ANGRA-II a 245 MWe PWR also to be operated by that company is under construction and will be connected to the grid in 1992. The competent authority for nuclear matters is the National Nuclear Energy Commission (*Comissao Nacional de Energia Nuclear* – CNEN) directly under the Presidency of the Republic since 1986 (Decree No. 93.337 of 6th October 1986).

Brazil is not a Party to the Vienna or the Paris Convention, but applies the principles of these international instruments in its national legislation.

The provisions governing nuclear third party liability in the country are contained in Act No. 6.453 of 17th October 1977 on civil liability for nuclear damage and criminal responsibility for acts relating to nuclear activities. A Circular, No. 26 of 22nd July 1982, issued by the Private Insurance Superintendence approves the general conditions of insurance policies for nuclear risks.

This chapter deals only with the provisions of the Act concerning civil liability for nuclear damage and does not cover those on criminal responsibility for acts relating to nuclear activities.

I. THIRD PARTY LIABILITY

A. SCOPE AND DEFINITIONS

The Act of 17th October 1977 on civil liability for nuclear damage (henceforth the Act) provides for compensation of damage due to a nuclear incident occurring in a nuclear installation and during transport of nuclear materials [Section 4]. The Act is effective on all the territory of Brazil.

Radioisotopes which have reached the final stage of fabrication so as to be usable for any scientific, medical, agricultural, commercial or industrial purpose are outside the scope of the Act [Section 1]. In addition, damage caused by emissions of ionizing radiation, where such an occurrence does not constitute a nuclear incident, is also excluded from its scope [Section 16].

It should be noted that the terms *operator, nuclear fuel, radioactive products or waste, nuclear installation* and *nuclear incident* have the same meanings as in the Vienna Convention [Section 13].

B. NATURE AND ASSIGNMENT OF LIABILITY

a) General – Nuclear Installations

The operator of a nuclear installation is exclusively liable, irrespective of fault, for compensation of damage due to a nuclear incident [Section 4]. Absolute and exclusive liability of the operator became part of the Brazilian Constitution promulgated on 8th October 1988 [Constitution, Section 21, Clause XXIII, letter C]. Where more than one operator is liable, and where it is not possible to verify the damage attributable to each of them, they are jointly and severally liable up to the ceiling of liability set by the Act [Section 5].

Several nuclear installations located on the same site and having the same operator may be considered by the CNEN as a single nuclear installation for the purposes of the Act [Section 2].

b) Transport

The operator of a nuclear installation is liable for nuclear damage caused by nuclear materials from that installation before liability has been assumed by a contract in writing by the operator of the nuclear installation to which the materials are being sent or, failing such contract, before that operator has effectively taken charge of the materials [Section 4.II].

c) Assumption of Liability

If a nuclear incident is caused by nuclear materials whose possession or use is unlawful and unconnected with any operator, the Federative Government (the State) takes responsibility for the damage up to the ceiling of liability set by the Act for a nuclear operator [Section 15].

d) Rights of Recourse

The operator has a right of recourse if this is expressly provided for by a contract in writing, and also if the person having caused the incident did so with intent to cause damage [Section 7].

Where the Federative Government has assumed liability for damage caused by nuclear materials whose possession or use are unlawful and unconnected with any operator, it may take proceedings against the person responsible for such damage [Section 15].

e) Exoneration from Liability

The operator of a nuclear installation is not liable for damage due to a nuclear incident arising from armed conflict, hostilities, civil war, insurrection or a case of force majeure [Section 8]. Also, when it is proved that the damage was caused exclusively by the victim, the operator is relieved of the obligation to pay compensation to that victim [Section 6].

C. AMOUNT OF LIABILITY

The liability of an operator is limited to an amount equal to 1.5 million adjustable Treasury Bonds (approximately $10 million in October 1989) for each nuclear incident [Section 9].

This ceiling is exclusive of legal costs, fees and interest for delays [Section 9].

D. NUCLEAR DAMAGE

The Act defines *nuclear damage* as: *personal injury or damage to property which arises out of or results from the radioactive properties or a combination of radioactive properties or other characteristics of nuclear materials that are in a nuclear installation or which come from or are sent to such installation* [Section 1.VII].

a) Damage Covered

As stated in the definition of nuclear damage above, personal injury and damage to property related causally to nuclear materials are covered by the Act. Furthermore, where damage has been caused by a nuclear incident jointly with other occurrences, if it cannot be reasonably separated from the non-nuclear damage, it is considered nuclear damage [Section 3].

b) Damage Excluded

The operator of a nuclear installation is not liable for nuclear damage to the installation itself or to any property on the site of that installation which is to be used in connection with it [Section 18.I and II]. Also, if a nuclear incident occurs in the course of carriage of nuclear materials, he is not liable for damage to the means of transport carrying the materials involved [Section 18.III].

The Act also provides that compensation for damage or injury suffered by persons working with nuclear materials or in a nuclear installation is governed by legislation relating to industrial accidents and not by its provisions [Section 17].

II. COVER AND COMPENSATION

A. INSURANCE OR OTHER FINANCIAL SECURITY

The Act [Section 13] provides that the operator of a nuclear installation must take out and maintain insurance or other financial security to cover his liability for nuclear damage. The National Nuclear Energy Commission (CNEN) determines, on a case-by-case basis, the nature and amount of the cover when it issues the construction or the operating licence for the installation; the nature and amount of the cover may be changed if alterations are made thereto.

When determining the nature and amount of such security, the CNEN takes into account the type, capacity, purpose and site of the installation, as well as all other foreseeable factors [Section 13(3)].

In the case of certain specific nuclear materials and installations which, in its view, involve only minor risks, the CNEN may relieve the operator of his obligation to take out insurance or other financial security [Section 13(5)].

The Circular of 22nd July 1982 (No. 26), which was published in the Official Gazette of 2nd August 1982, prescribes the general conditions of insurance policies for nuclear risks. These policies must in particular provide cover up to the amount insured, for compensation of damage of nuclear origin for which an operator licensed by the CNEN may be held liable. Only the risks expressly provided for in the policy are covered; in addition certain exclusions are listed, namely acts of war, civil war, insurrection and terrorism.

B. STATE INTERVENTION

The Federative Government guarantees up to the ceiling of the operator's liability – namely 1.5 million adjustable Treasury Bonds – the payment of compensation for nuclear damage for which he is liable; the Government also supplies the additional funds required if the insurance or financial security are insufficient [Section 14].

C. COMPENSATION

In cases where the amount due for compensation for damage caused by a nuclear incident exceeds the limit of liability set by the Act, compensation will be paid to the claimants concerned on a pro rata basis, according to their entitlement [Section 10]. Sums due for personal injury are paid separately and have priority over those due for damage to property; when claims for personal injury are settled, the balance remaining is distributed among those persons entitled to compensation for property damage [Section 10(1)].

The above provisions also apply when the Federative Government or a body provide funds for compensation for nuclear damage and such funds are insufficient to meet the claims in full [Section 10(2)].

D. TIME LIMITS FOR BRINGING CLAIMS

A right to compensation for nuclear damage in accordance with the Act may be exercised up to ten years from the date of the occurrence of the nuclear incident having caused such damage [Section 12].

Where the incident is caused by materials which have been stolen, lost or abandoned, the period will run as from the date of the incident, but can in no event exceed twenty years from the date of such theft, loss or abandonment [Section 12].

E. COMPETENT COURTS AND PROCEDURE

Proceedings for compensation of damage caused by a nuclear incident must be brought before the appropriate Federal Court; questions of jurisdiction are decided in accordance with the provisions of the Code of Civil Procedure [Section 100.V, letter a]. Before delivering judgment, the Court gives effect ex officio to the provisions of the Act concerning the apportionment of the compensation according to Section 10 in cases where the funds are insufficient [Section 11].

BULGARIA

INTRODUCTION

In the People's Republic of Bulgaria, five nuclear power plants are in operation with a total capacity of 2 760 MWe on the Kosloduj site. A further nuclear power plant of 1 000 MWe is under construction on the same site. Two power reactors of 1 000 MWe each are being constructed on the site of Belene; it is planned that this site will ultimately be equipped with four reactors.

The Act of 7th October 1985 on the Use of Atomic Energy for Peaceful Purposes (Atomic Energy Act), published in the Official Bulgarian Gazette of 11th October 1985 (No. 79, p. 953), governs all the peaceful uses of nuclear energy.

The Act provides that nuclear materials and equipment are the property of the State; other sources of ionizing radiation may be State property or be in co-operative or social ownership. The State makes available nuclear material and nuclear equipment for use by different State organisations [Atomic Energy Act, Section 2].

The Committee for the Peaceful Uses of Nuclear Energy, a State organisation set up by the Council of Ministers, is competent for all nuclear activities. The Committee, which is assisted by an Advisory Council for Nuclear Matters and Radiation Safety, exercises control and regulatory functions in the fields of nuclear safety and radiation protection, security control and licensing.

Bulgaria is not a Party to the Nuclear Third Party Liability Conventions. Chapter IV [Sections 33 to 38] of the Atomic Energy Act deals with civil liability for nuclear damage.

I. THIRD PARTY LIABILITY

A. SCOPE AND DEFINITIONS

The third party liability provisions of the Atomic Energy Act apply to nuclear incidents occurring and nuclear damage suffered in Bulgaria. If an incident occurs in Bulgaria and causes damage due to ionizing radiation in the territory of another State, liability for such damage is determined by an international agreement; failing such agreement, the principle of reciprocity applies [Section 36].

Definitions are contained in supplementary provisions to the Act as follows:

- *Source of ionizing radiation* means equipment, an installation, an apparatus or radioactive substances which emit directly or indirectly ionizing particles.
- *Radioactive substance* means material whose unstable nuclei produce ionizing radiation by transformation.
- *Nuclear material* is defined as material which, in sufficient quantity and configuration, is capable of producing a self-sustaining chain reaction.
- *Nuclear equipment* means a source of ionizing radiation in which such chain reactions can take place, or in which nuclear materials are stored or carried.
- *Radiation protection* is defined as the sum of different requirements, measures, means and methods of protecting man and the environment against the harmful effects of ionizing radiation.
- *Nuclear safety* means a state or quality of nuclear equipment preventing the occurrence of an incident by technical or organisational means.
- *Incident*, with respect to the terms radiation protection or nuclear safety, means an extraordinary occurrence which impedes the control of a source of ionizing radiation or makes such control completely impossible.

B. NATURE AND ASSIGNMENT OF LIABILITY

If radioactive damage is caused by a nuclear incident or an incident in nuclear equipment, liability lies with the organisation to which the nuclear material was made available, or which uses, carries or stores the nuclear material. This liability exists even in the absence of fault [Section 13(3)].

Matters which are not regulated by the Act are subject to the provisions of the Civil Code concerning unlawful acts. These provisions are equally applicable to liability for damage caused by other sources of ionizing radiation including their use for medical purposes, unless otherwise provided in other legal provisions [Section 37].

If the radiation was caused by several organisations, they are jointly liable, even in the case where each organisation has observed the limits for emissions of ionizing radiation as fixed by law [Section 37(3)].

C. AMOUNT OF LIABILITY

Liability for radiation damage is unlimited.

D. NUCLEAR DAMAGE

The Act covers damage due to ionizing radiation [Section 33(1)]; further details are to be found in the Civil Code [Section 37(1)].

If it is probable that damage is due to ionizing radiation, there exists a rebuttable presumption that such radiation has caused the damage [Section 37(2)].

II. COVER AND COMPENSATION

A. INSURANCE OR OTHER FINANCIAL SECURITY

The Act is silent on the question of whether liability according to the Act must be covered by insurance or other financial security.

B. STATE INTERVENTION

The State will compensate the damage which cannot be covered by the assets of the organisations mentioned in Section 33 of the Act. The State will also cover damage caused by force majeure [Section 35].

C. COMPENSATION

The nature, form and extent of compensation are governed by the Civil Code [Section 37(1)]. The Act specifies however that a person having suffered damage shall not be entitled to compensation if he has caused the incident intentionally [Section 33(3)].

D. TIME LIMITS FOR BRINGING CLAIMS

The time limit for bringing claims for compensation according to Section 33 starts on the date on which the damage is determined [Section 34]. The length of the limitation period is governed by the Civil Code.

E. COMPETENT COURTS AND PROCEDURE

Jurisdiction over actions based on incidents due to nuclear material or to nuclear equipment lies exclusively with the Bulgarian courts. The city court of Sofia is competent for such actions [Section 38].

CANADA

INTRODUCTION

In 1990, installed nuclear capacity in Canada amounted to some 12 000 MWe (18 reactors), with four other reactors in the course of being built. Canada possesses several other nuclear fuel cycle installations and is an important producer of uranium. In addition to the installations belonging to the Canadian Government, the operators of nuclear power plants are Ontario Hydro, Hydro Quebec and the New Brunswick Electric Power Commission. Canada also exports nuclear power plants.

The provisions relating to nuclear third party liability in Canada are contained in the Act Respecting Civil Liability for Nuclear Damage (Nuclear Liability Act), adopted on 19th June 1970. It forms Chapter 29, first Supplement of the Revised Statutes of Canada (CN 28, 1985). It was brought into force on 11th October 1976 by Proclamation of the Governor in Council, pursuant to Section 35.

Although Canada is not a Party to any of the international Conventions on nuclear third party liability, the Nuclear Liability Act is largely based on the principles laid down in those Conventions.

I. THIRD PARTY LIABILITY

A. SCOPE AND DEFINITIONS

In principle, a nuclear operator, that is to say the holder of a licence to operate a nuclear installation, issued pursuant to the Atomic Energy Control Act, is not liable for any injury or damage occurring outside Canada and attributable to a breach of the duty imposed upon him by the 1970 Act or for which he could be held liable under the domestic law of the country concerned. No Canadian court has jurisdiction to hear any claim for compensation of such damage [Section 34(1) of the Nuclear Liability Act].

Nevertheless, where the Governor in Council (the Government) is of the opinion that satisfactory arrangements exist in a foreign country for compensation of nuclear damage, including any such damage occurring in Canada, he may declare that such country shall be accorded reciprocal treatment for the purposes of the Act. The Governor in Council may make in relation to such country such rules as he considers necessary to implement any arrangements relating to compensation for nuclear damage [Section 34(2) and (3)].

The Governor in Council has made Rules implementing arrangements between Canada and the United States of America (Canada-United States Nuclear Liability Rules), which became effective on 11th October 1976. Under these Rules [Section 2], Canadian operators are liable for injury or damage suffered in the United States and resulting from a nuclear incident occurring in Canada.

Any court in Canada having jurisdiction in the place where the nuclear installation at the origin of the nuclear incident is situated, also has jurisdiction over actions relating to injury and damage suffered in the United States and caused by such incident in Canada [Section 3].

As regards definitions [Section 2 of the Act], *nuclear incident* means an occurrence resulting in injury or damage that is attributable to a breach of the duty imposed upon an operator by the Act (see "Nature and Assignment of Liability" below).

Nuclear installation is defined as a structure, establishment or place, or two or more structures, establishments or places at a single location, coming within any following description and designated as a nuclear installation for the purposes of the Act by the Atomic Energy Control Board, namely:

i) a structure containing nuclear material in such an arrangement that a self-sustaining chain process of nuclear fission can be maintained therein without an additional source of neutrons, including any such structure that forms part of the equipment of a ship, aircraft or other means of transportation;
ii) a factory or other establishment that processes or reprocesses nuclear material; or
iii) a place in which nuclear material is stored other than incidentally to the carriage of the material.

Nuclear material is defined as:

i) any material (other than thorium or natural or depleted uranium uncontaminated by significant quantities of fission products) that is capable of releasing energy by a self-sustaining chain process of nuclear fission,
ii) radioactive material produced in the production or utilisation of material referred to in subparagraph *i),* and
iii) material made radioactive by exposure to radiation consequential upon or incidental to the production or utilisation of material referred to in subparagraph *i),*

but does not include radioactive isotopes that are not combined, mixed or associated with material referred to in subparagraph *i).*

B. NATURE AND ASSIGNMENT OF LIABILITY

a) General – Nuclear Installations

The nuclear operator is under a duty to ensure that no damage is caused by nuclear material under his control as defined by the Act [Section 3]. The operator is absolutely (without the need to prove fault or negligence) liable for any breach of this duty [Section 4]. This liability is also exclusive [Section 11].

Where liability in respect of the same damage is incurred by several operators without being reasonably separable, they are jointly and severally liable [Section 5].

Where the Crown in right of Canada (the Canadian State) operates a nuclear installation, it is subject to the same liability regime as a nuclear operator [Section 33].

b) Transport

The nuclear operator is liable for damage caused by nuclear material which, having been in his installation, has not subsequently been in a nuclear installation operated under licence by another operator. He is also liable for damage caused by nuclear material in the course of carriage from outside Canada to his nuclear installation, or in a place of storage incidental to such carriage [Section 3].

c) Rights of Recourse

The nuclear operator has, in principle, no right of recourse or indemnity in respect of damage for which he is held liable under the Act [Section 10].

The operator nevertheless has a right of recourse against any person who has caused nuclear damage by virtue of an unlawful act or omission, intended to cause damage [Section 12(b)].

d) Exoneration from Liability

The nuclear operator is not liable for damage if the nuclear incident which caused it occurred as a direct result of an act of armed conflict in the course of war, invasion or insurrection [Section 7].

Neither is the operator liable for damage suffered by any person who has caused a nuclear incident by virtue of an unlawful act or omission, intended to cause damage [Section 8].

C. AMOUNT OF LIABILITY

The Act has no provision expressly limiting the legal liability of the operator for nuclear damage. However, it achieves the same result by limiting the financial obligations of the operator since it places a ceiling on the amount of insurance he is required to take out to cover his liability, and by discharging him, in certain circumstances, from liability by means of a proclamation by the Governor in Council (see "Insurance or Other Financial Security" below).

D. NUCLEAR DAMAGE

a) Damage Covered

For the purposes of the Act, damage comprises firstly, loss of life and personal injury and, secondly, any loss of or damage to property or damage resulting from such loss or damage [Section 2(b)].

The Act covers any damage resulting from any incident caused by the fissionable or radioactive properties or a combination of those properties with other hazardous properties of nuclear material under the nuclear operator's control as defined by the Act. Radioactive isotopes in the final stage of production are not considered nuclear material for the purposes of the Act [Sections 2 and 3].

Any damage which, although not nuclear damage, is not reasonably separable from such damage is deemed to be nuclear damage for the purposes of the Act [Section 6].

b) Damage Excluded

The liability regime introduced by the Act does not, where a nuclear incident occurs in a nuclear installation, cover damage to such installation or to property on the site intended for use in connection with the operation of the installation [Section 9(1)].

Where a nuclear incident occurs in the course of the carriage of nuclear material, any damage caused to the means of carriage or to the place where the material is stored incidental to such carriage is not covered by the Act [Section 9(2)].

II. COVER AND COMPENSATION

A. INSURANCE OR OTHER FINANCIAL SECURITY

The nuclear operator must, with respect to each installation for which he is liable, maintain with an insurer approved by the competent Minister (Minister of Energy, Mines and Resources), insurance covering his liability under the Act [Section 15(1)].

This does not apply to the Canadian State operating a nuclear installation [Section 33(2)].

The competent Minister may designate as an approved insurer any insurer or association of insurers who, in his opinion, fulfill the conditions necessary to cover such risks [Section 15(2)]. A Ministerial Designation of Approved Insurers and a Ministerial Approval of Terms and Conditions of Insurance were issued on 1st October 1976.

The insurance consists of basic insurance for such period and amount as are prescribed by the Atomic Energy Control Board, with the approval of the Treasury Board, not exceeding 75 million Canadian dollars (some 50 million Special Drawing Rights of the International Monetary Fund – SDRs), and supplementary insurance for the same period and for an amount equal to the difference, if any, between the amount prescribed for the basic insurance and the ceiling of 75 million Canadian dollars [Section 15(1)]. This system makes it possible for the financial burden of the basic insurance subscribed by each operator to be fixed in accordance with the seriousness of the risks presented by his installation.

The competent Minister may, with the approval of the Treasury Board, enter into an agreement in relation to the supplementary insurance with an approved insurer, reinsuring the risk assumed by that insurer under such terms and conditions as the Minister shall deem appropriate. Such an agreement must be laid before Parliament within fifteen days [Section 16]. All sums payable by the Government under such an agreement are charged to a special account of the Consolidated Revenue Fund known as the Nuclear Liability Reinsurance Account, and all amounts received by the Government under any such agreement are paid into that Account [Section 17].

On 1st October 1976, the Competent Minister and the Nuclear Insurance Association of Canada concluded such a reinsurance agreement.

B. STATE INTERVENTION

The Act provides that special measures for compensation, requiring active State intervention, must be taken where the amount of insurance taken out by the operator (75 million Canadian dollars) is likely to be insufficient to cover the amount of the damage or where, as a result of a nuclear incident, it is in the public interest to take such measures. In these circumstances, the Governor in Council initiates this special procedure by way of proclamation [Section 18].

The first consequence of the proclamation is that the liability of the operator who would normally be liable for the nuclear damage ceases and that any proceedings are permanently suspended, the State being substituted for the operator [Section 19].

The operator nevertheless remains accountable to the Canadian State for an amount equal either to the basic insurance which he has been required to take out, or to the aggregate compensation paid by the State under the special procedure, whichever is the lesser. In case of default by the operator, the approved insurer is liable for the payment of such amount, which may not in any year exceed the aggregate of the amounts paid by the State during that year in respect of any damage caused by the nuclear incident in question [Section 20]. These provisions do not apply to the Canadian State operating a nuclear installation [Section 33(2)].

Except as otherwise authorised by Parliament, the aggregate of compensation paid by the State must not, for any one nuclear incident, exceed 75 million Canadian dollars [Section 32].

C. COMPENSATION

a) Special Compensation Measures

In cases where special measures for compensation are proclaimed, the Governor in Council must establish a Nuclear Damage Claims Commission to deal with claims for compensation arising out of the nuclear incident to which the proclamation relates. The members of the Commission are all chosen by the Governor from among judges of Canadian courts or Canadian barristers or advocates. The Chairman is responsible for the control and direction of the Commission [Section 21].

The Commission, which may employ such staff as it considers necessary for the proper conduct of its activities [Section 22], has exclusive jurisdiction to hear and determine, in accordance with the provisions of the Act, every claim brought before it for compensation arising out of the nuclear incident in respect of which it was established or out of any other nuclear incident with which it is authorised to deal, and to decide the amount of compensation to be awarded in respect of each claim [Sections 23 and 24(1)].

The Commission is also empowered to make rules regarding its own procedure, notably as concerns the investigation of claims and the carrying out of all necessary investigations and examinations [Sections 24(3) and 25].

When the Commission gives a favourable decision in respect of a claim, it issues an order specifying the amount of compensation awarded and the amount of any payment that may already have been made by or on behalf of the operator liable to the person named in the order [Section 27]. Such orders must be sent to the competent Minister.

Upon receipt of an order for the payment of compensation, the competent Minister may, subject to any special regulations applicable to the payment of compensation, pay out of the Consolidated Revenue Fund to the person entitled thereto, an amount equal to that specified in the order. Such amount may be subject to the deduction of any sum already paid to the person entitled either by the operator or by way of interim financial assistance [Section 28].

The Governor in Council may, with respect to compensation payable under an order, make regulations providing for payment by instalments or for pro rata payments. Such regulations may also establish priorities among persons claiming compensation or exclude, temporarily or permanently, certain categories of injuries or damage from the payment of compensation. These regulations must be laid before Parliament within the shortest possible time [Section 29].

The Act preserves all rights or obligations of any person arising under any contract of insurance, including any insurance the operator of a nuclear installation is required to carry under the Act, schemes for health insurance, for hospitalisation, or for occupational disease compensation, or under any retirement or pension plan [Section 12].

b) Interim Financial Assistance

Provision may be made by the Governor in Council for interim financial assistance where this proves to be necessary by reason of the distress or suffering of the victims of a nuclear incident. The Governor shall, in such cases, make regulations providing for the payment of such assistance by the Minister out of the Consolidated Revenue Fund and specifying the persons who are to benefit. The Governor in Council may instruct a special commission to carry out this task [Section 31].

D. TIME LIMITS FOR BRINGING CLAIMS

No action for compensation may be brought in the case of a claim for injury other than loss of life, or for damage to property, more than three years after the earliest date upon which the person making the claim had knowledge or ought reasonably to have had knowledge of the injury or damage. In the case of a claim for loss of life, the period of prescription is also three years from the date of death or, where conclusive evidence of the death is not available, from the date of an order of presumed death made by a court having jurisdiction in such matters [Section 13].

In any event, no claim for compensation may be brought after ten years from the date on which the cause of action arose [Section 13].

E. COMPETENT COURTS AND PROCEDURE

Actions for compensation must be brought before the court exercising jurisdiction either in the place where the damage was suffered or, when this would give rise to the jurisdiction of several courts, in the place where the installation was situated. The court having jurisdiction in accordance with this provision is deemed to have jurisdiction throughout Canada [Section 14(1)].

It is pointed out that in the context of the Canada-United States Arrangement, Canadian courts are competent to settle claims for the compensation of damage suffered in the United States (see "Scope and Definitions" above).

All laws enforceable in Canadian provinces where actions for compensation are brought, continue to apply except insofar as they are incompatible with the provisions of the Act [Section 14(2)].

Rules made under the Act relating to the jurisdiction of courts may be modified by special arrangements made by the Governor in Council with countries to which reciprocity is accorded, as concerns the payment of compensation for injuries and damage of nuclear origin [Section 34(4)].

CHILE

INTRODUCTION

The Nuclear Energy Commission of Chile is carrying out a programme on the development of the uses of nuclear energy which includes research reactor operation. On the other hand, for the time being, Chile has no nuclear power reactors.

The Executive Board of the Atomic Energy Commission (*Comisión Chilena de Energia Nuclear*) is also the competent authority for the regulation of nuclear activities.

Since 1989, Chile is a Party to the Vienna Convention and has also ratified the Joint Protocol relating to the Application of the Vienna and Paris Conventions.

The provisions on nuclear third party liability are contained in Nuclear Safety Act No. 18302 of 16th April 1984, published in Official Gazette No. 31860 of 2nd May 1984.

I. THIRD PARTY LIABILITY

A. SCOPE AND DEFINITIONS

The Nuclear Safety Act, 1984 ("The Act") includes no special provisions concerning its territorial scope.

Chilean legislation is, in general, closely based on the Vienna Convention. In particular, the definitions of a *nuclear incident*, *nuclear installation*, *nuclear substances*, *fuel* and *waste* are similar to the corresponding provisions of the Convention [Section 3 of the Act].

The operator of a nuclear installation is defined as the physical person or the legal entity licensed to operate a nuclear installation by the Chilean Nuclear Energy Commission ("the Commission") [Section 3.11].

B. NATURE AND ASSIGNMENT OF LIABILITY

a) General – Nuclear Installations

Third party liability for nuclear damage is absolute and limited in accordance with the conditions set by the Act [Section 49].

The holder of a licence issued by the Commission, and who is therefore the operator of a nuclear installation, plant, centre, laboratory or establishment as the case may be, is held liable for damage caused by an incident on the premises concerned [Section 50] (see also under "Transport" below).

As regards nuclear substances which have been abandoned, diverted, stolen or lost, the operator of the nuclear installation from which such substances came is also held directly liable for nuclear damage caused by them. However, the Act provides that the third party liability of third parties guilty of these actions is governed by the rules of common law [Section 52].

Where several operators are liable for nuclear damage, and insofar as it is not possible to determine the portion of liability attributable to each of them, they are jointly and severally liable up to the maximum amount of compensation, without prejudice to the possibility that they may finally contribute in equal shares to compensating the damage [Section 53].

Where, following a nuclear incident, nuclear damage and damage attributable to another cause occur and they cannot be separable with certainty, all the damage will be considered nuclear damage [Section 55].

A person other than a nuclear operator who has caused damage with intent to cause harm, for which the nuclear operator is not definitely liable under the Act, will be held liable for the damage resulting from his action or his omission to act [Section 59].

b) Transport

The operator is liable for nuclear damage caused by nuclear substances coming or originating from the nuclear installation for which he is responsible, provided that the nuclear incident has occurred under one of the following conditions:

- before the operator of another nuclear installation has assumed liability therefor by written contract;
- failing such written contract, before the operator of another nuclear installation has actually taken in charge the nuclear substances concerned, or before those substances have reached that operator's installation;
- before the nuclear substances despatched abroad have left the national territory and have been taken in charge by another operator, unless otherwise provided in a bilateral agreement concluded by Chile on the subject;
- before the operator of a nuclear reactor used as a source of power for a means of transport has taken in charge the nuclear substances intended for that reactor [Section 50].

In the cases listed above, liability lies with the nuclear operator when he has assumed it in writing or when he has taken in charge the nuclear substances sent to his installation or when those substances have arrived from abroad onto the national territory [Section 51].

Carriers of nuclear substances or the persons handling radioactive wastes may be assimilated to a nuclear operator in respect of such substances or wastes, subject to an agreement in writing approved by the Commission providing that the operator holding the licence has entrusted them with the substances or wastes. As from the time the substances or wastes have been handed over, those persons are considered liable, as a nuclear operator, for any nuclear damage likely to be caused by such substances or wastes [Section 54]. In the event that several such persons are involved in the same incident, they will be jointly and severally liable but only up to the maximum amount set by this Act (see "Amount of Liability" below) [Section 54].

c) Rights of Recourse

This Act contains no special provisions in this respect.

C. AMOUNT OF LIABILITY

The nuclear operator's maximum liability for each nuclear incident is set at the equivalent of $75 million in the national currency. This amount must be automatically adjusted according to the variations of the dollar against the Special Drawing Right of the International Monetary Fund between the date of this Act and that of the nuclear incident [Section 60]. The fact that the nuclear operator's liability limit is expressed in $ clearly does not affect the courts, which must award compensation in the national currency.

This amount does not include any interest or costs which may be set by the court having jurisdiction for the matter [Section 60].

D. NUCLEAR DAMAGE

a) Damage Covered

Nuclear damage is defined as loss of life, personal injury, including somatic, genetic and psychological effects as well as damage to property which is the direct or indirect result of:

- the radioactive properties or a combination of radioactive properties with toxic, explosive or other hazardous properties in a nuclear installation or of nuclear substances coming or originating from, or sent to this installation;
- ionizing radiation emitted by any other source of radiation inside a nuclear installation [Section 3].

b) Damage Excluded

The nuclear operator is not liable for damage to the means of transport carrying the nuclear substances having caused the incident while on board [Section 57].

II. COVER AND COMPENSATION

A. INSURANCE OR OTHER FINANCIAL SECURITY

Each nuclear operator must cover his liability by insurance or other financial security up to the above mentioned maximum amount of liability [Section 62].

The operator must submit to the Commission's approval, the conditions of insurance as well as the name of the insurance company or the conditions of financial security, as the case may be [Section 62].

When he has fulfilled these conditions, the operator may obtain the licence to operate a nuclear installation [Section 62].

Without prejudice to the attributions of the Securities and Insurance Superintendence (*Superintendencia de valores y seguros*), insurance companies must, to be entitled to cover the risks referred to in this Act, submit to the Commission's approval model policies and their operating conditions, in particular, regarding coinsurance and reinsurance. The same procedure applies when liability is covered by other financial security [Section 63].

When the operator cannot obtain, in whole or in part, insurance to cover his liability, he may request a State guarantee. This may be granted for that part which is not covered by insurance or for the entire amount. The form and conditions of the guarantee are to be laid down by regulation [Section 65].

As regards the transport of nuclear substances, the operator liable must supply the carrier with a certificate issued by the insurer or body having provided the financial security so as to show that insurance or financial security do exist [Section 64].

B. STATE INTERVENTION

This Act contains no provision for State intervention either in place of the operator in case of the latter's default or to make an additional contribution if the damage exceeds the financial security.

C. COMPENSATION

Nuclear damage suffered by persons employed as workers occupationally exposed to nuclear hazards in a nuclear installation is not compensated according to this Act in so far as the nuclear damage involved is covered by a social security scheme or an industrial accidents and occupational diseases scheme [Section 58].

Payment of compensation is governed by the following rules:

- personal injury is compensated at a minimum up to twice the amount of the official scales of compensation for industrial accidents;
- damage to property, if the maximum amount of liability is insufficient, is compensated on a prorata basis [Section 61].

A victim may amend his initial claim if the damage suffered worsens until a final judgment is rendered on appeal. In that case the court decides by summary procedure [Section 66].

D. TIME LIMITS FOR BRINGING CLAIMS

Actions for compensation of nuclear damage are extinguished after a period of ten years from the date of the incident or the date on which an inspector has reported such incident [Section 66].

E. COMPETENT COURTS AND PROCEDURES

This Act contains no special provisions concerning the determination of a competent court in case of a nuclear incident. However, according to the principle of *territoriality*, the competent court to hear an action for compensation for nuclear damage would be that of the domicile of the operator liable.

PEOPLE'S REPUBLIC OF CHINA

INTRODUCTION

The Chinese nuclear power programme currently consists of a unit of 300 MWe under construction at the Quinstan power plant and two units of 950 MWe each at the Daya Bay power plant. The use of nuclear energy for peaceful purposes in the People's Republic of China comes under the authority of the Ministry of Energy and, with respect to safety and regulatory matters, the National Nuclear Safety Administration is the competent body.

In the absence of any specific legislation on nuclear third party liability, it was necessary for the purposes of the contract for the construction of the Daya Bay power plant to clarify the official position of the Chinese authorities on this matter: this was done by a written declaration of the Council of State published in April 1986.

In addition, a framework Act on atomic energy is currently being prepared and should soon be published. Chapter 10 of this draft Act sets down provisions on compensation of nuclear damage. Both texts are analysed in this chapter.

I. COUNCIL OF STATE DECLARATION ON HOW TO DEAL WITH NUCLEAR THIRD PARTY LIABILITY QUESTIONS

The above-mentioned 1986 declaration includes the following points:

Any entity operating a nuclear power plant or other nuclear installation for the supply, processing or transportation of nuclear material for a nuclear power plant, situated in the territory of the People's Republic of China will, upon designation by the Government, be a nuclear operator with a legal personality.

The operator is *absolutely and exclusively* liable for nuclear damage caused by a nuclear incident which occurs on the site of the installation or which occurs on Chinese territory after the operator has taken charge of nuclear material sent by another person or as long as another person has not taken charge of material sent by the operator.

The *limit of liability* of the operator with respect to victims of a nuclear incident is set at 18 million RMB (approximately $4 million). However, should the damage exceed this amount the Government undertakes to provide financial aid up to 300 million RMB (approximately $64 million).

The operator has a *right of recourse* against any person who causes nuclear damage by an intentional act or omission. In addition, the operator is exonerated from liability for nuclear damage caused by acts of armed conflict, hostilities, rebellions or grave natural disasters.

The *time limit* for bringing actions for compensation is three years from the date on which the victim knew – or should have known – of the damage, subject to an additional limitation of ten years from the date of the nuclear incident.

Actions for compensation of damage caused by a nuclear incident occurring on Chinese territory, are to be brought before the courts of the People's Republic. The *competent court* is that of the place where the incident occurred.

II. PROVISIONS OF THE DRAFT ACT ON ATOMIC ENERGY

In accordance with Chapter 10 of the Draft Law, compensation of nuclear damage is to be governed by the following principles:

The operator of a nuclear installation is liable for nuclear damage caused by a nuclear incident occurring in his installation. In the case of transport between two nuclear installations, the sending operator remains liable until this liability is transferred to the receiving operator either pursuant to the terms of a written contract or – in the absence of such a contract – when the receiving operator takes charge of the material [Section 42].

If nuclear damage gives rise to the liability of more than one operator to the extent that it is not possible to distinguish the damage attributable to each operator, the operators will be jointly and severally liable in equal shares [Section 42].

The operator of a nuclear installation is liable to compensate nuclear damage when such damage results from negligence or an intentional act. He is not, however, liable for damage caused by acts of war, hostilities or grave disasters. He must, nevertheless, take the necessary measures to prevent aggravation of the damage and will be held liable for such aggravation if he fails to take them [Section 43].

If the operator proves that a nuclear incident within the meaning of Section 42 mentioned above was caused by the fault of another person, he has a right of recourse against that person for the compensation that he has paid to the victims of the incident [Section 44].

Compensation for nuclear damage should correspond to damage actually suffered by the victims, but is not to exceed the maximum amount (not specified by the Draft Act) of the liability fixed by the State [Section 45].

The operator of a nuclear installation must take out and maintain insurance to cover his liability, or establish another form of financial security [Section 45].

To the extent that claims for the compensation of nuclear damage exceed the amount of the financial security, the victims will only be compensated after the department responsible for atomic energy matters has submitted a report concerning the financing of the compensation [Section 45].

The courts of the People's Republic of China are the only courts competent to hear actions concerning nuclear damage caused by a nuclear incident occurring in China and attributable to foreign undertakings, other organisations or individuals, or concerning a nuclear incident occurring in China and causing damage in foreign territories [Section 46].

The time limit for the bringing of actions for compensation is three years from the date on which the victim knew – or should have known – of the damage suffered, but not exceeding a period of ten years from the date of the incident [Section 46].

CZECHOSLOVAKIA

INTRODUCTION

Czechoslovakia had 3 264 MW of installed nuclear capacity as at 31st December1988, representing approximately 28 per cent of its total energy production.

The Atomic Energy Commission has general responsibility for questions of nuclear third party liability.

Czechoslovakia is not a Party to either the 1960 Paris Convention or the 1963 Vienna Convention.

Czechoslovakia does not have legislation directed specifically to addressing questions of nuclear third party liability. Rather, nuclear third party liability is covered under provisions concerning liability in relation to specially dangerous operations. The basic legislation is contained in Part VI, Chapter II of the Civil Code (Act No. 40 of 26th February 1964 as amended by Act No. 58 of 5th June 1969 and Act No. 131 of 9th November 1982.

I. THIRD PARTY LIABILITY

A. SCOPE AND DEFINITIONS

The Civil Code covers liability for damage including liability for damage caused by a particularly dangerous operation [Part VI, Chapter II of the Civil Code]. This includes the operation of a nuclear power plant and the transport of nuclear substances. The Civil Code applies to nuclear damage suffered within Czechoslovakia.

B. NATURE AND ASSIGNMENT OF LIABILITY

a) General – Nuclear Installations

The operator is liable for damage due to the character of a particularly dangerous operation [Section 432].

He is so liable regardless of fault if the damage was due to the hazardous nature of the operation. In other cases, he will be relieved of his liability if he can prove that the damage could not have been prevented in spite of all possible care [Sections 428 and 432].

If damage is caused by several operators, they are jointly and severally liable [Section 438(1)]. However, if a case so warrants, a court may rule that those who caused the damage are to bear liability separately according to their involvement in the damage [Section 438(2)]. Where liability is jointly and severally borne, the contribution of each is to be determined according to their role in the incident which caused the damage.

b) Transport

In the case of transport, the person in charge of the means of transport is liable for damage due to the character of a particularly dangerous operation [Section 432].

This liability is subject to the same conditions concerning fault and joint liability as described above in relation to nuclear installations.

c) Rights of Recourse

The operator or the person in charge of the means of transport, as the case may be, is entitled to seek recourse against any person who caused the damage [Section 440].

d) Exoneration from Liability

As stated above, if the damage is not due to the circumstances of the operation or transport itself, the operator or the person in charge of the means of transport, will not be liable if he can prove that the damage could not have been prevented in spite of all reasonable efforts [Sections 428 and 432].

If the damage is due in whole or in part to the fault of the person suffering the damage, he is to bear the loss entirely or proportionately, as the case may be [Section 441].

C. AMOUNT OF LIABILITY

The Civil Code makes no provision for a limit to the liability of the operator.

D. NUCLEAR DAMAGE

Damage to human health, including death, or to property, including loss of property, is covered by the Civil Code [Section 429].

II. COVER AND COMPENSATION

A. INSURANCE OR OTHER FINANCIAL SECURITY

The Civil Code imposes no obligation to hold insurance to cover liability for damage due to an especially dangerous operation nor does the Act provide for any special conditions in relation to insurance for such liability.

B. STATE INTERVENTION

The Civil Code contains no provisions for State intervention to compensate damage.

C. COMPENSATION

For reasons meriting special regard, the court may reduce the amount of compensation. In doing so, it is to take into account, in particular, the social impact of the damage, the manner in which the damage occurred, as well as the personal and material situation of the individual who caused the damage; the court shall also take into consideration the situation of the injured. No reduction may be granted if the damage was caused intentionally by the injured [Section 450].

D. TIME LIMITS FOR BRINGING CLAIMS

A right to compensation will be extinguished two years after the date on which the person suffering the damage knew of the damage and of the identity of the person liable [Section 106(1)]. In any case, apart from cases of damage to health, the right will be extinguished three years after the incident causing the damage or ten years after that incident where the damage was caused intentionally [Section 106].

E. COMPETENT COURTS AND PROCEDURE

The Code of Civil Procedure (Act No. 99 of 1963 as amended by Act No. 36 of 6th April 1967, Act No. 158 of 18th December 1969 and Act No. 49 of 26th April 1973) enables claims for compensation to be brought in the court within whose jurisdiction the operator has his place of business or the incident took place [Sections 84, 85 and 87]. District courts have competence in the first instance, appeals from district courts being heard by regional courts [Sections 9 and 10].

DENMARK

INTRODUCTION

Denmark has no nuclear power programme. It does, however, have two research reactors, one of 2 kW and one of 10 MW, operated by the Research Establishment Risø. Responsibility for matters concerning nuclear installations and radioactive substances and materials, including the transport and storage thereof and the issue of liability and financial security for damage caused by a nuclear accident, is vested in the Minister of the Interior and the Minister of Justice.

Denmark is a Party to the Paris Convention and the Brussels Supplementary Convention and to the 1982 Protocols to amend these Conventions. It is also a Party to the 1971 Brussels Convention Relating to Civil Liability in the Field of Maritime Carriage of Nuclear Material. In addition, Denmark has ratified the Joint Protocol Relating to the Application of the Vienna Convention and the Paris Convention.

Nuclear third party liability is governed by Act No. 332 of 19th June 1974 on Compensation for Nuclear Damage. (The text of this Act, translated into English, has been reproduced in Nuclear Law Bulletin No. 15). This Act implements the Paris Convention, the Brussels Supplementary Convention and the 1971 Brussels Convention. It was amended by Act No. 732 of 7th December 1988 (published in *Lovtidende for Kongeriget Danmark*, Part A, 13th December 1988) to comply with the 1982 Protocols to amend the Paris Convention and the Brussels Supplementary Convention and the Joint Protocol. The amendments came into force on 1st July 1989, with the exception of the provision increasing the amount of compensation to be paid from public funds in accordance with the 1982 Protocol Amending the Brussels Supplementary Convention which awaits the coming into force of that Protocol.

I. THIRD PARTY LIABILITY

A. SCOPE AND DEFINITIONS

In general, nuclear damage occurring in a non-Contracting State (i.e. a State which is not a Party to the Paris Convention) is not covered by the Act, unless such damage was caused by an incident occurring in Denmark [Section 5(1)].

However, the Minister of Justice may direct that a State which is not a Party to the Paris Convention be dealt with as though it were such a Party [Section 6].

Furthermore claims for compensation for damage caused by an incident occurring in a non-Contracting State against a nuclear operator in Denmark, may be brought on condition that:

- the damage arose either in a Contracting State or on the high seas on board a vessel registered in such State, and
- the incident occurred either during carriage of nuclear substances to a non-Contracting State before the substances in question were unloaded from the means of transport by which they arrived in the territory of that State, or during carriage from such State after the substances were loaded onto the means of transport by which it was to be carried from the territory of that State [Section 5(2)].

The Act provides that the territorial scope of the liability of the operator of a nuclear installation situated within the territory of another Contracting State shall be governed by the domestic legislation of such State [Section 5(3)].

Where the relevant legislation of a non-Contracting State provides, with respect to nuclear damage which occurs in Denmark, for less compensation than is provided for under the Danish Act, the Minister of Justice may direct that corresponding rules be applied to compensation for damage occurring in such State, for which a Danish operator is liable [Section 5(4)].

The Act applies to Greenland. It does not at the present time apply to the Faroe Islands but may be made applicable by Royal Order [Section 43].

The terms *nuclear installation, operator, radioactive products* and *nuclear substances* are used in the same sense as in the Paris Convention. Where more than one installation is situated on the same site and belongs to the same operator, the Minister of the Interior can determine that they be treated as one installation [Section 3].

B. NATURE AND ASSIGNMENT OF LIABILITY

a) General – Nuclear Installations

The operator of a nuclear installation is responsible for nuclear damage caused by an incident occurring in such installation, except in cases where the damage is due to nuclear substances stored in the installation incidentally to their carriage to or from a nuclear installation situated in the territory of a Contracting Party [Section 7].

Liability to pay compensation falls exclusively on the operator unless otherwise provided by an international agreement concerning damage during transport to which Denmark is a Party [Sections 16(1), 17(1) and 18]. He is liable even if the damage is fortuitous [Section 13(1)].

Where the operators of several installations are held liable for the same nuclear damage under this Act or the legislation of any other Contracting State, they are jointly and severally liable for the payment of compensation up to the liability ceiling applicable to each of them [Section 22(1)]. This liability is to be apportioned between the operators having regard to the share of each installation in the damage and any other relevant circumstances [Section 22(2)].

b) Transport

Subject to the territorial limitations described above, an operator whose installation is situated in Denmark or in the territory of any other Contracting State is liable for nuclear damage occurring in the course of carriage of nuclear substances from his installation [Section 8(1)].

Nevertheless, an operator of an installation situated in Denmark or in the territory of any other Contracting State is liable for nuclear damage occurring in the course of carriage of nuclear substances to his installation if he has assumed liability by contract in writing and the incident occurs after the time stipulated for transfer of liability or, in other cases, where the incident occurs after he has taken charge of the substances [Section 8(2)]. The Minister of Justice may direct in which cases and under what conditions operators of installations in Denmark must or may make such an agreement concerning transfer of liability [Section 8(4)].

Where nuclear substances are sent from a State which is not a Party to the Paris Convention to an installation in Denmark or in any other Contracting State with the written consent of the operator of that installation, that operator is, subject to the territorial limitations described above, liable to compensate nuclear damage caused by an incident in the course of the carriage [Section 9(1)].

In the case of damage caused by nuclear substances in transit on Danish territory and for which no operator is otherwise held liable under the Act, liability is borne by the person authorised to effect such transport under the Danish Act on the Use of Radioactive Substances [Act No. 94 of 1953] [Section 9(3)].

The above provisions determining liability for nuclear damage caused by an incident in the course of carriage also apply to any incident occurring during storage of the substances incidental to such carriage [Section 10].

Where nuclear substances outside an installation, but not in the course of carriage, cause damage, liability attaches to the operator who at the time of the incident had the substances in his charge or, if the substances were not in the charge of any operator at the time of the incident, the operator who last had them in his charge before the incident. However, if by written agreement an operator has assumed liability for such damage, he shall be liable in accordance with such agreement [Section 11].

Where the above-described provisions covering cases where several operators are liable under this Act or the legislation of any other Contracting State apply to an incident occurring in the course of carriage of nuclear substances either in the same means of transport or, in the case of storage incidental to the carriage, in the same nuclear installation, the total liability of the operators shall not exceed the highest amount applicable with respect to any one operator [Section 22(1)].

A carrier in possession of the necessary financial security may, at his request and with the agreement of the operator, be authorised by the Ministry of Justice to assume liability in place of such operator for any nuclear damage occurring in the course of transport [Section 12].

c) **Rights of Recourse**

Where a person has had to pay compensation for nuclear damage by virtue of an international transport agreement to which Denmark is a Party or under the legislation of a foreign State, that person has a right of recourse against the operator liable pursuant to this Act [Section 19(1)].

In addition, any person whose principal place of business is in the territory of a Contracting State and who has had to pay compensation for nuclear damage where the nuclear operator involved was not liable by virtue of the provisions of the Act relating to its territorial scope, has a right of recourse against such operator. This provision does not apply with respect to damage caused by an incident occurring, in the case of carriage from a non-Contracting State, before the nuclear substances were loaded onto the means of transport or, in the case of carriage to a non-Contracting State, after the nuclear substances were unloaded from the means of transport [Section 19(2)].

In the case of wilful nuclear damage caused by a third party and for which an operator is held liable under the Act, the operator has a right of recourse against the person causing the damage. He may also exercise any right of recourse expressly provided by contract [Section 24(1)].

A right of recourse may also be exercised by the State, in respect of any sums which it has paid, against an insurer who by express agreement has accepted liability for the damage, as well as against any other operator jointly liable, and lastly against the operator himself where any insufficiency in financial security is attributable to his default [Section 35(2)].

d) **Exoneration from Liability**

The operator of an installation is exonerated from any liability under this Act where a nuclear incident is directly due to an act of armed conflict, hostilities, civil war, insurrection or a grave natural disaster of an exceptional character. The liability in such cases of an operator of an installation situated in any other Contracting State is determined by the legislation of that State [Section 13(2)]. In these cases, unless otherwise provided by an international agreement concerning damage during transport to which Denmark is a Party, only a person who has intentionally caused the damage will be liable to pay compensation [Sections 16(2) and 18].

In cases where a person has contributed to the damage intentionally or through gross negligence, the operator may be relieved in whole or in part of his obligation to pay compensation to that person [Section 15].

C. AMOUNT OF LIABILITY

The aggregate liability of the operator of a nuclear installation situated in Danish territory is limited to 60 million Special Drawing Rights of the International Monetary

Fund (SDRs) for any one nuclear incident. Nevertheless, having regard to the size and type of the installation or the nature of the carriage to which liability relates and any other relevant circumstance, the Minister of Justice may fix some other maximum amount, but not less than 5 million SDRs [Section 21(1)].

With respect to installations situated in the territory of any other Contracting State, the limits of liability laid down in the legislation of that State are applicable [Section 21(1)].

These limits do not include any interest or costs [Section 21(2)].

D. NUCLEAR DAMAGE

a) Damage Covered

The liability of the operator arises under the Act in the above-described cases for any damage which arises out of or results from either radioactive properties or a combination of radioactive properties with toxic, explosive or other hazardous properties of nuclear fuel or radioactive products in a nuclear installation or of nuclear substances coming from, originating in, or sent to, a nuclear installation or any other ionizing radiation emitted by any source of radiation inside a nuclear installation [Section 1(h)].

Where non-nuclear damage is caused jointly with nuclear damage without it being possible to separate one from the other with any certainty, the non-nuclear damage is treated in the same way as the nuclear damage. Nevertheless, where nuclear damage and damage caused by an emission of ionizing radiation not covered by the Act, occur jointly, the provisions of the Act do not affect liability for such latter damage in accordance with the rules of tortious liability [Section 20].

An operator of an installation situated in Denmark is only liable for damage caused to the means of transport upon which the nuclear substances involved were at the time of the incident, insofar as the payment of compensation does not reduce compensation for other damage to a sum less than 5 million SDRs [Section 14(2)]. Where liability for such damage attaches to the operator of an installation situated in the territory of any other Contracting State, the legislation of that State shall determine whether or not this damage is covered [Section 14(2)]. If the damage is not covered, unless otherwise provided in an international agreement concerning damage during transport to which Denmark is a Party, an individual who caused the damage intentionally may be required to compensate the damage and the operator may be held liable under the rules of tortious liability [Sections 16(2) and 18].

b) Damage Excluded

Nuclear damage sustained by the installation itself or another installation, including an installation under construction, on the site where that installation is located or any property on that site which is used or is to be used in connection with that installation is excluded from the liability of the operator under the Act [Section 14(1)]. An individual who has caused the damage intentionally may, however, be required to compensate the damage [Section 16(2)].

The Minister of the Interior is empowered to exclude, wholly or in part, from the scope of application of the Act, any nuclear installation, nuclear fuel or radioactive products, if in his view this is warranted by the small extent of the risks involved [Section 2].

II. COVER AND COMPENSATION

A. INSURANCE OR OTHER FINANCIAL SECURITY

The operator of a nuclear installation situated in Denmark must have insurance to cover his liability [Section 26(1)]. In addition, he must obtain the approval of the Minister of Justice in relation to such insurance [Section 26(2)]. The Minister may approve separate insurance to cover liability resulting from nuclear damage caused in the course of transport [Section 26(2)].

The Minister of Justice is also empowered to make regulations concerning the types of insurance which an operator may have [Section 28].

In the case of termination of the insurance contract without any new insurance taking effect, the obligations of the insurer under the contract continue for two months from the date of notification by the insurer of the termination of such contract to the Minister of Justice. Where the insurance relates to the carriage of nuclear substances, the obligations of the insurer under the contract continue until the carriage has been completed [Section 27].

The obligation to insure does not extend to installations for which the State is liable [Section 29(1)].

The Minister of Justice may relieve the operator of the obligation to insure if he provides such security as the Minister considers equally adequate [Section 29(2)]. Where the security is furnished by a person other than the operator, the provisions of the Act shall apply accordingly [Section 29(3)].

In the case of the international transport of nuclear substances, the operator liable must deliver to the carrier a certificate issued by the insurer or by the person who has furnished any other financial security to cover the liability. In the absence of this certificate the carrier will not be authorised to effect the carriage in Denmark. The form of the certificate is to be prescribed by the Minister of Justice. In particular it must contain a declaration by the Ministry of the Interior or, in the case of foreign operators, the foreign competent authority certifying that the operator named in the certificate is a nuclear operator within the meaning of the Paris Convention [Section 38].

B. STATE INTERVENTION

Where it is apparent that the operator's insurance or other financial security is insufficient for the payment of compensation for damage for which he is liable, the State will provide financial assistance up to the liability ceiling of the operator in question [Section 30].

Where claims for compensation exceed the liability ceiling of the operator in question, the State will grant financial assistance on the following conditions:

i) that the incident did not occur exclusively in a State not a Party to the Brussels Supplementary Convention;

ii) that the Danish Courts have jurisdiction to hear the claim for compensation;

iii) that liability attaches to the operator of a nuclear installation for peaceful purposes situated in Denmark or in the territory of another State which is a Party to the Brussels Supplementary Convention; and

iv) that the damage was suffered in Danish territory or in that of another State which is a Party to the Brussels Supplementary Convention, or on or over the high seas on board a vessel or aircraft registered, at the time of the incident, in Denmark or in another State which is a Party to the Brussels Supplementary Convention, or on or over the high seas by a State which is a Party to the Brussels Supplementary Convention, or by any of its nationals [Section 31(1)] provided that, in the case of damage to a ship or aircraft, the ship or aircraft is registered in a Brussels State [Section 31(2)].

In the case of State intervention beyond the limits of the liability ceiling of the operator in question, the aggregate compensation payable by the operator and the State by reason of a single nuclear incident is not to exceed 120/300 million SDRs [Section 32(1)]*. This is not to include any interest or costs [Section 32(2)].

Where an action for compensation of nuclear damage may not be brought as a result of the provisions of the Act concerning prescription, the State will pay compensation for the damage on condition that there exist valid reasons to justify the fact that proceedings were not brought against the operator before his liability was extinguished. The action for compensation is nevertheless still subject to the rule that claims are barred thirty years after the date on which the nuclear incident occurred [Section 34(1)].

The Minister of Justice is empowered to direct that such compensation shall also be paid for damage suffered outside of Denmark [Section 34(2)].

Where the State intervenes on any of the above bases, it has a right of recourse against a person who has intentionally caused the damage [Section 35(1)].

C. COMPENSATION

Where a claim for compensation of nuclear damage cannot be brought against the operator owing to his death or the fact that his undertaking has ceased operations, the claim may be brought against the insurer [Section 16(1)].

Where the nuclear damage caused by a single incident for which compensation is payable under the Act exceeds the liability ceiling of the operator, the compensation and any interest accruing thereon, which is not included in the ceiling, are reduced proportion-

* Section 1(11) of Act No. 732 of 7th December 1988, in accordance with the 1982 Protocol to amend the Brussels Supplementary Convention, replaces the amount of 120 million SDRs with the amount of 300 million SDRs. This amendment is not yet in force. The Act specifies that it is to come into force on a day to be decided by the Minister of Justice, thus allowing its coming into force to be co-ordinated with the coming into force of the Protocol [Section 2 of Act No. 732 of 7th December 1988].

ally. Such a reduction is subject to the requirement, mentioned above, that any compensation for damage to the means of transport of nuclear substances in carriage is not to reduce the compensation available for other damage below 5 million SDRs [Section 23(1)]. Where, as a result of an incident, there is reason to believe that such a reduction will be necessary, the Minister of Justice may direct that, for the time being, only a specified proportion of the compensation shall be paid [Section 23(2)]. Similar reductions may be applied when compensation is to be paid from public funds, under the Brussels Supplementary Convention [Section 32(3)].

D. TIME LIMITS FOR BRINGING CLAIMS

Claims for compensation are subject to the Statute of Limitation Act of 22nd August 1908, with the period of limitation being set at three years [Section 25(1)]. As regards actions brought against the operator by a party entitled by subrogation to the rights of persons injured by nuclear damage, such period of limitation commences to run from the time when that party would normally have been able to institute legal proceedings against the operator [Section 25(1)].

Where a claim for compensation is not so barred, the claim is extinguished at the end of a period of ten years from the date of the nuclear incident which caused the damage, unless before such date, the damage is acknowledged by the operator or legal proceedings have already been commenced by the person injured in relation to his claim [Section 25(2)].

However, where the substances causing the damage had been stolen, lost or abandoned and not recovered at the time of the incident, the period of limitation for actions for compensation shall in no case exceed twenty years from the date of the theft, loss of abandonment [Section 25(2)].

Where, pursuant to its powers under Article 17 of the Paris Convention, the European Nuclear Energy Tribunal is to decide whether an action is to be brought in Denmark or in another Contracting State, the above limitation periods shall not operate if, before limitation has become effective under the legislation of the Contracting State concerned, a request has been made to initiate a decision of the Tribunal or, provided no such decision has been taken, an action is brought in any of the States where this may be done under the Paris Convention. In such cases, the limitation period applicable shall be that determined by the Tribunal [Section 25(3)].

E. COMPETENT COURTS AND PROCEDURE

In order for the Danish courts to have jurisdiction to hear an action against the operator of a nuclear installation in a Contracting State, either the incident causing the damage must have occurred wholly or in part in Denmark, or the claim must be made against the operator of an installation situated in Denmark in cases where the incident occurred outside the territory of any Contracting Party or in an undetermined place [Section 36(1)].

Nevertheless, where the European Nuclear Energy Tribunal decides, pursuant to the Paris Convention, that an action is to be brought in another Contracting State, jurisdiction over that action no longer lies with Danish courts [Section 36(2)].

The particular Danish court having jurisdiction is determined, not by the Act, but by the general rules of civil procedure. Under these rules, an action against an operator can be brought in the jurisdiction where the main office of the operator is located [Procedural Act – No. 567 of 1st September 1986 – Section 238], where the incident occurred or where the damage was suffered [Section 243]. In addition, the parties to an action may agree to the case being brought before a court which would not otherwise be competent under the law [Section 245] and several plaintiffs may sue the defendant in one action before a court which has jurisdiction for at least one of the claims [Section 250]. Cases are heard in the first instance by the relevant city court, unless the claim is for 500 000 Danish kroner or more and one of the Parties demands that the case is tried by the High Court as the court of first instance [Section 227 as amended by Act No. 273 of 3rd May 1989].

According to the 1974 Act on Compensation for Nuclear Damage any judgment, other than an interim judgment, of a Court of a Contracting State concerning compensation for nuclear damage under the Paris Convention is enforceable in Denmark. The application for enforcement must be accompanied by a certified copy of the judgment and a declaration by the competent authority of the State concerned certifying that the judgment concerns a claim for compensation for damage covered by the Paris Convention and that it is enforceable under the legislation of that State [Section 37].

FINLAND

INTRODUCTION

There are four nuclear power plants supplying electricity in Finland as of 1990, with a total electricity capacity of 2 300 MWe. These plants are operated by a national electric power company "IVO" (*Imatran Voima Oy*) and a private electric power company "TVO" (*Teollisuuden Voima Oy*). Approximately 30 per cent of Finland's electricity production is nuclear.

The Minister of Trade and Industry and the Minister of Social Affairs and Public Health are responsible for nuclear third party liability questions.

Finland is a Party to the Paris Convention and the Brussels Supplementary Convention as amended by the 1982 Protocols. It is also a Signatory of the 1971 Brussels Convention relating to Civil Liability in the Field of Maritime Carriage of Nuclear Material. In addition, Finland has signed the Joint Protocol relating to the Application of the Vienna Convention and the Paris Convention.

The basic legislation on nuclear third party liability in Finland is contained in the Nuclear Liability Act of 8th June 1972 (published in the Official Gazette, 27th June 1972, No. 484/72, p. 1153). This legislation was amended by an Act of 7th January 1977 (published in the Official Gazette, 3rd February 1977, No. 128/77, p. 225), an Act of 23rd May 1986 (published in the Official Gazette, 30th May 1986, No. 388/86, p. 901) which implemented the Montreal Protocol No. 4 to the Warsaw Convention concerning Carriage by Air, and an Act of 15th September 1989 (published in the Official Gazette, 22nd September 1989, No. 820/89, p. 1458) which implemented the 1982 Protocols to the Paris Convention and the Brussels Supplementary Convention and raised the limit of the nuclear operator's liability to 100 million Special Drawing Rights of the International Monetary Fund (SDRs). This latter amendment came into force on 1st January 1990, except for those provisions implementing the 1982 Protocol to the Brussels Supplementary Convention which will come into force when the Protocol itself comes into force. (The text of this Act as amended has been reproduced in the Supplement to Nuclear Law Bulletin No. 44.)

I. THIRD PARTY LIABILITY

A. SCOPE AND DEFINITIONS

As a general rule, the Act does not apply to nuclear damage resulting from nuclear incidents occurring in the territory of a non-Contracting State to the Paris Convention [Section 4(1)].

Conversely, the Act does apply to nuclear damage suffered in the territory of a non-Contracting State if the incident causing the damage occurred in Finland and liability lies with the operator of an installation situated in Finland [Section 4(2)]. However, the Government may determine that compensation for nuclear damage suffered in the territory of a non-Contracting State is to be payable only to the extent that compensation for nuclear damage suffered in Finland would also be payable under the law of that State [Section 4(3)].

Having due regard to Finland's obligation under the Paris Convention, the Government may decide that, on the basis of reciprocity, a non-Contracting State to the Paris Convention is to be treated as a Contracting State to the Paris Convention for the purposes of the Act [Section 5].

The terms *nuclear installation, operator, radioactive products, nuclear substances* and *nuclear incident* are used in the same sense as in the Paris Convention.

The Government is empowered to determine that two or more nuclear installations operated by one and the same operator and located on the same site in Finland are deemed to be a single nuclear installation for the purposes of the Act [Section 3].

B. NATURE AND ASSIGNMENT OF LIABILITY

a) General – Nuclear Installations

The operator of a nuclear installation is liable to pay compensation for nuclear damage caused by a nuclear incident in his installation. The liability of the operator is subject to certain exceptions in the case of nuclear substances stored temporarily in his installation in the course of carriage (see below under "Transport") [Section 6].

The operator of a nuclear installation is liable even if there is no fault or negligence on his part [Section 12(1)].

Furthermore, claims for compensation for nuclear damage covered by the provisions of the Act, or by the corresponding legislation of another Contracting State to the Paris Convention, may not be brought against any person other than the operator or the person providing insurance covering the liability of the operator [Section 15(1)].

However, claims for compensation for which the operator is exonerated by the Act or the corresponding provisions of the law of another Contracting State to the Paris Convention can be brought against an individual who has caused the damage by an act or omission done with intent to cause damage [Section 15(2)].

Where nuclear damage gives rise to the liablity of two or more operators, they are jointly and severally liable to pay compensation; provided that the liability of each operator is limited to the liability ceiling applicable to him [Section 19(1)].

b) Transport

An operator whose installation is situated in Finland or in the territory of another Contracting State to the Paris Convention is liable to pay compensation for nuclear damage caused by a nuclear incident occurring in the course of carriage of nuclear substances from his installation [Section 7(1)]. However, the consignee operator is liable from any time fixed by a written contract between him and the consignor or, in the absence of such contract, when the nuclear substances are taken in charge by him [Section 7(1)].

In the case of carriage of nuclear substances from a non-Contracting State to the Paris Convention to a nuclear installation situated in Finland or in the territory of another Contracting State to the Paris Convention, the operator of the latter installation is liable [Section 8(1)].

In the case of carriage of nuclear substances from a nuclear reactor, with which a ship or any other means of transport is equipped as a source of power, to a nuclear installation situated in Finland or in the territory of another Contracting State to the Paris Convention, the operator of that installation is liable from the time when the nuclear substances are taken in charge by him [Section 8(2)]. In the converse circumstances, the consignor operator of the installation is liable until the time when the nuclear substances are taken in charge by the person duly authorised to operate or be in charge of the reactor [Section 7(3)].

In the case of damage caused by nuclear substances in transit through Finland and which are not being transported to or from another Contracting State to the Paris Convention, the person authorised to perform such carriage is liable [Section 8(3)].

The foregoing provisions also apply to a nuclear incident occurring while nuclear substances are stored incidentally to carriage, unless the operator, under a contract in writing, accepts liability for nuclear damage which may occur during such storage in his installation [Section 9].

Where nuclear substances outside an installation but not in the course of carriage cause damage, liability attaches to the operator who at the time of the incident had the substances in his charge or, if the substances were not in the charge of any operator, the operator who last had them in his charge before the incident. However, if by written agreement an operator has assumed liability for such damage, he is to be liable in accordance with such agreement [Section 10].

Where damage has arisen in the course of carriage of more than one consignment of nuclear substances carried on one and the same means of transport, or while more than one consignment has been stored in one and the same nuclear installation incidental to its carriage, the aggregate liability of the operators is not to exceed the highest amount established with respect to any of them [Section 19(1)]. The apportionment of the aggregate liability between the operators is to be determined in a reasonable manner taking into account the proportions in which the damage is attributable to each of the involved nuclear installations as well as any other relevant circumstances [Section 19(2)].

The Government may determine, on the request of a carrier of nuclear substances and with the consent of the operator concerned, that the carrier is to be liable, in place of the operator of a nuclear installation situated in Finland, for nuclear damage caused by a nuclear incident occurring in the course of or in connection with the carriage [Section 11(1)].

c) Rights of Recourse

Any person, who has been held liable to pay compensation for nuclear damage under the Air Transport Act, or the law of any foreign State, or an international transport agreement in force, open for signature, ratification or accession on 29th July 1960 (date of adoption of the Paris Convention), acquires, by subrogation, the rights of the person suffering damage against the operator liable for the damage under the Act. If such rights have been reduced or annulled by a decision of the Government that compensation for nuclear damage suffered in that territory shall be payable under the Act only to the extent that compensation for nuclear damage suffered in Finland would be payable under the law of that State [Section 4(3)], the person who has been held liable to pay the compensation is to have a right of recourse against the operator who would have been liable for the damage if no such decision had been taken [Section 16(1)].

Such a person also has a right of recourse against the State in respect of compensation paid for damage for which additional compensation is payable out of public funds under Section 30 of the Act [Section 31(2)].

In addition, any person who has his principal place of business in Finland or in the territory of another Contracting State to the Paris Convention and who has been held liable to pay compensation for nuclear damage for which the person suffering damage, by virtue of the provisions limiting the territorial scope of the Act, has no right to compensation under the Act, has a right of recourse against the operator who, but for the provisions limiting the territorial scope of the Act, would have been liable for the damage. However, this does not apply with respect to damage caused by a nuclear incident occurring, in the case of carriage of nuclear substances to a non-Contracting State, after the substances have been unloaded from the means of transport, or, in the case of carriage of nuclear substances from a non-Contracting State, until the substances have been loaded on to the means of transport [Section 16(2)].

An operator, who has paid compensation under the Act or the corresponding legislation of another Contracting State to the Paris Convention, has a right of recourse against any individual who has caused the damage by an act or omission done with intent to cause damage and against any person who has assumed liability for the damage under the express terms of a contract in writing with the operator [Section 21].

Where the State has stepped in to provide compensation due to the default of the operator or his insurer [Section 29], the State has a right of recourse against the operator, his insurer, and any person against whom the operator would have had such a right under the above provision [Section 36(1)].

Where the State has stepped in to provide additional compensation because the damage exceeds the maximum liability of the operator [Sections 30 and 34], the State acquires by subrogation any right to obtain compensation from the operator that the person suffering the damage would have had [Section 36(2)].

d) Exoneration from Liability

The operator of a nuclear installation situated in Finland is not liable under the Act for nuclear damage caused by a nuclear incident directly due to an act of war, armed conflict, civil war or insurrection, or caused by a grave natural disaster of an exceptional character [Section 12(2)].

This exclusion also applies to compensation paid by the State [Section 35].

Where the person suffering damage has contributed thereto by wilful act or omission or gross negligence, the compensation payable may be reduced [Section 14(2)].

C. AMOUNT OF LIABILITY

The liability of an operator of a nuclear installation situated in Finland is not to exceed 100 million SDRs in respect of nuclear damage caused by any one nuclear incident. The Government may, taking into account the size or character of a nuclear installation, the extent of carriage or any other circumstances, fix a lower amount of no less than five million SDRs. In the case of a nuclear incident occurring in the course of carriage of nuclear substances, the liability of the operator for damage other than damage to the means of transport is not to be limited to an amount less than five million SDRs [Section 18(1)].

D. NUCLEAR DAMAGE

a) Damage Covered

The Act defines *nuclear damage* as:

- any damage caused by the radioactive properties of nuclear fuel or radioactive products or a combination of radioactive properties with toxic, explosive or other hazardous properties of such fuel or products;
- any damage caused by ionizing radiation emitted from any source of radiation inside a nuclear installation other than nuclear fuel or radioacive products [Section 1].

The right to compensation for nuclear damage extends to other damage insofar as such damage cannot reasonably be separated from the nuclear damage [Section 17(1)].

b) Damage Excluded

The Government is empowered to exclude any nuclear installation, nuclear fuel or radioactive products from the application of the Act, if the small extent of the risks involved so warrants [Section 2]. By Council of State Decision of 22nd June 1978, certain kinds and small quantities of nuclear substances, which are excluded from the Paris Convention in accordance with the Decisions of 27th October 1977 of the OECD Steering Committee for Nuclear Energy, were excluded from the coverage of the Act.

The operator of a nuclear installation is not liable under the Act for damage to the nuclear installation itself or to another nuclear installation, completed or under construction, on the same site or to any property which, at the time of the nuclear incident, is on the site of the installation referred to above and is used or intended to be used in connection with such installation [Section 13(1)].

II. COVER AND COMPENSATION

A. INSURANCE OR OTHER FINANCIAL SECURITY

The operator of a nuclear installation situated in Finland is required to take out and maintain insurance to cover his liability for nuclear damage under the Act or the corresponding legislation of another Contracting State to the Paris Convention, up to the amount of liability established with respect to him. The insurance is to be approved by the Ministry for Social Affairs and Public Health [Section 23(1)].

Liability for damage arising in the course of carriage of nuclear substances may be covered by a separate insurance [Section 23(3)].

Insurance may be taken out either to cover the maximum liability of the operator for each nuclear incident that may occur or to cover at any time the nuclear installation by an amount exceeding the maximum amount of liability of the operator by not less than one-fifth [Sections 23(2) and 24(1)].

Where insurance has been taken out on the latter basis and an insurance contingency occurs which itself or together with one or more earlier contingencies is likely to entail a reduction of the insurance amount below the maximum amount of liability of the operator, the operator must without delay take out such supplementary insurance as will bring the insurance amount back up to an amount exceeding the maximum amount of his liability by not less than one-fifth [Section 24(2)].

The insurance policy taken out by the operator must enable any person entitled to compensation for nuclear damage to bring an action for such compensation directly against the insurer [Section 25].

If the insurance policy is cancelled or otherwise ceases to be valid, the insurer is nevertheless required to honour the policy in respect of nuclear damage caused by a nuclear incident occurring within two months from the date on which the Ministry of Trade and Industry had been notified in writing of the time of expiry of the policy. Moreover, where an insurance policy covers liability for nuclear damage caused by a nuclear incident occurring in the course of carriage of nuclear substances and such carriage has started before the expiry of the policy, the insurer is required to honour the policy in respect of damage caused by a nuclear incident at any stage in the carriage [Section 26(1)].

The provisions concerning the right to bring an action for compensation and the duration of the insurance mentioned above apply where the action for compensation may, under the Act, be brought in Finland, notwithstanding the fact that the law of a foreign State may be applicable to the relationship between the insurer and the liable operator or that the involved nuclear installation is situated outside Finland [Section 27].

The Government is empowered to relieve an operator from the obligation to take out insurance, provided that the operator furnishes adequate financial security to cover his obligations under the Act and the corresponding legislation of any other Contracting State to the Paris Convention and shows that he has taken satisfactory measures to ensure the settlement of any claims for compensation [Section 28(2)].

The State is exempted from the obligation to take out insurance [Section 28(1)].

B. STATE INTERVENTION

a) State Guarantee

If a person who is entitled under the Act or the corresponding legislation of another Contracting State to the Paris Convention to obtain compensation for nuclear damage from the operator of a nuclear installation situated in Finland shows that he has been unable to recover the compensation due from the operator's insurer, compensation is to be paid by the State [Section 29(1)].

This compensation is not, however, to exceed the maximum amount of the relevant operator's liability [Section 29(2)].

If a nuclear incident, in respect of which liability lies with the operator of a nuclear installation situated in Finland, has caused nuclear damage by way of personal injury in Finland which has not come to light until after the rights of compensation against the operator have been extinguished by virtue of the time limits set by the Act or the corresponding provisions of the legislation of another Contracting State to the Paris Convention but within thirty years after the date of the incident, compensation for such damage is to be paid by the State. The State is also to be liable to pay compensation for nuclear damage for which, although it has come to light before the rights of compensation have been extinguished, the person suffering the damage has failed to bring an action against the operator or to take other appropriate measures to preserve his rights within the applicable periods, if that person had a reasonable excuse for not bringing such action or taking such measures [Section 33].

The Government is also empowered to decide that such compensation will be payable in respect of damage occurring outside of Finland for which an operator of an installation situated in Finland is liable [Section 33(3)].

b) Supplementary Payments

Where:

- liability for nuclear damage lies with the operator of a nuclear installation used for peaceful purposes which is situated in Finland or in the territory of another State Party to the Brussels Supplementary Convention and appears at the time of the nuclear incident on the list referred to in Article 13 of the Brussels Supplementary Convention;
- jurisdiction over actions for compensation lies with Finnish courts; and
- the maximum amount of liability established with respect to the operator is insufficient to satisfy the claims for compensation,

compensation is to be paid out of public funds up to a total, including that payable by the liable operator, of 300 million SDRs [Section 32] (120 million SDRs until the 1982 Protocol amending the Brussels Supplementary Convention enters into force [Section 43]). It is to be afforded for nuclear damage suffered:

- in Finland or in the territory of another State Party to the Brussels Supplementary Convention; or
- on or over the high seas on board a ship or aircraft registered in Finland or in the territory of another State Party to the Brussels Supplementary Convention; or
- in any other case on or over the high seas by a State Party to the Brussels Supplementary Convention or by a national of such State; provided, however, that compensation is to be payable for damage to a ship or an aircraft only if it was, at the time of the nuclear incident, registered in the territory of a State Party to the Brussels Supplementary Convention [Section 30(1)].

If the maximum amount of liability established with respect to the operator is insufficient to satisfy the claims for compensation with respect to damage suffered in Finland and additional compensation is not payable pursuant to the above provision, additional compensation is to be paid according to criteria confirmed by the State Council, subject to the consent of Parliament [Section 34(1)].

C. COMPENSATION

If the maximum amount of liability established with respect to the operator is not sufficient to satisfy in full the claims of those who are entitled to compensation, their compensation and any interest accruing thereto is to be reduced proportionally [Section 20(1)]. The same is to apply when compensation is awarded out of public funds [Section 32(2)]. If, following a nuclear incident, there are reasons to believe that such reduction will prove necessary, the Ministry for Social Affairs and Public Health is empowered to decide that the payable compensation is to be reduced to a fixed percentage until further notice [Section 20(2)].

D. TIME LIMITS FOR BRINGING CLAIMS

The right to bring an action for compensation under the Act is extinguished if a claim for compensation has not been made within three years from the date on which the person suffering damage had knowledge or, by observing due diligence, ought reasonably to have known both of the fact that he has suffered damage entitling him to compensation under the Act and of the identify of the liable operator [Section 22(1)].

In any event, the right to compensation is extinguished if an action is not brought against the operator or his insurer within ten years from the date of the nuclear incident [Section 22(2)] or in the case of nuclear damage caused by a nuclear incident involving nuclear substances which have been stolen, lost or abandoned and have not yet been recovered, twenty years after the date of the theft, loss or abandonment [Section 22(2)].

E. COMPETENT COURTS AND PROCEDURE

Finnish courts have jurisdiction over actions for compensation against the operator of a nuclear installation or his insurer if:

- the nuclear incident has occurred wholly or partly in Finland; or

– the relevant nuclear installation is situated in Finland, and either the nuclear incident has occurred wholly outside the territory of any Contracting State to the Paris Convention, or the place of the nuclear incident cannot be determined with certainty [Section 37(1)].

Such actions and actions for compensation against the Finnish State lie with the general court of first instance of the jurisdictional area within which the nuclear incident occurred [Section 38(1)].

If there is no competent court under the preceding paragraph, the action lies with the City Court of Helsinki [Section 38(2)].

FRANCE

INTRODUCTION

In 1990, France had 53 reactors, with a nuclear power capacity of some 55 200 MWe. The main nuclear operators are *Electricité de France* (EDF), *Société Nersa, Société d'énergie nucléaire franco-belge des Ardennes* (SENA), Cogema and the Atomic Energy Commission (*Commissariat à l'énergie atomique* – CEA). The main supervisory authorities in the field of nuclear energy are the Ministry for Industry and Regional Development and the Ministry for Research and Technology.

France is Party to the Paris Convention and the Brussels Supplementary Convention, as amended in 1982. It has also signed the Joint Protocol relating to the Application of the Vienna Convention and the Paris Convention. In addition, it has ratified the Brussels Convention of 17th December 1971 relating to Civil Liability in the Field of Maritime Carriage of Nuclear Material.

The provisions regulating liability for nuclear damage are contained in the Act of 30th October 1968 on third party liability in the field of nuclear energy (published in the Official Gazette of the French Republic – *Journal officiel de la République française* – JORF of 31st October 1968). This Act has been amended by Act No. 90-488 of 16th June 1990 (published in the JORF of 17th June 1990), in particular, to take into account the ratification by France of the Protocols adopted in 1982.

The present Act was drafted in such a way as to fit into the legal framework established by the Paris Convention and the Brussels Supplementary Convention, its main purpose therefore being to enact the provisions which, under these Conventions, are left to the initiative of the Contracting Parties. Moreover, it is to be completed by implementing decrees.

In the field of third party liability for nuclear damage, note should also be made of the Decree of 15th March 1973 (published in the JORF of 22nd March 1973), which deals with the insurance and reinsurance by the Central Reinsurance Fund (*Caisse Centrale de Réassurance*) of nuclear risks and other risks of an exceptional nature, and the Decree of 20th September 1983 (published in the JORF of 24th September 1983), which amends the provisions of the Insurance Code relating to the Central Reinsurance Fund.

I. THIRD PARTY LIABILITY

A. SCOPE AND DEFINITIONS

Given that the Act of 30th October 1968 on third party liability in the field of nuclear energy, as amended, ("the Act") does not contain any specific provisions on those aspects which are already sufficiently clear under the Paris Convention, its scope is determined by the relevant provisions of that Convention, as specified by the OECD Steering Committee for Nuclear Energy in its Recommendation of 25th April 1968. In accordance with this Recommendation, the Act applies to nuclear incidents on the high seas and to damage occurring on the high seas. It does not, on the other hand, apply to nuclear incidents occurring on the territory of States which are not parties to the Paris Convention, or to damage suffered on such territory.

The Act (Section 20) specifies that its provisions are applicable to the Overseas Territories (Wallis and Futuna, French Polynesia, New Caledonia and French Southern and Antarctic Territories) and to the Territorial Commune of Mayotte.

The definitions of the terms *nuclear incident, nuclear installation, nuclear fuel, radioactive products or waste, nuclear substances* and *operator* must be understood as being the same as those of the Paris Convention. In accordance with the Decisions of 27th October 1977 of the OECD Steering Committee for Nuclear Energy, published by Decree No. 79-623 of 13th July 1979, certain categories of nuclear substances as well as certain small quantities of nuclear substances are excluded from the scope of the Act.

B. NATURE AND ASSIGNMENT OF LIABILITY

a) General – Nuclear Installations

Section 2 specifies that the provisions of the Act apply to public or private natural or legal persons operating a civil or military nuclear installation to which the Paris Convention applies. The installations in question are also listed in Section 2 of Decree No. 63-1228 of 11th December 1963 concerning nuclear installations, as amended by Decrees in 1973 and 1990. They are:

- nuclear reactors, with the exception of those comprised in a means of transport;
- particle accelerators, the characteristics of which are specified by joint Order of the Minister of Education, the Minister for Industrial and Scientific Development and the Minister for Public Health;
- plants for the preparation, manufacture or processing of radioactive substances, i.e. all natural or artificial substances emitting radiation which is directly or indirectly ionizing, including: plants for the manufacture of nuclear fuels, isotopic separation of nuclear fuels, reprocessing of irradiated nuclear fuels or processing of radioactive waste;
- facilities for the storage, deposit or use of radioactive substances, including waste, and notably those substances intended for irradiation.

As regards the latter two categories of installation, the thresholds for quantities of substances held and for activity above which such plants or installations are considered as large nuclear installations are fixed by Ministerial Decrees of 6th December 1966 and 23rd January 1967.

As allowed by Article 1(a)(ii) of the Paris Convention, several nuclear installations, or a nuclear installation and any other installation in which radioactive materials are held, are, if they have the same operator and are on the same site, considered for the purposes of the Act as a single nuclear installation [Section 2, paragraph 2].

b) Transport

As regards the rules for liability during transport, the Act does not add to the relevant provisions of the Paris Convention. The operator of a nuclear installation is therefore liable for all damage caused by a nuclear incident outside the installation and involving nuclear substances in the course of carriage therefrom, provided no other operator has assumed liability, or in the course of carriage thereto, after liability has been transferred to him by another operator. The operator must give the carrier a certificate of financial security issued by the insurer or guarantor.

In accordance with Article 4(d) of the Paris Convention, it is provided that a carrier of nuclear substances may apply to be substituted for the operator liable, with the agreement of such operator, provided he meets the requirements relating to financial security, in accordance with the procedure to be laid down by Decree [Section 2].

In the case of the carriage of nuclear substances between France and a country in which the Brussels Supplementary Convention does not apply, the operator of the nuclear installation in France is held liable for nuclear incidents in the course of carriage on French territory, whether he is sending or receiving the substances involved [Section 9, paragraph 1]. In this way, even in the case of an incident for which another operator in a country in which the Paris Convention alone applies could otherwise be liable, victims in the territory of a country Party to the Brussels Supplementary Convention can benefit from the additional funds provided for under the Supplementary Convention. As soon as the Joint Protocol relating to the application of the Vienna Convention and the Paris Convention enters into force in France, the same protection will apply to victims of an incident occurring in French territory in the course of carriage between France and a Contracting Party to the Vienna Convention which has ratified the Joint Protocol.

c) Rights of Recourse

The nuclear operator enjoys the rights of recourse accorded him under the Paris Convention, i.e. in cases of wilful damage or express contractual stipulation. In addition, the Act recognises the principle of direct action against the insurer or financial guarantor [Section 14].

Where the victims of nuclear damage are indemnified directly by the insurer or person who has provided financial security, these latter may exercise the right to recourse given to the nuclear operator by the Paris Convention. In such circumstances, priority is given to the repayment of any amounts provided by the State [Section 14] (see under "State Intervention" below).

d) Exoneration from Liability

In accordance with the provisions of the Paris Convention, the nuclear operator cannot be held liable for damage caused by a nuclear incident resulting from acts of armed conflict, hostilities, insurrection or civil war, or a grave natural disaster of an exceptional character.

C. AMOUNT OF LIABILITY

The maximum liability of the operator is fixed at FF 600 million (approximately 80 million SDRs) per nuclear incident. This amount may be reduced to FF 150 million per nuclear incident when the installations operated on a given site present a reduced risk only. The characteristics of installations for which an operator may benefit from a reduction in his liability amount remain still to be defined by decree, to be adopted after the opinion of the Interministerial Committee on Large Nuclear Installations has been made public [Section 4].

For the transport of nuclear substances, the maximum liability of the operator is FF 150 million per nuclear incident [Section 9]. Before carrying nuclear substances in transit through French territory, the carrier must, if the transport operation is regulated by the Paris Convention, prove that he is insured for the same amount, or has an equivalent security, covering any damage which could be caused by a nuclear incident in the course of carriage. Over and above FF 150 million, the State will pay compensation in accordance with the Brussels Supplementary Convention. However, if the transport operation is not regulated by the Paris Convention, the carrier is obliged to prove the existence of a guarantee equivalent to FF 1 500 million [Section 9, paragraph 2], which corresponds approximately to the compensation ceiling of the first tier of the Brussels Supplementary Convention [Article 3(b)(ii)]. Thus, victims of a nuclear incident occurring in course of carriage will benefit from the amounts provided for under the first two tiers of the Brussels Supplementary Convention, whether or not the transport operation was regulated by these Conventions.

Furthermore, compensation will be paid by the State, up to a maximum of FF 2 500 million per incident, to the victims of damage caused by incidents in installations used for purposes other than peaceful ones, where such victims would have been entitled to invoke the Brussels Supplementary Convention had the installation been one used for peaceful purposes [Section 5]. Thus, account is taken of the increase in the amount of compensation, which will be applicable as soon as the 1982 Protocol to amend the Brussels Supplementary Convention enters into force.

D. NUCLEAR DAMAGE

a) Damage Covered

Damage giving rise to liability on the part of the nuclear operator, for the purposes of the Act, is that set out in the Paris Convention, i.e. damage resulting from the radioactive properties, or from a combination of radioactive properties and toxic, explosive or other dangerous properties, of nuclear fuels, radioactive substances or radioactive waste. The Act also covers damage due to ionizing radiation emitted by any source of radiation within a nuclear installation and damage caused to any means of transport carrying nuclear substances at the time the incident occurs.

In French law, the concept of damage covers, in addition to expenses relating to personal injury as such (medical expenses, hospital expenses, disability payments, pensions paid to the heirs of persons killed), the cost of evacuating and lodging the local population and any resulting loss of salary, loss of production caused by contamination, clean-up costs, notably those involved in decontaminating property in the short or medium term, and loss of income suffered by any neighbouring enterprises obliged to interrupt their activities.

b) Damage Excluded

In accordance with the Paris Convention, the operator of a nuclear installation is not liable for any damage caused to the nuclear installation itself or to any other nuclear installation, even under construction, on the same site, or for damage to property on this site, which is used or to be used in connection with any such installation.

II. COVER AND COMPENSATION

A. INSURANCE OR OTHER FINANCIAL SECURITY

The nuclear operator is required to provide and maintain insurance or other financial security in order to cover his liability under the Act. Any such financial security must be approved by the Minister for Economic Affairs and Finance [Section 7, paragraph 1].

Upon the proposal of the Minister responsible for atomic energy, the Minister for Economic Affairs and Finance may provide a complete or partial State guarantee for operators of nuclear installations, which thus takes the place of the insurance or other financial security [Section 7, paragraph 2]. The Central Reinsurance Fund is empowered, with State guarantee, to cover the risks for which operators of nuclear installations are liable [Decree No. 73-322 of 15th March 1973 relating to the insurance and reinsurance by the Central Reinsurance Fund of nuclear risks and other risks of an exceptional nature].

Insurers and guarantors are required to give two months' written notice to the Minister responsible for atomic energy before suspending or terminating the insurance [Section 7, paragraph 3].

As regards international transport operations, the carrier is required to prove the existence of financial security by means of a certificate issued by the insurer or any other person providing an equivalent financial guarantee. When the transport operation falls within the scope of the Paris Convention, the certificate must be established in accordance with Article 4(c) of the Convention. For international transport operations not covered by the Paris Convention, the certificate must specify the name and address of the insurer or guarantor, the amount, type and duration of the security as well as the nuclear substances and the itinerary involved [Section 9(3), paragraphs 1 and 2]. Model certificates are established by joint Order of the Minister responsible for atomic energy and the Minister of Transport [Section 9(3), paragraph 3].

All operators and carriers must, within three months of the entry into force of the present Act, be able to prove that their liability is covered in the circumstances prescribed by the Act [Section 15 of Act No. 90-488 amending Act No. 68-943 of 30th October 1968 on third party liability in the field of nuclear energy]. Any breach of the provisions relating to the constitution and maintenance of the financial security by operators or to the production of the required transport certificate, gives rise to administrative and criminal penalties [Section 18]. In particular, if the official records show that the operator or carrier is unable to prove the existence of insurance or the required financial security, the competent administrative authority may suspend the operation of the installation or the performance of the transport operation until production of the required proof. If the transport operation is suspended, any measures required to ensure the safety of persons and property may be taken at the expense of the operator [Section 18.II].

B. STATE INTERVENTION

The State may intervene in a subsidiary or complementary capacity in the compensation of nuclear damage. Moreover, it is responsible for the payment of compensation when it is itself the operator of the installation in question.

In the event of the victims of a nuclear incident being unable to recover compensation because of the failure to pay of the financial guarantor, insurer or operator, the State, in a subsidiary capacity, pays compensation up to the limits established by the Act [Section 8]. In such a case, the State has the rights of recourse to which the operator is entitled under the Conventions and has priority in recovering such sums as it may have disbursed [Section 14, paragraph 1].

In addition, compensation in excess of the operator's liability is paid by the State out of public funds and under the conditions and within the limits specified in the Brussels Supplementary Convention i.e. 300 million Special Drawing Rights (SDRs) when the 1982 Protocol enters into force [Section 5].

Lastly, after expiry of the ten-year time limit, and during a further five years, the State intervenes to compensate damage in respect of which the right to compensation from the operator liable has been extinguished [Section 15, paragraph 2] (see under "Time Limits for Bringing Claims" below).

C. COMPENSATION

The provisions for the payment of compensation to victims of nuclear incidents do not affect the rules established by the legislation on social insurance and compensation for industrial accidents and occupational diseases [Section 16, paragraph 1].

Where the victim was employed by the operator at the time of the nuclear incident and has received compensation for an industrial injury or occupational disease, and such incident was caused by a person other than the operator or his agents, the victim and the organisation having paid the social benefits may, in accordance with the principle of channelling of liability, exercise against the operator the rights of recourse they have against the person who caused the incident [Section 16, paragraph 3].

Where the victim was not employed by the operator and has not received compensation for an industrial injury or occupational disease, rights of recourse may be exercised against the operator, or even directly against his insurer or the person having provided financial security [Sections 14 and 16].

Because of its financial obligations in this field, the State, in the person of the law agent to the Treasury, must be informed by nuclear operators of all claims for compensation [Section 6].

When the maximum sums available under the Act appear insufficient to compensate for the whole of the damage suffered as a result of a nuclear incident, a decree made in Council of Ministers and published within six months of the day when the incident occurred, is to lay down the conditions of allocation of the amounts available [Section 13, paragraph 1], and may subject the population to control measures for the purpose of identifying the victims. The rules for calculating the compensation payable to each victim may also be laid down in this decree, in the light of the insufficiency of the sums available and of the priorities established in the present Act [Section 13, paragraph 2]. The rules specify that priority is to be given to the payment of compensation for bodily injury on terms similar to those laid down by the legislation on industrial accidents, the balance remaining being shared among the victims in proportion to any uncompensated bodily injury and any damage to property, evaluated in accordance with the rules of the ordinary law [Section 13, paragraph 3].

As regards bodily injury, a decree issued after a report by the Minister responsible for atomic energy and the Minister for Social Affairs is to establish, having regard to the amounts of irradiation and contamination received, a non-restrictive list of the disorders which will be presumed to have been caused by the nuclear incident in question [Section 10].

No repayment of compensation paid to victims, whether on a provisional or final basis, may be claimed on the grounds of the limits of liability provided for in the Act [Section 11].

D. TIME LIMITS FOR BRINGING CLAIMS

As regards the period of time within which actions for compensation must be commenced, French law distinguishes between damage which becomes apparent within a normal time and deferred damage.

Actions for compensation must be brought within three years from the date when the victim knew or should reasonably have known of the damage and of the identity of the operator liable, but can in no event be brought later than ten years from the date of the incident [Section 15, paragraph 1].

However, when the incident has occurred on French territory and a French Court has jurisdiction under the Paris Convention, the State will pay compensation, within the limits of the Act, for damage which only became apparent more than ten years from the date of the incident and in respect of which no claim for compensation can therefore be made. In this event, proceedings against the State for such compensation must be commenced within a maximum period of five years after the expiry of the initial ten-year period [Section 15, paragraph 2].

These specific provisions exclude the application of the special rules concerning the prescription of claims against the State, *départements*, communes, and public bodies [Section 19].

E. COMPETENT COURTS AND PROCEDURE

The Act provides for a single court – the *Tribunal de grande instance de Paris* – as being the only one competent to hear actions brought in respect of incidents occurring on French territory when, under the Paris Convention, jurisdiction is granted to a French court. However, emergency measures may be taken by the public prosecutor (*Procureur de la République*) or the examining magistrate (*juge d'instruction*) of the court within whose jurisdiction the nuclear incident occurred. Proceedings are subsequently transferred to the competent court. In no case may a criminal court in which proceedings have been instituted entertain a civil claim [Section 17].

FEDERAL REPUBLIC OF GERMANY

INTRODUCTION

The Federal Republic of Germany has an important nuclear research and power programme. At present, 23 nuclear power plants are in operation with a total capacity of 22 635 MWe, representing approximately 34 per cent of the country's electricity production.

The Federal Republic of Germany is a Party to the Paris Convention and to the Brussels Supplementary Convention and is also a Party to the 1971 Brussels Convention relating to Civil Liability in the Field of Maritime Carriage of Nuclear Material. It has furthermore signed the 1962 Convention on the Liability of Operators of Nuclear Ships as well as the Joint Protocol relating to the Application of the Vienna Convention and the Paris Convention.

The legislation on nuclear third party liability in the Federal Republic of Germany forms part of the Act on the Peaceful Uses of Atomic Energy and Protection against its Hazards (Atomic Energy Act) of 23rd December 1959. This Act, which entered into force on 1st January 1960, was amended several times, notably by the Third Act amending the Atomic Energy Act of 15th July 1975, which, inter alia, adapted the Act to the Nuclear Liability Conventions. The revised version of the Act of 15th July 1985, takes account of all amendments up to that date; it was published in the Federal Gazette (*Bundesgesetzblatt*, BGBl) 1985 Part I, p. 1565. (The text of this Act, translated into English, has been reproduced in the Supplement to Nuclear Law Bulletin No. 36.) The third party liability provisions of the Act are supplemented by the Nuclear Financial Security Ordinance (*Atomrechtliche Deckungsvorsorge - Verordnung*) of 25th January 1977 (BGBl. I, p. 220). (The text of the Ordinance, translated into English, has been reproduced in the Supplement to Nuclear Law Bulletin No. 18.)

*

* *

According to Article 3 in conjunction with Annex II, Section III, No. 2 of the Agreement of 18th May 1990 on the Establishment of a Monetary, Economic and Social Union between the Federal Republic of Germany and the German Democratic Republic, the Atomic Energy Act of the Federal Republic of Germany and its implementing Ordinances are applicable, as of 1st July 1990, in the German Democratic Republic.

I. THIRD PARTY LIABILITY

A. SCOPE AND DEFINITIONS

The operator of a nuclear installation situated in the Federal Republic of Germany is liable wherever the incident occurs or the damage is suffered, provided that German law is applicable under the Paris Convention, an international agreement, or the rules of private international law [Section 25(4)] (unless otherwise indicated, all references are to the Atomic Energy Act in the version published on 15th July 1985). The amount of his liability is, however, subject to reciprocity, if the damage was suffered in other States [Section 31(2)].

The Atomic Energy Act constitutes the general legal framework for all nuclear activities. It contains provisions not only relating to third party liability but also to surveillance, licensing, competent authorities, offences and penalties. Two sets of definitions are therefore used, a general one applicable to all provisions, and a special one applicable to the provisions on liability and financial security. For the purpose of the latter, the terms *nuclear incident, nuclear installations, operator of a nuclear installation, nuclear substances* and *Special Drawing Rights* are defined in conformity with the Paris Convention [Section 1(3) and Annex 1].

The Atomic Energy Act declares the provisions of the Paris Convention as directly applicable (self-executing) without incorporating them. The Act makes use, however, of the options left by the Convention to national legislation as well as of certain reservations made by the Federal Republic of Germany. The Brussels Supplementary Convention, on the other hand, is treated as establishing rights and obligations between the Contracting Parties only and not affecting those between the nuclear operators and the victims of a nuclear incident; similarly, the provisions on State intervention are construed independently from that Convention.

B. NATURE AND ASSIGNMENT OF LIABILITY

The Act distinguishes between the liability of operators of nuclear installations in accordance with the Paris Convention which, as already mentioned, is directly applicable and completed by a number of provisions [Sections 13 to 15, 25 and 27 to 40], on the one hand, and liability in cases not covered by the Paris Convention [Section 26], on the other. This latter provision, discussed below, is construed as a catch-all clause comprising damage due to nuclear substances, installations or activities falling outside the special regime of the Paris Convention.

1. *LIABILITY ACCORDING TO THE PARIS CONVENTION*

a) General – Nuclear Installations

The operator is absolutely and exclusively liable for damage caused by a nuclear incident in his nuclear installation, which may consist of several installations if they are operated by the same person or persons and are located on the same site [Sections 25(1), 2(2) and Annex 1].

If several operators are liable to pay compensation for nuclear damage, their liability is joint and several. In that case, the amount of compensation is to be apportioned between the operators according to the circumstances and the extent to which the damage was caused by one or the other, except as otherwise provided in Article 5(d) of the Paris Convention. However, no operator is required to pay compensation exceeding the maximum amount of his liability [Section 33].

b) Transport

The operator of a nuclear installation is liable for damage caused by a nuclear incident outside that installation and involving nuclear substances in the course of carriage therefrom or thereto, pursuant to Article 4(a) and (b) of the Paris Convention [Section 25(1)].

The carrier may assume liability by a contract in writing in place of the operator of a nuclear installation situated in the Federal Republic of Germany. Such assumption of liability must be authorised by the authority competent for the granting of transport licences, the Federal Office for Radiation Protection (*Bundesant für Strahlenschutz*), provided that the carrier is licensed or has his main place of business in the Federal Republic of Germany and that the operator has declared his consent to the authority [Sections 25(2) and 4].

c) Rights of Recourse

Articles 6(d) to (g) of the Paris Convention on the rights of recourse of and against the operator are directly applicable [Section 25(1)].

d) Exoneration from Liability

The operator is liable even if the damage was caused by a nuclear incident directly due to an act of armed conflict, hostilities, civil war, insurrection, or a grave natural disaster of an exceptional character. Article 9 of the Paris Convention is declared inapplicable in accordance with the reservation of the Federal Republic of Germany with respect to that Article. However, if the damage is suffered in another State, this provision applies only to the extent that, at the time of the nuclear incident, the other State has provided an equivalent system of compensation, in relation to the Federal Republic of Germany [Section 25(3)].

2. *LIABILITY IN OTHER CASES*

In cases to which the provisions of the Paris Convention in conjunction with Section 25 of this Act do not apply, the holder of radioactive substances (this term is wider than *nuclear substances* within the meaning of the Paris Convention) or of a particle accelerator is liable for damage to persons and property caused by the effect of any nuclear fission process or radiation from such substances or an accelerator [Section 26(1)]. The same applies if damage is caused by the effects of nuclear fusion [Section 26(2)].

Any person who has lost possession of the substances without having transferred them to a person entitled to such possession under the Act or any statutory ordinance made thereunder, shall be liable as if he were the holder [Section 26(3)].

There is, however, no liability to pay compensation if the damage was caused by an event which the holder could not avoid, even by taking every reasonable precaution, and if the damage is due neither to a defective safety device nor to a failure in its performance [Section 26(1)].

There is equally no liability to pay compensation for damage [Section 26(4)]:

- where radioactive substances or accelerators have been applied to the injured person by or under the supervision of a physician or dentist in the course of medical treatment, and such substances and accelerators as well as the necessary measuring apparatus, have complied with the current state of science and technology and the damage is not due to the fact that such substances, accelerators or measuring apparatus have not been sufficiently maintained;
- where a legal relationship exists between the holder and the injured person under which the latter has accepted the risk associated with the substances.

The exonerations under Section 26(1) – unavoidable event – and Section 26(4) – acceptance of risk in case of a legal relationship – do not apply if radioactive substances are applied to persons in the course of medical research. The holder of the radioactive substance denying a causal connection between such application and a damage suffered has the burden of proof that in the light of existing medical science there is no sufficient probability of such a causal connection [Section 26(5)].

Whoever carries radioactive substances on behalf of a third party is not liable to pay compensation. The consignor, whether or not he is the holder of such substances, remains liable until the consignee has taken charge thereof [Section 26(6)].

The above provisions do not affect the application of legal provisions pursuant to which the holder of radioactive substances or an accelerator is liable to a greater extent (e.g. those of the Civil Code) or pursuant to which another person (e.g. a tort-feasor) is liable [Section 26(7)]. In other words, in cases to which the provisions of the Paris Convention in conjunction with Section 25 do not apply, the holder is not exclusively liable, as not all liability is legally channelled onto him.

C. AMOUNT OF LIABILITY

The liability of the operator of a nuclear installation situated in the Federal Republic of Germany is unlimited. However, if the damage is caused by nuclear incidents directly due to an act of armed conflict, hostilities, civil war, insurrection, or a grave natural disaster of an exceptional character, the operator's liability is limited to the maximum amount of the State guarantee, i.e. at present DM 1 000 million [Section 31(1)].

If the nuclear damage occurs in other States, the maximum amount of compensation is subject to reciprocity as follows:

- for damage suffered in a Contracting State to the Brussels Supplementary Convention, any compensation exceeding 300 million Special Drawing Rights (SDRs);
- for damage suffered in any other State (including Contracting Parties to the Paris Convention only) any compensation exceeding 15 million SDRs;

will be payable only if the other State concerned has, at the time of the nuclear incident, provided an equivalent system of compensation in relation to the Federal Republic of Germany [Section 31(2)]. By the Agreement of 22nd October 1986 (BGBl. II, p. 598) which entered into force on 21st September 1988 (BGBl. II, p. 955), the Federal Republic of Germany and Switzerland, which also provides for the operator's unlimited liability, have established full reciprocity.

D. NUCLEAR DAMAGE

a) Damage Covered

The Act, in direct application of the Paris Convention, covers damage to persons and property caused by a nuclear incident as defined in Article 1(a)(i) of the Paris Convention as amended by the 1982 Protocol, i.e. including damage arising out of or resulting from ionizing radiations emitted by any other source of radiation inside the nuclear installation as well as damage to the means of transport upon which the nuclear substances involved were at the time of the nuclear incident [Section 25(1)].

b) Damage Excluded

Damage to the nuclear installation itself and to any property on the site of that installation which is used or to be used in connection with that installation is not covered by the Act [Section 25(1)].

Furthermore, the operator of a nuclear installation is not liable under the Paris Convention for damage caused by a nuclear incident involving small quantities of or low-level nuclear substances [Section 25(6) and Annex 2]. He may, however, be liable as the holder of such substances [see above Section 26(1)].

II. COVER AND COMPENSATION

A. INSURANCE OR OTHER FINANCIAL SECURITY

a) General

Every holder of a licence under the Atomic Energy Act must provide financial security to cover his legal liability to pay compensation for damage. The type, terms and amount of financial security are to be fixed by the licensing authority and reviewed every two years [Section 13(1)].

In the case of installations and activities involving liability under the Paris Convention in conjunction with Section 25 of the Act, the financial security must be in due proportion to the hazards of the installation or activity. As a general rule, it shall not fall short of the maximum insurance cover obtainable on the insurance market at reasonable conditions but may not exceed DM 500 million. These higher limits must be reviewed every five years with a view to maintaining the real value of the financial security [Section 13(2)].

With respect to other activities requiring a licence, the financial security must ensure fulfilment of the legal liability to pay compensation for damage to the extent appropriate to the circumstances.

The *Bund* (Federal State) (with the exception of the Federal German Railways in the case of public transport) and the *Länder* (States forming the Federal Republic of Germany) are not required to provide financial security. However, insofar as a *Land* may be held liable under the Paris Convention in conjunction with the Act, the licensing authority shall establish the terms and conditions of a guarantee which is considered equal to the financial security [Section 13(4)].

b) Financial Security in Case of Transport

In the case of carriage of nuclear substances the necessary financial security may not exceed DM 50 million [Financial Security Ordinance, Section 8(4)].

The carrier must carry a certificate which conforms to the requirements of Article 4(c) of the Paris Convention; it must be produced, on request, to the competent authorities [Section 4(5)].

Financial security and a certificate are not required for the carriage of small quantities of or low-level nuclear substances [Sections 4(3) and 4a(2), Annex 2].

In the case of international carriage between Contracting Parties to the Paris Convention, the financial security required is considered as provided if the certificate referred to above relates to an operator of a nuclear installation situated in such Contracting State [Section 4a(1)].

The insurer within the meaning of Article 4(c) of the Paris Convention must be licensed to carry on his business within the realm of the Atomic Energy Act. In case of a foreign insurer, a domestic insurer or association of insurers must undertake jointly to assume the obligations of a third party liability insurer. Some other form of financial security may be permitted if it is ensured that the guarantor will be able to meet his obligations [Section 4a(2)].

However, special provisions apply with respect to States Party to the Paris Convention but not to the Brussels Supplementary Convention [Section 4a(3), (4)]:

- In the case of transit of nuclear fuel, the granting of a transit licence may be made subject to the condition that the operator's maximum amount of liability be increased to DM 50 million with respect to nuclear incidents occurring during carriage within the Federal Republic of Germany, if this is necessary in view of the amount and nature of the nuclear fuel and the safety measures applied. Proof of such increased financial security is to be furnished by a certificate issued by the competent authority of the State concerned.
- In the case of import or export of nuclear fuel, it may be required that the receiving or sending domestic operator assume liability for nuclear incidents occurring during carriage within the Federal Republic of Germany, if the foreign operator's maximum amount of liability is not adequate in view of the amount and nature of the nuclear fuel and the safety measures applied.

c) Type and Amount of Financial Security

In this respect, detailed provisions are laid down in the Nuclear Financial Security Ordinance.

i) Type

As to the type of financial security, it may be provided by third party liability insurance, by indemnification or guarantee furnished by a third person, or by a combination of both [Ordinance, Section 1].

Financial security by means of a third party liability insurance may be furnished only if the insurer is licensed to carry on business within the realm of the Atomic Energy Act. In the case of international carriage, insurance may be taken out with an insurer licensed outside the realm of the Act, provided that a domestic insurer or association of insurers undertake to assume jointly the obligations of a third party liability insurer [Ordinance, Section 2].

In case of indemnification or guarantee it must be ensured that the third person will be able to meet his obligations. If such person has his domicile or main place of business outside the realm of the Act, he must have sufficient property within the Federal Republic of Germany to cover his obligations, or it must be ensured that a decision of a court situated in the realm of the Act can be executed, by virtue of an international agreement, in the State where he has his property. Another State may provide an indemnification or guarantee, if it submits to the jurisdiction of the courts of the Federal Republic of Germany or if it is otherwise ensured that it will fulfil its obligations [Ordinance, Section 3].

ii) Amount

The amount of the financial security (coverage) depends on the nature of the installation or activity. Such coverage is fixed either directly or based on a standard coverage [Ordinance, Section 8].

If the standard coverage does not appear to be justified in the individual case at hand, the licensing authority may, within the maximum amounts established by Section 13(2) of the Atomic Energy Act, either increase the coverage to double the amount or reduce it to one-third of the standard coverage [Ordinance, Section 16]. Factors to be taken into account in arriving at this decision include:

- the extent of the hazards to persons and property other than the licensee and his employees and their property;
- the degree of safety obtained by protective measures and safety equipment;
- the extent of dispersion of radioactive substances in view of the particular meteorological or hydrological situation;
- the expected duration of the hazards in view of the half-life of the radioactive substances;
- the possibility of excluding nuclear damage due to nuclear fission even under the most adverse circumstances;
- in case of transport, the extent of the hazards, in view of the means and route of transport, the packaging and the nature of the radioactive substances.

In the case of handling of nuclear fuel and other radioactive substances, the standard coverage is to be determined according to the type, mass, activity or nature of the radioactive substances. The same applies to the transport of radioactive substances, up to a maximum of DM 50 million [Ordinance, Section 8(1), Annexes 1 and 2].

If radioactive wastes are handled in the agency of a *Land* for the collection of radioactive wastes [*Landessammelstelle*, Section 9a(3) of the Act], or in another installation licensed for the disposal of radioactive wastes, the standard coverage amounts to DM 10 million, and to DM 100 million if such other installation handles wastes originating from an installation for the production, treatment, processing or fission of nuclear fuel, or for the reprocessing of irradiated nuclear fuel [Ordinance, Section 8(3)].

In the case of reactors, the standard coverage is to be determined according to the maximum thermal power and amounts to DM 5 million for up to 1 MW and DM 1 million for each additional MW up to DM 500 million. However, the standard coverage is to be calculated according to the licensed type and mass of nuclear fuel, if this calculation results in a higher amount than under the first formula, but not exceeding DM 500 million. Consequently, all reactors having a maximum thermal power of 496 MWth and above require the maximum amount of financial security of DM 500 million pursuant to Section 13(2) of the Atomic Energy Act [Ordinance, Section 9].

In the case of installations for the production, treatment or processing of nuclear fuel, the standard coverage is to be determined in view of the nature and mass of the nuclear fuel which may be handled in the installation according to the terms of the licence. The maximum coverage in the case of installations for the fabrication of fuel elements and for uranium enrichment may, however, not exceed DM 200 million [Ordinance, Section 11(1), Annex 1].

The standard coverage for installations for the reprocessing of irradiated nuclear fuel is to be calculated according to the annual licensed output, as follows [Ordinance, Section 11(2)]:

- up to 50 tonnes, DM 100 million;
- more than 50 tonnes and up to 500 tonnes, DM 300 million;
- more than 500 tonnes, DM 500 million.

Installations for the production of ionizing radiation (accelerators) whose construction and operation are subject to a licence (large installations), require a standard coverage of DM 50 million. Where only the operation is subject to a licence (small installations), the standard coverage is DM 10 million if the installation is destined for medical treatment, and DM 1 million in all other cases, unless more than 10^8 neutrons per second are produced or the final energy of the accelerated electrons exceeds 10 MeV or that of the accelerated ions exceeds 1 MeV per nucleon, in which latter case the coverage amounts to DM 3 million [Ordinance, Section 13].

Where radioactive substances are applied to human beings in the course of medical research, the coverage is DM 1 million for every such person [Ordinance, Section 15].

When installations for the production, treatment, processing or fission of nuclear fuel or for the processing of irradiated nuclear fuel are decommissioned, the standard coverage is to be determined according to the residual activity. If such determination is not possible or feasible, the coverage may be reduced to 5 per cent of the coverage during operation, if there are no radioactive substances present in the installation other than contaminated components and substances used for monitoring purposes [Ordinance, Section 12, Annex 2].

d) Financial Security for Nuclear Power Plants

The maximum amount of financial security of DM 500 million at present is provided by a system consisting of two layers. Up to DM 200 million financial security is furnished by a third party liability insurance taken out by each operator. Between this amount and DM 500 million, it is provided in the framework of a contract jointly subscribed to by all nuclear power plant operators.

For the purpose of implementing the second layer, the electricity generating companies operating nuclear power plants have set up a partnership under civil law (*Nuklear-Haftpflicht-Gesellschaft bürgerlichen Rechts*). The partnership concluded a co-operative agreement and, on the basis of the latter, a contract with the six leading insurance companies in the Federal Republic of Germany. This contract covers the difference between DM 200 million and DM 500 million, i.e. DM 300 million.

The operators have to pay an annual advance fee and a deferred premium. The advance fee is calculated on the basis of the nominal thermal power of the nuclear power reactors covered by the contract and distributed among the operators according to a scale fixed by the partnership agreement. The deferred premium (up to a total of DM 300 million) falls due if compensation for nuclear damage has to be paid in excess of DM 200 million and up to DM 500 million. The deferred premium has to be paid in cash by the operators (partners) according to the scale specified in the partnership agreement. Thus, the operators act as their own reinsurers.

B. STATE INTERVENTION

a) State Guarantee

The operator of a nuclear installation situated in the realm of the Atomic Energy Act is to be indemnified against liability to pay compensation for nuclear damage to the extent that his liability is not covered by or cannot be satisfied out of his financial security [Atomic Energy Act, Section 34(1)]. Accordingly, the indemnification covers the risk of insolvency of the insurer or financial guarantor, as well as non-insurable risks such as armed conflicts or damage arising after ten years from the date of the nuclear incident. The indemnification is limited to twice the maximum financial security, i.e. at present DM 1 000 million, and is to be borne as to 75 per cent by the *Bund* and 25 per cent by the *Land* where the nuclear installation at the origin of the nuclear incident is situated [Section 36].

If, after a nuclear incident, it is to be expected that an indemnification will be necessary, the operator must notify this without delay to the competent Federal Minister and authorities of the *Länder*. He must provide them with all necessary information and notify them of all claims raised and procedures initiated against him. He is to follow the instructions of the *Länder* authorities in case of negotiations with victims and must not acknowledge or satisfy claims without their consent except in cases of obvious inequity [Section 34(2)].

b) Recourse Against the Operator

Recourse may be had against the operator thus indemnified if [Section 37]:

- he has violated his obligations as to information or not complied with the authorities' instructions;

- he or his legal representative have caused the damage wilfully or by gross negligence;
- compensation has been paid because the financial security did not correspond to the determination by the competent authority.

c) Supplementary Payments

The *Bund* shall pay compensation up to the maximum amount of State indemnification (at present DM 1 000 million) to persons having suffered nuclear damage within the realm of the Act who cannot obtain compensation under the law of another State Party to the Paris Convention applicable to the incident, because [Section 38(1)]:

- the nuclear incident occurred in the territory of a non-Contracting State to the Paris Convention;
- the damage was caused by a nuclear incident directly due to an act of armed conflict, hostilities, civil war, insurrection or a grave natural disaster of an exceptional character;
- the applicable law excludes liability for damage to the means of transport upon which the nuclear substances involved were at the time of the nuclear incident;
- the applicable law does not provide for the operator's liability for damage caused by ionizing radiation emitted by another source of radiation inside the nuclear installation;
- the applicable law provides for a shorter period of limitation or extinction than the Act; or
- the total sum available for compensation falls short of the maximum amount of State indemnification.

The *Bund* shall further grant compensation up to the maximum amount of State indemnification if damage is suffered within the realm of the Act, but the applicable foreign law or international agreements provide for compensation falling considerably short of the compensation which the victim would have obtained had the Atomic Energy Act been applied [Section 38(2)].

The provisions described above are applicable irrespective of nationality, if the damage was suffered on the territory of the Federal Republic of Germany. However, with respect to foreign nationals who do not have their habitual residence in that territory, these provisions are applicable only if their own country has provided an equivalent system of compensation in relation to the Federal Republic of Germany [Section 38(3)].

Claims for compensation against the Bund are to be brought before the Federal Agency for Administration (*Bundesverwaltungsamt*); they are extinguished three years after the date on which the decision on compensation rendered under foreign law has become final [Section 38(4)].

d) Exceptions

The provisions relating to indemnification [Section 34] and supplementary compensation [Section 38] are not applicable to claims for damage suffered by (moral) persons which form, together with the operator of the nuclear installation, a combined enterprise, within the meaning of the Stock Corporation Act (*Aktiengesetz*) (e.g. if the nuclear installation and the enterprise having suffered damage are legally independent but are controlled by the same company). The same applies if the damage is caused to an industrial installation in the vicinity of the nuclear installation, if the former's site has been chosen to use energy originating from the latter for production processes (e.g. process steam) [Sections 39(1), 15(1) and (2)].

Claims for compensation of non-financial damage (pain and suffering) in case of personal injury will only be subject to State intervention if this is necessary to avoid serious inequity because of the particular gravity of the injury [Sections 39(2) and 29(2)].

C. COMPENSATION

a) Extent of Compensation

Compensation for damage to property is limited to its ordinary value, plus the cost of protection against radiation hazards originating therefrom. As regards damage to the means of transport upon which the nuclear substances involved were at the time of the nuclear incident, compensation shall be paid only if the satisfaction of other claims has been secured [Section 31(3)].

In the event of death, compensation covers the pecuniary loss sustained by the deceased before his death as well as the funeral costs. If the deceased was under legal obligation to provide maintenance to third persons, such persons may claim compensation for loss of maintenance, including persons conceived but not yet born at the time of the injury [Section 28].

In the case of personal injury, compensation comprises the victim's pecuniary loss, including that resulting from a temporary or permanent loss or reduction of his earning capacity as well as increase of his needs or a handicap in regard to his career. If the damage had been caused wilfully or by negligence, the victim may also claim adequate compensation for pain and suffering [Section 29].

Compensation for loss or reduction of earning capacity, increase of needs or any handicap in regard to the career of the victim, or for loss of maintenance is to be provided by means of an annuity [Section 30(1)].

Where a fault of the injured person has contributed to the injury sustained, the liable person's obligation to pay compensation and its extent depend on the circumstances of the case and in particular on whether he or the injured person has mainly caused the damage [Section 27].

b) Rank of Claims and Apportionment

If the person suffering nuclear damage and the liable operator are combined enterprises within the meaning of the Stock Corporation Act, the operator's financial security may be used to satisfy claims of that person only on condition that the satisfaction of claims of other victims is not thereby prejudiced. The same applies to the claims of an industrial installation in the vicinity of the nuclear installation if the former's site has been chosen to use energy originating from the latter for production purposes [Section 15(1) and (2)].

Actions for death and personal injury under the Paris Convention which are brought within ten years after the nuclear incident, have precedence over actions instituted after this period [Section 32(3)].

Where claims for compensation are likely to exceed the operator's maximum amount of liability, the apportionment of the sums available and the procedure are to be governed by an Act and, pending enactment, by statutory ordinance. Such ordinance may only provide provisional measures to avoid hardships and must ensure that satisfaction of all claims will not be unduly prejudiced by the satisfaction of individual claims [Section 35].

D. TIME LIMITS FOR BRINGING CLAIMS

Claims for compensation of nuclear damage are barred by limitation after three years from the date on which the person entitled to compensation had knowledge or ought reasonably to have known of both the damage and the person liable, and irrespective thereof, thirty years after the date of the incident [Section 32(1)].

Where the damage was caused by a nuclear incident involving nuclear substances which, at the time of the incident, had been stolen, lost, jettisoned or abandoned and had not been recovered, the period of limitation is twenty years from the date of the theft, loss, jettison or abandonment [Section 32(2)].

The running of the limitation period is interrupted by negotiations pending between the person liable and the person entitled to compensation until such time as either Party refuses to continue such negotiations [Section 32(4)].

E. COMPETENT COURTS AND PROCEDURE

The courts of the Federal Republic of Germany have jurisdiction in accordance with Article 13 of the Paris Convention. The venue is determined by the provisions of the Code of Civil Procedure (*Zivilprozeßordnung*) according to which several courts are competent concurrently: jurisdiction may lie either with the court of the place where the incident occurred or where the damage was suffered or where the legal person (the operator) has his residence (which may be different from the site of the nuclear installation having caused the damage).

If such a German court has jurisdiction over actions against the operator of a nuclear installation situated in another Contracting State to the Paris Convention, the operator's liability is governed by the provisions of the Atomic Energy Act [Section 40(1)]. However, the law of that other Contracting State prevails in the following respects [Section 40(2)]:

- who is to be considered as operator;
- whether the operator's liability extends to damage suffered in a non-Contracting State to the Paris Convention;
- whether the operator's liability extends to nuclear damage caused by ionizing radiation emitted by another source of radiation inside a nuclear installation;
- whether and to what extent the operator's liability extends to damage to the means of transport upon which the nuclear substances involved were at the time of the nuclear incident;
- what is the maximum amount of liability of the operator;
- after what period claims against the operator will become barred by limitation or be extinguished;

- whether and to what extent nuclear damage is compensated in the cases enumerated in Article 9 of the Paris Convention.

*

* *

As already mentioned, the Federal Republic of Germany and the Swiss Confederation concluded an Agreement on Third Party Liability in the Nuclear Field on 22nd October 1986. The Agreement declares the principle of equal treatment for the nationals of both States and is intended, in particular, to facilitate the settlement of disputes if they are due to an event which occurs on the territory of either State, causing damage on the territory of the other. A translation of the Agreement is reproduced in Nuclear Law Bulletin No. 39.

HUNGARY

INTRODUCTION

Hungary has an installed nuclear capacity of 1 760 MWe. The National Atomic Energy Commission has overall responsibility for nuclear matters.

Hungary became a Party to the Vienna Convention in 1989 and approved the Joint Protocol relating to the Application of the Vienna Convention and the Paris Convention in 1990.

Nuclear third party liability is governed by the Nuclear Energy Act of 5th April 1980 and, in particular, Chapter III of that Act (*Magyar Közlöny* 1980, No. 21, p. 293). It should be noted that this Act predates Hungary's ratification of the Vienna Convention.

I. THIRD PARTY LIABILITY

A. SCOPE AND DEFINITIONS

The 1980 Nuclear Energy Act (the Act) does not cover nuclear damage suffered by non-Hungarian nationals unless they are to be covered by virtue of an international agreement to which Hungary is a Party (e.g. the Vienna Convention) or if the State of the foreign victim provides reciprocal coverage for Hungarian nationals [Section 20(3)]. Such victims may seek compensation under the provisions of the Civil Code governing exceptionally hazardous activities [Section 22].

The Act does not expressly limit its territorial scope and can accordingly also be applied to damage suffered outside Hungary.

The Act covers damage resulting from the operation of a nuclear installation or the transport of nuclear material [Section 20(1)]. Damage caused by an event involving radiation or radioactive contamination not occurring in connection with the operation of a nuclear installation or the transport of nuclear material is covered by the provisions of the Civil Code governing exceptionally hazardous activities [Section 22].

The term *nuclear installation* is defined by the Act to mean a nuclear power plant, a nuclear critical assembly, a nuclear reactor for research or training purposes and any other installation referred to in paragraph 1 of Article 97 of the IAEA Safeguards Agreement with Hungary, [Executive Order of the Act on Nuclear Energy; Governmental Decree

No. 12/1980 (IV.5)]. The latter are: critical assemblies, laboratories and research reactors of the Central Research Institute for Physics; laboratories of the Institute of Isotopes; the training laboratory of the Budapest Technical University and the Paks nuclear power station (4x440 MWe). The term *nuclear material* is defined by the Act to mean uranium, thorium, plutonium and any material containing one or more of these, with the exception of products and residues of ore mining and milling [Executive Order of the Act on Nuclear Energy; Governmental Decree No. 12/1980 (IV.5)].

B. NATURE AND ASSIGNMENT OF LIABILITY

a) General – Nuclear Installations and Transport

The operator of a nuclear installation is liable to compensate nuclear damage caused by an incident occurring at his installation or during the transport of nuclear material carried out on his behalf [Section 20(1)].

This liability is absolute [Section 20(2)].

Any contractual provision purporting to exclude or limit liability for compensation of nuclear damage is rendered null and void by the Act [Section 20(4)].

b) Exoneration from Liability

An operator is not liable to pay compensation to a person who has wilfully caused the damage which he has suffered [Section 20(20].

C. AMOUNT OF LIABILITY

The Act does not limit the amount of the liability of the operator.

D. NUCLEAR DAMAGE

Liability on the part of the nuclear operator is incurred under the Act for damage which arises out of an incident involving radiation or radioactive contamination [Section 20(1)]. Provision is also made for damage arising out of government acts to prevent or minimise nuclear damage – for example evacuation, restrictions on the use of property and the destruction of property – to be compensated [Section 24]. Damage caused by restrictions on the use of an area and damage to real property is to be compensated under the regulations governing compensation for expropriation of property [Civil Code of the Hungarian People's Republic, Act No. IV of 1959, Sections 177 and 178; Decree-Law No. 24 of 1976; and Governmental Decree No. 33 of 1976 (IX.5)]. Damage to personal property is to be governed by the provisions of the Civil Code on compensation of damage [Civil Code of the Hungarian People's Republic; Act No. IV of 1959, Sections 345 and 346].

II. COVER AND COMPENSATION

A. INSURANCE OR OTHER FINANCIAL SECURITY

The Act does not impose any obligation on the operator to hold insurance or other financial security to cover his liability.

B. STATE INTERVENTION

Payment of compensation for nuclear damage is guaranteed by the State [Section 21(1)].

C. COMPENSATION

The manner and extent of compensation is to be governed by the provisions of Chapter XXXI of the Civil Code [Section 21(1)].

To facilitate and expedite the enforcement of claims for compensation, claims may be made against the State Insurance Company, the body designated for this purpose by the Council of Ministers.

D. TIME LIMITS FOR BRINGING CLAIMS

The right to compensation under the Act is extinguished after a lapse of ten years from the incident causing the damage [Section 21(2)].

E. COMPETENT COURTS AND PROCEDURE

The Act makes no special provisions as to the competent courts or rules of procedure with respect to claims brought under the Act. The Code of Civil Procedures [Act No. III of 1952] is thus applicable. Under this Act actions for compensation may be brought in the court having jurisdiction in relation to (i) the place where the incident occurred; (ii) the place where the damage was suffered; or (iii) the domicile of the defendant.

INDONESIA

INTRODUCTION

Indonesia currently has no nuclear power plants although the Government has officially announced plans to build one with a power in the order of 600 MWe. It currently has a reactor for research purposes of 30 MWe.

Responsibility for regulation of nuclear energy matters lies with the National Atomic Energy Agency (BATAN).

Indonesia is not a Party to either the 1960 Paris Convention or the 1963 Vienna Convention. Conversely, Indonesia is a Signatory of the 1962 Brussels Convention on the Liability of Operators of Nuclear Ships.

The basic legislation on nuclear third party liability is contained in Act No. 31 of 1964 concerning Basic Principles of Atomic Energy. Regulations pursuant to Section 20 of this Act making more specific provisions were under preparation at the time of publication of this study.

THIRD PARTY LIABILITY

The operator of a nuclear installation is responsible for all occurrences during the operation of that installation [Section 16]. He is subject to prosecution in the case of an accident [Section 16].

In the case of an accident during transport, the consignor operator is liable until the consigned material is delivered and received by the consignee operator, unless both parties have agreed on other conditions [Section 18(1)].

An operator is not subject to prosecution if the accident was caused by a natural disaster or other circumstances outside his control and responsibility [Section 16].

In the case of an accident due to an intentional act or due to negligence on the part of installation employees, the persons concerned are subject to prosecution [Section 17(1)].

The Government is authorised by the Act to set up a Committee of Experts to investigate any nuclear accident whether occurring at a nuclear installation or during transport [Section 19].

The Act provides for Regulations to be made concerning nuclear third party liability and compensation for nuclear damage caused by a nuclear accident occurring at a nuclear installation or in the course of transport [Section 20]. Regulations pursuant to this provision are currently being prepared. It is anticipated that these Regulations will cover matters such as: the liability of the operator to pay compensation to a specified amount, provision by the Government of compensation beyond this amount, a definition of the type of damage to be compensated and time limits for the bringing of claims and other procedural matters.

ITALY

INTRODUCTION

In 1990, Italy had an installed nuclear capacity of some 1 100 MWe (two units). To this must be added various other installations connected with the nuclear fuel cycle. The main operators of nuclear installations are the national electricity company ENEL, and the public body responsible for nuclear energy, ENEA.

Italy is a Party to the Paris Convention and the Brussels Supplementary Convention, as amended in 1982 (Act No. 131 of 5th March 1985 published in the Supplement to the Official Gazette No. 89 of 15th April 1985), and to the 1971 Brussels Convention relating to Civil Liability in the Field of Maritime Carriage of Nuclear Material. Moreover, the Italian Government has signed the Joint Protocol relating to the Application of the Vienna Convention and the Paris Convention.

The provisions governing nuclear third party liability are contained in Act No. 1860 of 31st December 1962 on the peaceful uses of nuclear energy, as amended (the text of this Act, translated into English, has been reproduced in the Supplement to Nuclear Law Bulletin No. 16). By Act No. 109 of 12th February 1974, authorising ratification of the Paris Convention and the Brussels Supplementary Convention, powers were given to the Italian Government to enact by decree the provisions necessary for implementing those Conventions internally. In implementation of this provision, Decree No. 519 of 10th May 1975 of the President of the Republic, published on 6th November 1975, amended Sections 1 and 15 to 24 of the Act of 31st December 1962. Italian legislation was not, on the other hand, amended following ratification of the 1982 Protocols.

I. THIRD PARTY LIABILITY

A. SCOPE AND DEFINITIONS

Act No. 1860, as amended in 1975 upon ratification of the Paris and Brussels Conventions, adopted the Paris Convention definitions for the terms *nuclear incident, nuclear installation, nuclear fuel, radioactive products or waste* and *nuclear materials (substances)* [Sections 1(a) to (e) of the Act].

The Act provides that the decisions of the NEA Steering Committee concerning the exclusion of certain nuclear installations or materials from the scope of the Paris Convention are to be implemented in Italy by Decree of the Minister of Industry, Commerce and Crafts after consultation with ENEA [Section 1]. Thus, a Decree was adopted on 20th March 1979 (published on 5th April 1979) in order to implement in Italy the Decisions of the OECD Steering Committee for Nuclear Energy of 27th October 1977 on the exclusion of certain kinds or quantities of nuclear substances from the application of the Paris Convention.

Operator in relation to a nuclear installation means the holder of a licence issued by the Minister of Industry, Commerce and Crafts for the operation of the installation in question [Act No. 1860, Section 1].

The Act does not contain any special provisions, as compared to the Paris Convention, relating to its territorial application.

B. NATURE AND ASSIGNMENT OF LIABILITY

a) General – Nuclear Installations

The operator of a nuclear installation is absolutely and exclusively liable for all nuclear damage occurring in or in connection with his installation [Sections 15 and 18].

If the nuclear incident at the origin of the damage is caused by nuclear fuel or radioactive products or waste which have been in more than one nuclear installation, liability lies with the operator who had possession of the materials in question at the time of the incident [Section 17]. If these materials were not in a nuclear installation at the time when the damage was caused, liability lies with the operator of the last installation in which they were held or with the operator who subsequently took charge of them [Section 17].

Where the operators of two or more installations are found liable for the same damage, they are jointly and severally liable for compensation [Section 17].

Nuclear operators are also liable in respect of damage caused by a combination of a nuclear incident and an incident other than a nuclear one, where the nuclear damage cannot be separated with certainty from the other damage. However, where the damage is caused by a combination of a nuclear incident and an emission of ionizing radiation, the Act neither limits nor otherwise affects the liability of the person responsible for the emission of ionizing radiation [Section 15].

Any damage caused directly by nuclear fuel or by radioactive products or waste which have been stored, abandoned, stolen or lost, is deemed connected with the nuclear installation from the standpoint of the liability of the operator [Section 15].

Any damage caused by ionizing radiation emitted by any radioactive source within a nuclear installation engages the liability of the operator of the said installation [Section 15].

b) Transport

Act No. 1860 closely follows the provisions of the Paris Convention by stipulating that in the event of an incident arising during the carriage, or storage in course of carriage, of nuclear materials, the consigning operator is liable for any damage caused by the nuclear materials until such time as they are taken in charge by another nuclear operator or until such time as the consigning operator's liability is assumed by another operator pursuant to the terms of a contract in writing [Section 16].

In the case of the carriage of nuclear materials intended for use in a reactor comprised in a means of transport, the consigning operator is liable for any damage occurring before the nuclear materials are taken in charge by the person duly authorised to operate such reactor [Section 16].

Where nuclear materials are exported, with the express consent of the consigning operator, to a non-Contracting State to the Paris Convention, the consigning operator is liable for any damage caused before the materials are unloaded [Section 16].

As for the consignee operator, he is liable for any nuclear damage arising in the course of carriage from the time that he takes charge of the nuclear materials carried or from the time that liability has been transferred to him under an agreement in writing [Section 16].

Furthermore, where the nuclear materials are from a reactor comprised in a means of transport, the consignee operator is also liable from the time that he takes charge of them [Section 16].

Lastly, the consignee operator is liable, in the case of an import with his written consent from a non-Contracting State, from the time that the nuclear materials concerned are loaded on the means of transport by which they are to be carried from the territory of that State [Section 16].

A carrier may, with the consent of the operator of a nuclear installation situated in Italy, be authorised by the Minister of Industry, Commerce and Crafts to assume, in place of the operator in question, liability for any damage [Section 16].

c) Rights of Recourse

No person other than the nuclear operator is obliged to compensate damage caused by a nuclear incident except that the operator liable under the Act has a right of recourse against any individual who has intentionally caused damage, or unless a right of recourse has been conferred on him by contract [Section 18].

The State has a right of recourse against the operator in respect of any damage attributable to him, up to the maximum amount due for such compensation. In such a case, the State has priority over the claims of insurers or any other person who has furnished financial security [Section 20].

Insurance companies providing insurance against industrial accidents or occupational diseases, and insurance companies providing optional insurance in respect of nuclear damage, have no right of recourse against the nuclear operator liable, for the recovery of amounts paid under any such insurance [Section 18].

d) Exoneration from Liability

The operator of a nuclear installation is not liable for damage caused by a nuclear incident directly due to an act of armed conflict, hostilities, civil war, insurrection or a natural disaster of an exceptional character [Section 15].

C. AMOUNT OF LIABILITY

The Italian Act sets the maximum liability of the operator of a nuclear installation for damage caused by a nuclear incident at L 7 500 million (approximately 5 million Special Drawing Rights of the International Monetary Fund – SDRs) [Section 19].

If the amount of damage exceeds the limit of the operator's liability, thereby necessitating intervention by the State, the total amount of compensation may not exceed L 43 750 million (approximately 30 million SDRs). Above this ceiling, compensation for damage is to be provided within the limits and according to the conditions laid down by the Brussels Supplementary Convention [Section 19].

D. NUCLEAR DAMAGE

a) Damage Covered

Damage covered is that caused by a nuclear incident and resulting from the radioactive properties or a combination of radioactive properties with toxic, explosive or other hazardous properties, of nuclear fuel or radioactive products or waste [Section 1].

Damage caused by ionizing radiation emitted by any radioactive source within a nuclear installation is also covered [Section 15].

b) Damage Excluded

Damage to the installation itself or to any property on the site of the installation which is used, or to be used, in connection therewith is excluded from the scope of the Act [Section 15].

Damage to the means of transport on which the nuclear materials were at the time of the incident is not covered by the Act if caused by a nuclear incident involving nuclear fuel or radioactive products or waste in the nuclear installation or coming from it [Section 15]. However, the Act covers damage affecting the carrier by rail, provided that the liability of the operator in respect of other damage is not reduced to an amount less than L 3 150 million (approximately 2 million SDRs) [Section 16].

II. COVER AND COMPENSATION

A. INSURANCE OR OTHER FINANCIAL SECURITY

The operator of a nuclear installation situated in Italy is required to take out and maintain an insurance policy approved by the Minister of Industry, Commerce and Crafts, in an amount equal to his maximum liability [Section 22]. A Decree promulgated jointly on 3rd March 1978 by the Minister of Industry, Commerce and Crafts and the Minister of Transport (published on 12th April 1978), lays down the general conditions for the third party liability insurance policies which operators of nuclear installations or persons responsible for the transport of nuclear materials are required to take out.

Operators may be authorised to furnish equivalent financial security in another form, subject to the approval of the Minister of Industry, Commerce and Crafts, in agreement with the Minister of the Treasury and after consultation with the Department of the State Procurator-General (*Avvocatura Generale*) [Act No. 1860, Section 22].

Any insurance or financial security used to pay compensation following a nuclear incident must be reconstituted by the operator, on pain of revocation of his licence to operate his installation [Section 19].

Authorisation for the transit of nuclear materials through Italy is subject to proof of the existence of financial security of an amount at least equal to the maximum amount of liability established by the Act [Section 21].

At least three months' notice must be given to the Minister of Industry, Commerce and Crafts of the suspension or cancellation of any insurance or financial security furnished in respect of any nuclear installation [Section 22].

In respect of any nuclear materials in course of carriage, no insurance or financial security relating thereto may be suspended or cancelled before such carriage is completed and the nuclear materials have been taken in charge by another person liable in accordance with the Act [Section 22].

The operator liable is required to provide the carrier with a certificate of financial security for the carriage of nuclear materials, issued by or on behalf of the insurer or other financial guarantor [Section 16]; this certificate has to be in the form laid down by the Minister of Industry, Commerce and Crafts, in agreement with the Minister of Transport, on the basis of the model recommended by the NEA Steering Committee (Decree of 16th February 1976).

B. STATE INTERVENTION

As stated above, if the amount of damage exceeds that of the financial security available to the operator, the State gives financial assistance to cover the difference, up to an amount of L 43 750 million. Above this amount, the Italian Act specifies that the damage will be covered, up to a maximum of L 75 000 million (approximately 45 million SDRs), by the Contracting Parties to the Paris and Brussels Conventions, ratified and brought into force by Act No. 109 of 12th February 1974 [Act No. 1860, Section 19].

C. COMPENSATION

Claims for compensation may be brought solely against the operator liable for the damage or against the insurer or other financial guarantor [Section 18].

Where there are several claims and the amount of compensation is likely to exceed the amount of financial security, the Court may order proceedings for the settlement of such claims to be joined. The Court may also rule that the amount of compensation due to each claimant be proportionately reduced [Section 25].

Any interest or costs awarded by the Court in actions for compensation are payable in addition to the amount of such compensation [Section 20].

Notice of any actions for compensation must also be given to the Minister of the Treasury, who is empowered to intervene in the proceedings [Section 25].

D. TIME LIMITS FOR BRINGING CLAIMS

Actions for compensation for nuclear damage are barred after three years from the date on which the person concerned knew or ought reasonably to have known of both the damage and the operator liable [Section 23].

The right to compensation for nuclear damage is extinguished ten years after the date of the incident if no action has been brought in the meantime [Section 23].

However, in the case of damage caused by nuclear materials which have been stolen, lost or abandoned, the time limit for the admissibility of claims is calculated from the date of the nuclear incident, provided that it in no event exceeds twenty years from the date of the theft, loss or abandonment [Section 23].

E. COMPETENT COURTS AND PROCEDURE

The Italian Courts have exclusive jurisdiction to hear actions brought under the Act in respect of a nuclear incident which has occurred in Italy. They also have jurisdiction to determine claims for compensation in respect of a nuclear incident which has occurred outside the territory of the Contracting States to the Paris Convention and the Brussels Supplementary Convention or, where the place of the incident cannot be determined with certainty, provided the claim is made against the operator of an installation situated in Italian territory [Section 24].

Actions for compensation must be brought in the Court within whose jurisdiction the nuclear installation is situated [Section 25].

JAPAN

INTRODUCTION

There are 37 nuclear power plants supplying electricity in Japan in 1990, with a total electrical power generation of 29 280 MWe. Those plants are operated by several private companies. Approximately 27 per cent of the total electricity is nuclear.

The Director-General of the Science and Technology Agency is the authority responsible for nuclear third party liability questions in Japan.

Japan is not a Party to the Paris Convention or the Vienna Convention.

The legislation governing nuclear third party liability is contained in Law No. 147 of 17th June 1961 on Compensation for Nuclear Damage as last amended on 31st March 1989 (the Compensation Law), the Ordinance for enforcement of the Compensation Law (Cabinet Order No. 44 of 6th March 1962 as last amended on 17th November 1989 and Law No. 148 of 17th June 1961 on Indemnity Agreements for Compensation of Nuclear Damage as last amended on 27th May 1988 (the Indemnity Agreement Law). (These texts are reproduced in the Supplement to Nuclear Law Bulletin No. 45.)

I. THIRD PARTY LIABILITY

A. SCOPE AND DEFINITIONS

There are no special provisions concerning the territorial scope of application of the Compensation Law, with the result that the common law is applicable.

The Compensation Law provides for compensation of nuclear damage caused by reactor operation, fabrication, reprocessing and use of nuclear fuel, radioactive waste disposal and disposal of nuclear fuel material or material contaminated by nuclear fuel material (including nuclear fission products) as well as during transport or storage of nuclear fuel material; it should be noted that the term *operation of the reactor, etc.* is used in the Law to define these activities [Section 2].

The definitions of *reactor*, *nuclear fuel material* and *radiation* have the meaning given to them in the Atomic Energy Basic Law (Law No. 186 of 19th December 1955 as amended) while *fabricating* and *reprocessing* are defined by reference to Law No. 166 of

10th June 1957 for the Regulation of Nuclear Source Material, Nuclear Fuel Material and Reactors as amended – known as the Regulation Law [Compensation Law, Section 2(4)].

The Law defines the *nuclear operator* as any person who has been granted a licence, authorisation or approval to operate nuclear installations or undertake nuclear activities as specified by the Regulation Law; it also specifically designates as nuclear operators the Japan Atomic Energy Research Institute (JAERI) and the Power Reactor and Nuclear Fuel Development Corporation (PNC) [Compensation Law, Section 2(3)].

B. NATURE AND ASSIGNMENT OF LIABILITY

a) General – Nuclear Installations

Where nuclear damage is caused as a result of reactor operation as defined by the Law, the nuclear operator who is engaged in the operation of the reactor on such occasion is exclusively liable, irrespective of fault, for the damage [Compensation Law, Sections 3 and 4].

b) Transport

Where nuclear damage occurs as a result of the transport of nuclear fuel from one nuclear operator to another, the nuclear operator who sends the fuel (the consignor) is liable for the damage unless there is a special agreement in writing between the consignor and the consignee [Compensation Law, Section 3].

When transport of nuclear fuel is effected between a Japanese nuclear operator and a foreign nuclear operator, the Japanese nuclear operator is liable, whoever is the consignor [Compensation Law, Section 3].

Before the Compensation Law was revised in 1971 [the Law amending the Compensation Law: Law No. 53, 1971] the consignee was liable, because transport was considered as a service supplied to the nuclear operator who received the material. The 1971 revision provided for the contrary, namely the consignor is liable because he is responsible for packaging the material for the transport. This is also more in conformity with the equivalent provisions of the Paris and Vienna Conventions.

c) Rights of Recourse

If nuclear damage is caused by the wilful act of a third party, the nuclear operator who has paid compensation for the nuclear damage retains a right of recourse against such a third party. In addition, a nuclear operator may enter into special arrangements giving him a right of recourse [Compensation Law, Section 5].

When the Compensation Law was adopted in 1961, the nuclear operator had a right of recourse also when the damage was caused by the fault of a third party. But in view of developments in the nuclear field, in particular, the frequency of nuclear fuel transports, the 1971 revision omitted damage caused by the fault of a third party from the cases where a nuclear operator retains a right of recourse.

d) Exoneration from Liability

A nuclear operator is exonerated from liability for nuclear damage where the damage is caused by a grave natural disaster of an exceptional character, an insurrection or hostilities of any type [Compensation Law, Section 3].

C. AMOUNT OF LIABILITY

On the legal level, the liability of a nuclear operator is not limited in Japan.

D. NUCLEAR DAMAGE

a) Damage Covered

The Law defines *nuclear damage* as any damage caused by the effects of the nuclear fission process of nuclear fuel material, by the effects of radiation of nuclear fuel material, or by the toxic nature of such materials [Compensation Law, Section 2(2)].

When the Compensation Law was adopted, the damage suffered by the nuclear operator's employees in the course of performing their duties, was also not covered. The reason for this was that the damage suffered by the employees had been considered as being covered primarily by the workmen's compensation system as an industrial accident or occupational disease. After a number of discussions in the Diet (Parliament), the damage suffered by the employees was covered by the revision in 1979 [the Law amending the Compensation Law: Law No. 44, 1979].

b) Damage Excluded

Nuclear damage suffered by the nuclear operator (i.e. damage to the installation itself and to on-site property used in connection therewith) is not covered by the Compensation Law and the Indemnity Agreement Law [Compensation Law, Section 2].

II. COVER AND COMPENSATION

A. INSURANCE OR OTHER FINANCIAL SECURITY

A nuclear operator cannot operate nuclear installations or carry out nuclear activities as defined by the Law unless financial security to cover his liability for nuclear damage has been provided [Compensation Law, Section 6]. Financial security is furnished by the conclusion of an insurance contract amounting to 30 billion yen (approximately 150 million Special Drawing Rights of the International Monetary Fund – SDRs) for liability for nuclear damage and an indemnity agreement for compensation of nuclear damage or by a deposit, which are approved by the Director-General of the Science and Technology Agency as an arrangement that makes available an equivalent amount for compensation of nuclear damage for each single site, or by an equivalent arrangement which is approved by the Director-General of the Science and Technology Agency [Compensation Law, Section 7].

An insurance contract for liability for nuclear damage is the contract under which an insurer undertakes to indemnify a nuclear operator for his loss arising from compensating nuclear damage due to specified cases, where such nuclear operator becomes liable for compensation of nuclear damage, and under which the insured (the operator) undertakes to pay a premium to the insurer [Compensation Law, Section 8].

As mentioned above, the amount of such financial security must be 30 billion yen for each single site, but, for certain categories of nuclear installations which present a lesser risk, a lower amount has been fixed by Cabinet Order No. 44 of 6th March 1962 as amended [Compensation Law, Section 7].

The amount of financial security has been revised several times as follows:

1961 originally:	5 billion yen,
1971 revision:	6 billion yen,
1979 revision:	10 billion yen,
1989 revision:	30 billion yen.

Where the amount available for compensation of nuclear damage falls below the amount of financial security because the nuclear operator concerned has paid compensation for damage, the Director-General of the Science and Technology Agency may order the nuclear operator to restore the amount up to the full amount of financial security by a given time [Compensation Law, Section 7(2)].

B. STATE INTERVENTION

The State provides for two measures to compensate nuclear damage: the first is a government indemnity agreement to complement the operator's insurance for liability, and the second is state aid providing compensation for any nuclear damage which exceeds the amount of financial security and that of the government indemnity agreement.

These measures apply to the nuclear damage arising from the operation of a reactor, etc. coming into operation through the end of 1999 [Compensation Law, Section 20]. This time limit is designed to allow the Compensation Law and the Indemnity Agreement Law to be revised as the need arises from considerations or assessments of further progress in the development and utilisation of nuclear energy, and also on the basis of availability of funds on the insurance market.

a) Indemnity Agreements

If a nuclear operator chooses to cover his liability by an insurance contract for liability for nuclear damage, he must, in addition, conclude an indemnity agreement for compensation of nuclear damage with the Government. The indemnity agreement is the contract under which the Government undertakes to indemnify a nuclear operator for his loss arising from compensating nuclear damage not covered by the liability insurance contract and other financial security, and under which the nuclear operator undertakes to pay an indemnity fee to the Government [Compensation Law, Section 10].

Under the indemnity agreement the Government undertakes to indemnify the nuclear operator for any losses suffered as a result of compensating nuclear damage mentioned below:

- nuclear damage caused by earthquake or volcanic eruption (natural catastrophe);
- nuclear damage caused by an unknown occurrence during normal operation;
- nuclear damage which, in so far as the occurrence that caused the damage is concerned, can be covered by a liability insurance contract and for which persons having suffered the damage have not claimed for compensation within the period of ten years from the date of the occurrence (with regard to the damage suffered, this shall apply only to the case where there is a justifiable reason for their failure to claim for compensation within such period) [Indemnity Agreement Law, Section 3 – see below under "Time Limits for Bringing Claims"].

b) State Aid

If nuclear damage occurs, the Government gives the nuclear operator who is liable such aid as is required for him to compensate the damage, when the amount required for full compensation exceeds the amount of financial security and when the Government deems it necessary to fulfil the purpose of the Compensation Law [Compensation Law, Section 16].

In the event of nuclear damage caused by a grave natural disaster of an exceptional character or by an insurrection, the Government takes the necessary measures to relieve victims and to prevent any increase of the damage [Compensation Law, Section 17].

C. COMPENSATION

Any person having suffered nuclear damage has priority over other creditors in respect of compensation provided by the operator's liability insurance contract and an indemnity agreement [Compensation Law, Section 9].

The right to claim compensation under a liability insurance contract or an indemnity agreement may not be assigned, mortgaged, or seized; however a person having a claim under the Compensation Law may make such a seizure [Compensation Law, Section 9].

D. TIME LIMITS FOR BRINGING CLAIMS

No claim for compensation of nuclear damage may be brought against a nuclear operator ten years after the occurrence of the incident [Indemnity Agreement Law, Section 3].

A nuclear operator's right to receive payment from an indemnity agreement is extinguished two years after he has paid compensation [Indemnity Agreement Law, Section 11].

E. COMPETENT COURTS AND PROCEDURE

There are no provisions concerning the competent court to decide claims for the compensation of nuclear damage under the Compensation Law. The general provisions of the Civil Law (Law No. 9, 1898) and the Civil Suit Law (Law No. 29, 1890) are applicable.

A Dispute Reconciliation Committee for Nuclear Damage Compensation may be established as an organisation attached to the Science and Technology Agency, to mediate in respect of reconciliation of disputes arising from the compensation of nuclear damage [Compensation Law, Section 18].

REPUBLIC OF KOREA

INTRODUCTION

The Republic of Korea has 6 666 MWe of installed nuclear capacity, representing approximately 46.9 per cent of its total electricity production. Its nuclear power plants are owned and operated by the Korea Electric Power Corporation (KEPCO) which is state-owned.

The Atomic Energy Commission, which reports to the Prime Minister, has responsibility for the general orientation of nuclear activities. It is served by the staff of the Atomic Energy Office in the Ministry of Science and Technology. Authorisation for nuclear activities is given by the Director General of the Office of Atomic Energy on the advice of the Atomic Energy Commission.

The Republic of Korea is not a Party to either the 1960 Paris Convention or the 1963 Vienna Convention.

The legislation on nuclear third party liability is Act No. 2094 of 24th January 1969 on Nuclear Damage Compensation as amended by Act No. 2765 of 7th April 1975. Additional, more detailed, provisions in relation to this Act are established by Presidential Decree No. 5396 of 3rd December 1970 as amended by Presidential Decree No. 7756 of 22nd August 1975. The legislation is supplemented by Act No. 2764 of 7th April 1975 on Nuclear Damage Compensation Indemnity Agreements. More detailed provisions in relation to this latter Act are provided by Presidential Decree No. 7755 of 22nd August 1975.

I. THIRD PARTY LIABILITY

A. SCOPE AND DEFINITIONS

The Act covers the operation of reactors, processing prescribed by Presidential Decree, reprocessing prescribed by Presidential Decree, use of nuclear fuel prescribed by Presidential Decree and the transportation, storage and disposal of nuclear fuel or goods contaminated by nuclear fuel [Section 2]*.

* All references, unless otherwise specified, are to Act No. 2094 of 24th January 1969 as amended by Act No. 2765 of 7th April 1975.

It designates persons authorised to install or operate a reactor, a processing facility or a reprocessing facility and to use or handle nuclear fuel or source materials, as well as atomic energy research institutes, atomic energy development organisations or atomic energy generating organisations, as operators.

B. NATURE AND ASSIGNMENT OF LIABILITY

a) General – Nuclear Installations

An operator is liable for nuclear damage arising from the carrying out of an activity covered by the Act. This liability is absolute and exclusive [Section 3(1) and (3)].

b) Transport

In the case of transport of nuclear material between operators, the sending operator is liable for any damage. This is, however, subject to any agreement to the contrary between the relevant operators [Section 3(2)].

c) Rights of Recourse

An operator has a right of recourse against a person who wilfully or erroneously caused the nuclear damage. However, in the case of a supplier of materials or services, this right only arises if the damage was caused deliberately by the supplier or his employees, or by their serious errors [Section 4(1)]. Furthermore, if there is a contract governing rights to claim compensation, such rights shall be subject to that contract [Section 4(2)].

d) Exoneration from Liability

An operator is not liable for damage caused by a serious disaster, earthquake, act of God, war or other comparable circumstances [Section 3(1)].

C. AMOUNT OF LIABILITY

The Act makes no express provision for a limit to the liability of the operator. Nevertheless, his obligation to hold insurance or other financial security to cover his liability is limited. (See below.)

D. NUCLEAR DAMAGE

a) Damage Covered

The nuclear damage covered by the Act is damage arising from the nuclear fission process, radioactivity or toxic properties of nuclear fuel or goods contaminated by nuclear fuel [Section 2(2)].

b) Damage Excluded

Damage suffered by the operator or his employees is not covered by the liability provisions of the Act [Section 2(2)].

II. COVER AND COMPENSATION

A. INSURANCE OR OTHER FINANCIAL SECURITY

The activities covered by the Act may not be carried out unless the operator either has an insurance contract covering nuclear damage for which the operator is liable under the Act and a nuclear damage compensation indemnity contract with the Government (see below under "State Intervention") or holds a deposit to cover his obligation to compensate nuclear damage [Section 5 and 7(1)].

The amount to be so covered by insurance and an indemnity contract or by deposit varies according to the risk posed by the activity as follows:

- for a reactor with a thermal output of more than 10 000 kw and related transport and storage, 3 billion won (approximately 3 million Special Drawing Rights of the International Monetary Fund – SDRs);
- for a reprocessing plant, 1 billion won;
- for a reactor with a thermal output of between 100 and 10 000 kw and related transport and storage, 500 million won;
- for a reactor with a thermal output of between 1 and 100 kw and related transport and storage, 100 million won; and
- for a reactor with a thermal output of less than 1 kw and related transport and storage; for a processing plant; for an installation using fissionable material and for the transportation and storage of fissionable materials, 10 million won [Section 6(1) and Decree No. 5396 of 3rd December 1970 as amended by Decree No. 7756 of 22nd August 1975, Section 3].

Before an operator enters into the insurance contract, he must obtain the approval of the Minister of Science and Technology as to the terms of the contract [Section 7(2)].

The right to claim insurance money under the insurance contract is not to be transferred, mortgaged or confiscated. However, a person suffering nuclear damage compensable under the Act may confiscate such money to the extent of his claim under the Act [Section 8(3)].

A deposit made to cover the operator's obligation to compensate nuclear damage is to be made in cash or securities at the district court having jurisdiction over the place where the main office of the operator is located [Section 11].

The Minister for Science and Technology is empowered to instruct an operator to take the necessary steps to replenish compensation funds expended for nuclear damage compensation up to the amount of financial security required under the Act by a given date if the amount available for future nuclear damage compensation is insufficient. In this case the installation may be operated up to that given date notwithstanding the insufficiency of the compensation funds available [Section 6(2) and (3)].

The above provisions do not apply where the relevant operator is the Government [Section 18].

B. STATE INTERVENTION

Unless the operator holds a deposit to cover his obligation to compensate nuclear damage, he must, in addition to holding an insurance contract, hold a nuclear damage compensation indemnity agreement with the Government [Section 5]. Under this agreement the Government is to cover any compensation payable under the Act up to the ceiling of the financial security required to be held by the operator that is not paid by the operator's insurance [Section 9(1)]. These provisions do not apply where the relevant operator is the Government [Section 18].

In addition, the Government will compensate under the indemnity agreement nuclear damage caused by tidal waves, floods, storms or thunderbolts or where the claim has not been made during the period of validity of the relevant insurance contract due to unavoidable circumstances [Law No. 2764 of 7th April 1975, Section 4(2) and Presidential Decree No. 7755 of 22nd August 1975, Section 2(2)].

Where nuclear damage exceeds the ceiling of the financial security required to be held by the operator, the Government may provide additional compensation as it deems necessary in accordance with authority granted by the National Assembly [Section 14(1) and (3)].

In the case of a nuclear incident, the Government is to take the necessary measures to rescue the injured and prevent any further damage [Section 14(2)].

C. COMPENSATION

A person suffering damage covered by the Act has priority over other creditors in claiming compensation from the insurance and under the nuclear damage indemnity agreement with the Government [Section 8(1) and 10]. These provisions do not apply where the relevant operator is the Government [Section 18].

D. TIME LIMITS FOR BRINGING CLAIMS

The Act provides no special time limits for bringing claims.

E. COMPETENT COURTS AND PROCEDURE

The Act makes no special provision with respect to courts competent to decide claims under the Act.

A Nuclear Damage Compensation Deliberation Committee within the Ministry of Science and Technology is provided for to co-ordinate extra-judicial settlement of claims for nuclear damage compensation and to survey and evaluate nuclear damage for this purpose [Section 15].

MALAYSIA

INTRODUCTION

Malaysia does not presently have a nuclear power programme. It does, however, have a research reactor, Triga Puspati, of 1 MWe.

The Atomic Energy Licensing Board has general responsibility for matters pertaining to nuclear third party liability.

Malaysia is not a Party to either the 1960 Paris Convention or the 1963 Vienna Convention. Conversely, Malaysia is a Signatory of the 1962 Convention on the Liability of Operators of Nuclear Ships.

The basic legislation on nuclear third party liability is contained in the Atomic Energy Licensing Act 1984 (Act No. 304). It is generally consistent with the provisions of the Vienna Convention.

I. THIRD PARTY LIABILITY

A. SCOPE AND DEFINITIONS

The Atomic Energy Licensing Act of 1984 (the Act) applies throughout Malaysia [Section 1(2)]. It does not apply to incidents occurring outside Malaysia nor to damage suffered outside Malaysia.

The terms *operator* and *nuclear installation* are used as those terms are used in the Vienna Convention [Section 2].

B. NATURE AND ASSIGNMENT OF LIABILITY

a) General – Nuclear Installations

The operator of a nuclear installation is liable for nuclear damage caused by a nuclear incident in his installation unless the incident involved nuclear material stored therein incidentally to its carriage and another operator is liable in accordance with the provisions concerning transport [Section 43(1)].

The liability of the operator is absolute and, as a general principle, exclusive [Section 45].

Where more than one operator is liable for nuclear damage and the damage attributable to each operator is not reasonably separable, all operators involved are to be jointly and severally liable [Section 52(1)].

Where several installations of one operator are involved in one nuclear incident, the operator is to be liable in respect of each installation up to the amount of the operator's liability established under the above provisions [Section 53] (see under "Amount of Liability" below). The Atomic Energy Licensing Board or, in the case of medical activities, the Director-General of Health is authorised to determine that several nuclear installations of one operator located at the same site are to be considered as a single nuclear installation [Section 56].

Where more than one operator is liable for damage caused by one nuclear incident, the liability of any one operator is limited to the amount of the operator's liability established under the above provisions [Section 52(3)].

b) Transport

An operator of a nuclear installation in Malaysia is liable for nuclear damage caused by an incident occurring in the course of carriage of nuclear material from his installation and before liability for such damage has been assumed, pursuant to the express terms of a contract in writing, by another operator of a nuclear installation in Malaysia or, in the absence of such express terms, before another such operator has taken charge of the nuclear material [Section 43(b)]. In the case of such carriage, the consignee operator is liable for nuclear damage caused by an incident occurring after he so assumes liability or takes charge of the nuclear material [Section 43(c)].

In the case of transport between an installation in Malaysia and a place outside Malaysia, the operator of an installation in Malaysia is liable for nuclear damage caused by any incident occurring during the part of the carriage within Malaysia [Section 43(2)]. This is subject to any contrary provision in any bilateral or multilateral arrangement or Convention to which Malaysia is a Party [Section 43(3)].

Where nuclear material is being carried through Malaysia in transit between places outside Malaysia and a nuclear incident occurs in Malaysia, the person licensed to transport the material by the competent authority in the country from which it is being carried is liable for any nuclear damage caused [Section 44(1)].

A carrier of nuclear material or a person handling radioactive waste may, at his request and with the consent of the operator concerned, be designated as operator by the Atomic Energy Licensing Board and shall thereupon be considered as an operator for the purposes of the Act [Section 51].

c) Rights of Recourse

The operator has a right of recourse against: (a) any person against whom such a right is provided by the express terms of a contract in writing; (b) if the nuclear incident results from an act or omission with intent to cause damage, against the person who has acted or omitted to act with such intent; and (c) if the nuclear incident involves stolen nuclear material, against the person who stole or unlawfully received that material [Section 47(1)].

d) Exoneration from Liability

No person is to be liable for any nuclear damage caused by a nuclear incident directly due to an act of armed conflict, hostilities, civil war, insurrection or a grave natural disaster of an exceptional character [Section 46(1)].

If the operator proves that the nuclear damage resulted wholly or partly either from the gross negligence of the person suffering the damage or from an act or omission of such person with intent to cause damage, the court may relieve the operator from paying compensation in respect of the damage suffered by that person [Section 49].

C. AMOUNT OF LIABILITY

The aggregate liability of the operator of a nuclear installation situated in Malaysia for any one nuclear incident is limited to an amount equivalent at 1st February 1985 to 50 million ringgit (approximately $18 million) [Section 59(1)]. The amount of the operator's liability is thus indexed against inflation. The Atomic Energy Licensing Board is authorised, taking into account the size and nature of the nuclear installation, the extent of the damage involved or any other circumstances, to prescribe a different limit but not lower than 12 million ringgit [Section 59(2)]. The amount of the operator's liability pursuant to either of these provisions is not to include any interest or costs awarded by the court in actions for compensation [Section 59(3)].

D. NUCLEAR DAMAGE

a) Damage Covered

Liability arises under the Act in the above described cases for any loss of life, bodily injury, loss of, loss of use of, or damage to property or loss of use of or damage to the environment, which arises out of or results from: (a) radioactive properties or a combination of radioactive properties with toxic, explosive or other hazardous properties of nuclear fuel or radioactive products or waste in, or of nuclear material coming from, originating in, or sent to a nuclear installation; or (b) ionizing radiation emitted by any source of radiation inside a nuclear installation [Section 2].

Whenever both such nuclear damage and other damage have been caused by a nuclear incident or jointly by a nuclear incident and one or more other occurrences, to the extent that the nuclear damage and the other damage are not reasonably separable, that other damage is to be treated as though it were such nuclear damage [Section 54].

b) Damage Excluded

The operator is not liable under the Act for nuclear damage to the nuclear installation itself or to any property on the site of the installation which is used or is to be used in connection with that nuclear installation nor, in the case of an incident during transport, to the means of transport in which the nuclear material involved was carried at the time of the incident [Section 46(2)]. However, this does not affect any liability which the operator may have other than under the Act for nuclear damage to the means of transport in which nuclear material involved in an incident was being carried [Section 50].

The competent Minister (presently the Prime Minister), if he determines that the small extent of the risks involved so warrants, may exclude any prescribed small quantities of any radioactive material, nuclear material or prescribed substance from the application of the provisions of the Act concerning liability for nuclear damage [Section 66].

II. COVER AND COMPENSATION

A. INSURANCE OR OTHER FINANCIAL SECURITY

The operator of a nuclear installation situated in Malaysia or any other person importing or exporting nuclear material must have financial security to cover his liability for nuclear damage under the Act [Section 60(1)]. Such financial security may include private insurance, private contractual indemnity, self-insurance or a combination thereof or other evidence of financial ability to pay compensation under the Act [Section 60(2)]. The type and terms of the financial security are to be prescribed by the Atomic Energy Licensing Board [Section 60(2)]. No financial guarantor may suspend, cancel or vary the type and terms of the financial security without giving notice in writing of at least two months to the Atomic Energy Licensing Board of its intention to do so, nor, in so far as the financial security relates to the carriage of nuclear material, may it do so during the period of the carriage [Section 60(3)].

No person is to carry nuclear material in transit through Malaysia unless that person provides such financial security as may be required by the Atomic Energy Licensing Board and furnishes proof to the satisfaction of the Board that he is authorised by the country from which it is being carried to do so [Section 44(2)].

With respect to carriage to or from an installation in Malaysia, the operator must provide the carrier with a certificate issued by or on behalf of the financial guarantor [Section 55(1)]. This certificate is to state the name and address of the installation operator and the amount, type and duration of the financial security [Section 55(2)]. The financial guarantor is barred from disputing these particulars [Section 55(2)]. The certificate is also to indicate the nuclear material in respect of which the financial security applies and include a statement by the Atomic Energy Licensing Board or, in the case of carriage related to medical activities, the Director-General of Health that the person designated is an operator under the Act [Section 55(3)].

B. STATE INTERVENTION

To the extent that the financial security held by the operator is inadequate, the Government may, where it considers it necessary to do so, provide the necessary funds for the payment of compensation claims up to the maximum liability of the operator under the Act [Section 61(1)].

Where it appears that claims for compensation for nuclear damage caused by a nuclear incident may exceed the limit of the operator's liability under the Act, the Atomic Energy Licensing Board is to furnish a report to the competent Minister with recommendations for the appropriation of additional funds for the payment of claims for such compensation and the Minister is to have the report immediately laid before the *Dewan Rakyat* (the House of Representatives of the Parliament) [Section 61(2)]. Upon such report being laid before it, the *Dewan Rakyat* may, by resolution, appropriate additional funds to provide compensation as it considers necessary in the interests of the nation [Section 61(3)].

Any nuclear incident involving the application of the Act is to be immediately reported to the Atomic Energy Licensing Board and the operator is to provide all the information which the Board requires to evaluate the extent of the nuclear damage involved [Section 57(1)]. The Board is to investigate the cause and extent of the nuclear damage and, if it deems it to be in the public interest, it may make its findings available to the public and to the parties involved [Section 57(2)].

After the occurrence of a nuclear incident the Board is authorised to adopt such measures as are appropriate to determine the persons who were or might have been exposed to ionizing radiation [Section 58(1)]. For the purposes of carrying into effect such measures, the Board is authorised to: require any person likely to be affected by exposure to ionizing radiation to be medically examined or to be removed to a hospital or other place specially designated for the treatment, detection or observation of any nuclear damage and to detain such person until he can be discharged without danger to himself or others. It may also cause a post-mortem examination to be made on any corpse where the death is suspected to have been due to a nuclear incident or exposure to ionizing radiation [Section 58(2)].

C. COMPENSATION

Where it appears that the nuclear damage from a nuclear incident may exceed the limit of liability under Section 59 of the Act and the Federal Government intends to act pursuant to Section 61 of the Act, the court having jurisdiction in the matter is to issue such orders as may be necessary to assure the equitable distribution of compensation, including orders apportioning the payments to be made to claimants and orders permitting partial payments to be made before final determination of the total claims [Section 65].

Where there is any nuclear damage to the environment, a claim for compensation against the operator is to be made by the Federal Government, the Government of one of the States of Malaysia or both, according to whether the segment of the environment that is damaged is within the jurisdiction of the Federal Government, a State of Malaysia or both [Section 48].

D. TIME LIMITS FOR BRINGING CLAIMS

Actions for compensation under the Act are barred if not brought within twenty years after the nuclear incident or twenty years from the date on which the person suffering nuclear damage had knowledge or should reasonably have had knowledge of such damage, providing that this date is within twenty years after the date of the accident [Section 63]. Nevertheless, a person who has brought an action for compensation within the period applicable may amend that claim to take into account any aggravation of the damage even after the expiry period provided that final judgment has not been entered in the case [Section 63].

Even in the case where the nuclear incident involves nuclear material which had at any time been stolen, lost, jettisoned or abandoned, the period within which to bring actions for compensation is to be calculated from the date of the incident and not from the date when the material had been stolen, lost, jettisoned or abandoned [Section 64(1)].

E. COMPETENT COURTS AND PROCEDURE

The Act makes no special provision with respect to the courts competent to hear claims under the Act. Under the general law the High Courts of Malaysia would have jurisdiction.

MEXICO

INTRODUCTION

Mexico has one nuclear power plant (Laguna Verde), the first unit of which began operating in 1989, while the second is still under construction. Installed capacity will be some 1 300 MWe. The operator is the Federal Electricity Commission.

Mexico is one of the Contracting Parties to the Vienna Convention. Provisions to implement the Convention are contained in the Act on Third Party Liability for Nuclear Damage, promulgated on 29th December 1974 and published in the Official Gazette on 31st December 1974.

I. THIRD PARTY LIABILITY

A. SCOPE AND DEFINITIONS

The purpose of the Act is to regulate third party liability for any damage caused by the use of nuclear reactors and nuclear substances, fuel and the resulting radioactive waste [Section 1].

The nuclear installations covered by the Act are:

- nuclear reactors, except those used in a means of transport;
- industrial installations using nuclear fuel for the production of hazardous nuclear substances, and plants in which such substances are processed, including any plant for the reprocessing of irradiated fuel;
- facilities for storing hazardous nuclear substances, unless such substances are stored there temporarily in course of carriage [Section 3(f)].

As for hazardous nuclear substances, they are defined as nuclear fuel (other than natural or depleted uranium) capable of producing a self-sustaining nuclear fission reaction outside a nuclear reactor, and radioactive products or waste, other than radioisotopes which are used or are to be used for medical, scientific, agricultural, industrial or commercial purposes and which are outside a nuclear installation [Section 3(j)].

A group of nuclear installations situated on the same site is considered as a single installation for the purposes of the Act [Section 3(f)].

B. NATURE AND ASSIGNMENT OF LIABILITY

a) General – Nuclear Installations

The third party liability of the operator for nuclear damage is absolute (strict) [Section 4]. The operator of a nuclear installation is defined as the person designated or authorised by the competent authority of the State (of the United Mexican States) within whose jurisdiction the installation is situated [Section 3(e)].

The operator is liable for all damage caused by a nuclear incident (an occurrence or series of occurrences having the same origin which causes nuclear damage) occurring in a nuclear installation for which he is responsible, or by an incident involving hazardous nuclear substances produced in such an installation, unless such substances form part of a consignment of nuclear materials [Sections 3(a) and 5].

Where nuclear damage engages the liability of more than one operator, the operators involved are jointly and severally liable [Section 8]. The cumulative liability of all the operators involved may not, however, exceed the maximum limits laid down by the Act [Section 9].

Where damage was caused both by a nuclear incident and by other events, and it is not possible to distinguish the proportion of damage resulting from the different causes in question, the whole damage is deemed to have been caused by the nuclear incident [Section 12].

Any agreements or contracts excluding or limiting the operator's liability as defined by the Act, are null and void [Section 28].

b) Transport

The operator of a nuclear installation is liable for all damage caused by a nuclear incident occurring during the carriage of nuclear substances until such time as the substances are unloaded from the means of transport at the agreed location or upon delivery, or until such time as the operator of another nuclear installation has assumed liability under contract for the consignment [Section 6]. These provisions also apply to consignments of nuclear reactors.

The carrier or shipping agent may take over the operator's liability with regard to the nuclear substances, provided he satisfies the requirements of the Act and any applicable regulations [Section 7]. In particular, he must cover the risks of transport in the same way as the operator himself [Section 15].

Before each shipment of nuclear substances, the operator must supply a certificate indicating his name and address as well as the nature and quantity of the substances transported, and specifying the statutory amount of his liability. The certificate must be accompanied by a declaration by the competent authority that the person concerned meets the conditions required for a nuclear operator, and by a certificate from his insurer or financial guarantor. Public bodies are not required to comply with this formality [Section 10].

Where nuclear damage arises from simultaneous incidents involving two or more consignments of hazardous nuclear substances on the same means of transport or which were being stored in course of carriage in the same facility, the total obligations of the persons jointly and severally liable may not exceed the higher of the individual liabilities, nor may the liability of each person concerned exceed the limits laid down for his particular transport operation [Section 16].

c) Exoneration from Liability

The operator is not liable when a nuclear incident is the direct consequence of war, invasion, insurrection or other warlike acts, or of natural disasters [Section 11].

C. AMOUNT OF LIABILITY

The maximum amount of the operator's third party liability is established at 100 million pesos for each nuclear incident [Section 14]. However, in view of Mexico's commitments following its accession to the Vienna Convention, account should be taken of the fact that the nuclear operator's liability cannot amount to less than $5 million, which corresponds to the minimum set by that Convention.

Subject to the above, the Act provides that, in the event of several nuclear incidents occurring in the same installation within a consecutive twelve month period, this amount is established at 150 million pesos [Section 14].

The figure of 150 million pesos covers the case of transport incidents occurring during the said period and involving nuclear substances coming from or going to an installation, and for which the operator is liable [Section 14].

The said amounts of maximum liability do not include interest payable in accordance with the law or the legal costs fixed by the court [Section 17].

D. NUCLEAR DAMAGE

a) Damage Covered

Nuclear damage is defined in the Act as being loss of life, personal injury, or any damage or material loss resulting directly or indirectly from the radioactive properties or a combination of such properties with toxic, explosive or other properties of nuclear fuel or radioactive products or waste in, or of hazardous nuclear substances produced in, coming from or sent to, a nuclear installation [Section 3(c)].

b) Damage Excluded

If the operator liable shows that the nuclear damage resulted wholly or partly from the fault or deliberate omission of the person suffering the damage or from his gross negligence, the competent court may decide to relieve the operator wholly or partly from his obligation to compensate such person [Section 13].

II. COVER AND COMPENSATION

A. INSURANCE OR OTHER FINANCIAL SECURITY

The Act has no special provision as regards the type of insurance or financial security the operator has to take out to cover his liability. However, the existence of such an obligation, also referred to in transport documents, appears indirectly in Section 23 which provides that public bodies are exempt from the requirement to obtain insurance or financial security to cover the damage referred to in the Act.

B. STATE INTERVENTION

The Act has no special provision on this topic other than to state that the Secretary of the Interior is responsible for co-ordinating action by the authorities concerned and by private services, in order to arrange for assistance, evacuation and safety measures in the event of a nuclear incident [Section 29].

C. COMPENSATION

The amount of compensation payable in the event of personal injury is calculated as follows:

- in case of death, the amount of the minimum salary applying in the Federal District concerned, multiplied by one thousand;
- in case of total disablement, the said amount multiplied by one thousand, five hundred;
- in case of partial disablement, the said amount multiplied by five hundred [Section 18].

D. TIME LIMITS FOR BRINGING CLAIMS

The right to claim compensation from the operator for nuclear damage is subject to a prescriptive period of ten years from the date of the incident in the case of deferred personal injury of which the victim was unaware and which does not involve loss of life [Section 21].

When nuclear damage is caused by nuclear fuel or radioactive products or waste which were stolen, lost, jettisoned or abandoned, the prescriptive period of ten years runs from the date of the incident [Section 20].

Actions for compensation of nuclear damage brought before a court may be revised in the event of any aggravation of damage, provided that final judgment has not been entered [Section 22].

E. COMPETENT COURTS AND PROCEDURE

In accordance with the provisions of the Federal Code of Civil Procedure, the Federal courts of the domicile of the claimant will have jurisdiction to hear proceedings concerning the implementation of the Act [Section 25].

The Act also provides that judgments entered abroad in respect of nuclear damage will be neither recognised nor executed in Mexico in the following circumstances:

- the judgment was obtained by the fraud or collusion of the parties to the proceedings;
- there was a violation of the defendant's individual rights or the judgment was iniquitous;
- the judgment was contrary to public policy;
- the case in question should have been brought before the Federal Courts of the Mexican Republic [Section 26].

Under the Act, the operator of a nuclear installation is required to inform the competent Federal authorities of any nuclear incident and of any loss or theft of radioactive substances or materials [Section 27].

NETHERLANDS

INTRODUCTION

In 1990, the installed nuclear capacity in the Netherlands amounts to 507 MWe, which is approximately 3 per cent of the total electricity capacity from all sources. This nuclear electricity is generated by two nuclear power plants, Borssele (PWR-452 MWe) and Dodewaard (BWR-55 MWe), respectively operated by EPZ and GKN. Both operators are private companies with public shareholders. In the Netherlands, responsibility for nuclear activities is not centralised. It is shared by several Ministers who consult each other and issue regulations jointly, as the case may be, according to their duties. The Ministers of Justice and of Finance are the competent authorities in connection with nuclear third party liability and compensation of nuclear damage.

The Netherlands is a Party to the 1960 Paris Convention and the 1963 Brussels Convention, Supplementary to the Paris Convention. The Netherlands has also signed the 1988 Joint Protocol relating to the Application of the Vienna Convention and the Paris Convention and it is a Party to the 1962 Convention on the Liability of Operators of Nuclear Ships.

The basic legislation governing nuclear third party liability in the Netherlands is contained in the Nuclear Incidents (Third Party Liability) Act of 17th March 1979 (Stb.*1979, No. 225) which entered into force on 28th December 1979 (the text of the Act is reproduced in the Supplement to Nuclear Law Bulletin No. 24).

The Netherlands is expected to ratify the 1982 Protocols to amend the Paris and Brussels Conventions in the near future, and amendments to the 1979 Act have been submitted to Parliament implementing the changes made by the Protocols and introducing improvements with regard to, amongst others, exonerations from liability, time limits, claims procedure and additional compensation from public funds.

In the meantime, this study is based on the present text of the 1979 Act. When adopted, the text of the new legislation will be reproduced in the Nuclear Law Bulletin.

* Stb. = Staatsblad = Bulletin of Acts, Orders and Decrees.

I. THIRD PARTY LIABILITY

It should be noted that the Paris Convention and the Brussels Supplementary Convention are directly applicable as national law in the Netherlands.

A. SCOPE AND DEFINITIONS

The operator of a nuclear installation situated in the Netherlands is liable for damage suffered in the Netherlands wherever the nuclear incident occurs, as well as for damage suffered outside the Netherlands and resulting from a nuclear incident occurring in the Netherlands [Section 26(1)].

As regards the liability of the operator of a nuclear installation situated in the Netherlands, further extensions of the geographical scope of the liability of the operator may be made under a general administrative order which must be confirmed within three months by an Act [Section 26(2) and 3].

The terms *nuclear incident*, *nuclear installation*, *nuclear substances, operator* and *damage* have the same meaning as in the Paris Convention [Section 1(1)].

B. NATURE AND ASSIGNMENT OF LIABILITY

a) General – Nuclear Installations

The operator of a nuclear installation situated in the Netherlands is absolutely and exclusively liable for nuclear damage involving nuclear material in his installation, including damage arising out of or resulting from ionizing radiations emitted by any source of radiation in his installation [Section 4].

Any person who is duly authorised to construct or operate a nuclear installation in the Netherlands is considered as an operator [Section 1(2)]. The loss of his licence does not affect his liability for damage caused by a nuclear incident involving nuclear material for which he was liable at the time of such loss [Section 1(2)].

The Minister of Finance may, in agreement with other competent Ministers, determine that several nuclear installations operated by the same operator on the same site shall be regarded as a single nuclear installation [Section 7(2)].

b) Transport

The operator is also absolutely and exclusively liable for nuclear damage involving material being carried to or from his installation. However, at the request of a carrier and with the operator's consent the Minister of Finance may decide that, subject to conditions to be fixed by him, the carrier will be liable in place of the operator [Section 5].

In case of a nuclear incident occurring in the Netherlands, both the consignor (in most cases the operator) and the carrier of the nuclear substances involved in the incident, as well as the persons storing such substances at the time of the incident, will be deemed to be the operator of a nuclear installation and liable for the damage up to the maximum amount stated in Article 3(a) of the Brussels Supplementary Convention, namely 120 million Special Drawing Rights – SDRs* (approximately 295 million guilders) [Section 28(1)]. This provision could, in particular, be applied in the following cases:

- the transit through the territory of a Contracting Party to the Paris Convention of nuclear substances in course of carriage to or from a person in a non-Contracting State;
- the consignment of nuclear substances by a person in the territory of a non-Contracting State to an operator of a nuclear installation situated in a Contracting State, without the written consent of such an operator;
- the *unauthorised* operator, i.e. the case where the person constructing or operating the nuclear installation is neither designated nor recognised as such by the competent authority.

The above provision does not apply:

- to persons who did not know or could not reasonably be expected to know of the nuclear nature of the substances consigned;
- to persons transporting the nuclear substances at the time of the nuclear incident under a transport agreement or storing them in connection with such transport, if such persons could reasonably assume that another person would be liable for the damage under the Paris Convention or under Section 28(1) of the Act and that, in the latter case, such a person was covered by insurance or financial security approved by the Minister of Finance [Section 28(3)].

c) Rights of Recourse

The Act does not contain special provisions on this subject; Article 6(f) of the Paris Convention applies (wilful fault or contractual clause). (For recourse by the State see under "State Intervention" below.)

d) Exoneration from Liability

The operator is not liable for damage caused by a nuclear incident directly due to an act of armed conflict, hostilities, civil war, insurrection and a grave natural disaster of an exceptional character [Section 2, 1979 Act; Article 9, Paris Convention].

C. AMOUNT OF LIABILITY

Originally, the maximum liability of the operator of a nuclear installation in the Netherlands was limited to 100 million guilders; the Act provides, however, that this maximum amount may be raised by administrative order, taking into account the available possibilities of obtaining financial cover [Section 3(2)]. This amount was raised for the first time to 200 million guilders by General Administrative Order of 21st June 1984 (Stb. 1984, No. 341) and once again to 400 million guilders (approximately 160 million SDRs) by General Administrative Order of 27th April 1987 (Stb. 1987, No. 190). This is the present maximum liability of a nuclear operator in the Netherlands [Section 3(1)].

* The Convention, as amended by the 1982 Protocol, raises this amount to 300 million SDRs (this amendment, however, is not yet in force).

With respect to nuclear installations which do not appear on the list of nuclear installations established pursuant to Article 2(a)(i) and 13 of the Brussels Supplementary Convention, the maximum amount is 120 million SDRs [Section 27]. This provision is intended to give effect to the Annex to the Brussels Supplementary Convention; this Annex contains a declaration stating that compensation for damage caused by a nuclear incident and not covered by that Convention because the installation concerned, on account of its utilisation, is not on that list, will be provided without discrimination to the nationals of Contracting Parties up to the maximum limit of compensation.

D. NUCLEAR DAMAGE

a) Damage Covered

The Act covers any damage to persons or property caused by a nuclear incident involving nuclear substances in a nuclear installation situated in the Netherlands or in the course of carriage thereto or therefrom [Section 1(1)]. As already mentioned, damage arising out of or resulting from ionizing radiations emitted by any other source of radiation in a nuclear installation is also within the scope of the Act [Section 4], as is damage due to nuclear installations not included in the list established pursuant to the Brussels Supplementary Convention [Section 27].

The Act equally covers damage to the means of transport upon which the nuclear substances involved were at the time of the nuclear incident provided that the operator's liability in respect of other damage is not reduced to less than five million SDRs [Section 3(3)].

b) Damage Excluded

The Act does not cover damage to the nuclear installation itself and to any property on the site of that installation which is used or to be used in connection therewith [Section 1(1), 1979 Act; Article 3, Paris Convention].

II. COVER AND COMPENSATION

A. INSURANCE OR OTHER FINANCIAL SECURITY

The operator is required to have and maintain insurance or other financial security covering his liability under the Act, pursuant to Article 10(a) of the Paris Convention.

Any action by an insurer or other financial guarantor which is contrary to the provisions of Article 10(b) of the Paris Convention, in particular, concerning the notice to be given before suspending or cancelling cover shall be null and void [Section 12].

If the Minister of Finance is of the opinion that the operator of a nuclear installation situated in the Netherlands is unable to obtain any, or any adequate financial security, or that it can be obtained only at unreasonable conditions, he is authorised to enter into insurance contracts on behalf of the State as insurer or to provide other State guarantees [Section 8(1)].

The Minister of Finance is further authorised to determine, if the small extent or nature of the risks involved so warrant, that the required financial security will consist wholly or partly of public funds [Section 8(2)].

Where the operator of a nuclear installation situated in the Netherlands may be held liable for nuclear damage under provisions other than the Paris Convention and the Act (e.g. in the case of transport through the territory of a State which is not a Party to the Paris Convention), the Minister of Finance is empowered to conclude insurance contracts on behalf of the State as insurer or to provide other State guarantees up to a maximum amount of 1 000 million guilders per nuclear incident [Section 32].

B. STATE INTERVENTION

a) Extent of Compensation

To the extent that insurance or financial security are inadequate to provide compensation, the State may make public funds available to the operator of a nuclear installation situated in the Netherlands up to the maximum amount of his liability [Section 9(1)].

If it is likely that the State will have to make available public funds to compensate nuclear damage, the Minister of Finance may order that he will exercise all rights and obligations regarding the settlement of the claims on behalf of the operator concerned [Section 11(1)]. Any agreements concluded between the operator and any financial guarantor which are in conflict with such an order shall have no effect [Section 11(1)].

If the maximum amount of liability of an operator of a nuclear installation situated in the Netherlands under the Act is insufficient to provide compensation for damage under the Brussels Supplementary Convention, the public funds referred to in Article 3(b)(ii) and (iii) and (f) of that Convention will be made available by the State as cover for the liability of the operator [Section 19].

If such public funds have to be made available, the Minister of Finance will pay them to persons who have suffered damage within the meaning of Article 2 of the Brussels Supplementary Convention and are entitled to compensation under the Paris Convention according to a final judgment by the competent court or a written acknowledgement of the operator; the State will not enter into any consideration of the merits of such judgment or acknowledgement [Section 20].

If there is reason to believe that public funds have to be made available this is announced by the Minister of Finance in the Government Gazette [Section 21(1)].

As from the date of such announcement, persons entitled to claim compensation pursuant to Article 2 of the Brussels Supplementary Convention must address a written application to the Minister of Finance justifying their claim [Section 21(2)].

Furthermore, if damage is suffered on Netherlands territory as a result of a nuclear incident for which compensation is payable pursuant to the Brussels Supplementary Convention or to the Act, and the funds for such compensation from other sources are insufficient to compensate the damage to an amount of 1 000 million guilders, the State will make available the public funds needed up to this amount [Section 28a(1)]. This provision also applies to such damage suffered in States Parties to the Brussels Convention in which the regulations in force at the time of the incident were equivalent to those of the Act in nature, scope and amount [Section 28a(4)].

b) Recourse by the State

To the extent that the inadequacy of financial security is due to the operator's fault and the State has paid compensation in connection therewith, the State has a right of recourse against the operator [Section 9(3)].

The State acquires the operator's right of recourse under Article 6(f) of the Paris Convention to the extent that it has made available public funds [Section 9(1)]. In the exercise of such right the State has priority over insurers and guarantors who have provided financial security [Section 9(3)].

The same priority applies with respect to other Contracting States to the Brussels Supplementary Convention which have made public funds available pursuant to Article 3(b)(ii) and (iii) and (f) of that Convention [Section 24].

The State has further a right of recourse against the operator if it has paid compensation out of public funds and the operator has not notified the Minister of Finance of the nuclear incident or claim concerned, or of any compensation paid [Section 29(3)].

In effect, the State has a right of recourse regarding any disbursements it has made and any related costs against the persons liable therefor under the Act [Section 28a(2)].

C. COMPENSATION

Acknowledgement and satisfaction of claims for compensation of nuclear damage as well as all actions and arrangements in relation to such claims may be made only with the approval of the Minister of Finance; any acts contrary to this provision shall be null and void [Section 10].

Upon application by an interested party, the competent court may rule that insurers and financial guarantors must pay compensation directly to the parties concerned. Such a ruling may be made only after the Minister of Finance and the operator have been heard. This ruling is provisionally enforceable even if appealed against. If the ruling is reversed on appeal, payments made in accordance with such ruling shall remain valid and binding [Section 14].

If the total compensation exceeds the operator's maximum amount of liability, the claims for compensation shall be reduced proportionally [Section 15]. If it seems likely that this will occur and the amount of individual claims has not yet been established, any interested party may apply to the competent court to enjoin payments for compensation. This application must be notified to the operator, the Minister of Finance and the insurers or financial guarantors [Section 16(1)].

After having filed, or been notified of, such an application, the operator and guarantors must not make any payment until a final ruling is made [Section 16(2) and (3)].

If the Brussels Supplementary Convention is applicable and the total damage is in excess of the total amount pursuant to Article 3(a) of that Convention, claims for compensation will be reduced proportionally [Section 22(1)].

The Minister of Finance may make advance payments to persons who have suffered nuclear damage. Such advance payments shall be deducted from the amount of compensation due to such persons. The Minister of Finance may require insurers and guarantors to pay the equivalent of the advance payments directly to him as soon as compensation has been recognised or awarded [Section 31].

If a right to compensation for damage exists under the Netherlands social legislation, the right to compensation for this damage pursuant to the Paris and Brussels Supplementary Conventions and under the Act shall accrue to those who have made payments under the social legislation. In all other respects the provisions of that legislation remain applicable [Section 30].

D. TIME LIMITS FOR BRINGING CLAIMS

Claims for compensation are barred by limitation three years after the date on which the victim or his legal representative had knowledge or should reasonably have known of the damage and the operator liable [Section 6]. Also, as provided by the Paris Convention, claims are extinguished ten years after the nuclear incident. If the nuclear incident involved nuclear substances that had been stolen, lost, jettisoned or abandoned and not been recovered at the time of the incident, this period shall not exceed twenty years from the date of the theft, loss, jettison or abandonment.

E. COMPETENT COURTS AND PROCEDURE

The District Court of The Hague has exclusive jurisdiction as court of the first instance in the Netherlands [Section 13].

NORWAY

INTRODUCTION

Norway has no nuclear power programme. It does, however, have a nuclear research programme and two reactors for this purpose: a 2 MWe reactor and a 20 MWe reactor. These reactors are operated by the Institute for Energy Technology (*Institutt for Energiteknikk*). Overall responsibility for nuclear policy matters is vested in the Ministry of Petroleum and Energy.

Norway is a Party to the Paris Convention and the Brussels Supplementary Convention and to the 1982 Protocols to amend these Conventions. It is also a Party to the 1971 Brussels Convention relating to Civil Liability in the Field of Maritime Carriage of Nuclear Material. In addition, Norway has signed the Joint Protocol relating to the Application of the Vienna Convention and the Paris Convention.

The basic legislation on nuclear third party liability in Norway is contained in Act No. 28 of 12th May 1972 concerning nuclear energy activities (published in the Official Gazette, *Norsk Lovtidend* 1972, p. 606). This Act implements the Paris Convention and the Brussels Supplementary Convention. It was amended by Act No. 26 of 25th May 1973 (*Norsk Lovtidend* 1973, p. 586), Act No. 37 of 8th June 1973 (*Norsk Lovtidend* 1973, p. 659) which implements the 1971 Brussels Convention, and Act No. 103 of 20th December 1985 (*Norsk Lovtidend* 1985, p. 1392) which implements the 1982 Protocols. (The text of this Act has been reproduced in the Supplement to Nuclear Law Bulletin No. 41.) Furthermore, Regulations were adopted on 15th November 1985 [Regulation No. 1912, *Norsk Lovtidend* 1985, p. 1189] to exclude small quantities or certain kinds of nuclear substances from the application of the Paris Convention.

The Norwegian legislation was originally drafted in such a way as to enable Norway to become a Party to the Paris Convention and the Brussels Supplementary Convention, as well as the Vienna Convention. However, Norway has not become a Party to the Vienna Convention and is at present not likely to do so. Accordingly, for greater clarity, to the extent that the operation of a provision of the legislation is subject to Norway being a Party to the Vienna Convention, it is not referred to in this study.

I. THIRD PARTY LIABILITY

A. SCOPE AND DEFINITIONS

As a general rule, the Act* applies to nuclear damage caused by a nuclear incident occurring in a State which is a Party to the Paris Convention – including Norway – or on or above the high seas, provided that the damage is suffered in such a State or on or above the high seas. In addition to mainland Norway, the Act applies to Svalbard (Spitsbergen), Jan Mayen and the Norwegian non-metropolitan territories, except as otherwise provided by the King. This general rule derives from the following specific provisions of the Act as to the limitations on its territorial scope. Firstly, the Act does not apply to damage caused by an incident occurring in a State which is not a Party to the Paris Convention [Section 18(1)]. The King may decide, however, that in such cases the Act shall apply, in whole or in part, to nuclear damage suffered in Norway or in another State Party to the Paris Convention or on the high seas. Such a decision may be made conditional upon reciprocity between Norway and the State where the damage is suffered or where the injured person is domiciled [Section 18(2)].

Secondly, as regards nuclear damage suffered in a State which is not a Party to the Paris Convention, the Act does not apply unless the nuclear incident occurred in Norway and the operator of a nuclear installation in Norway is liable under the other provisions of Chapter III of the Act [Section 18(1)]. Compensation for damage suffered in such a State may also be made subject to reciprocity [Section 18(3)].

If a foreign operator is liable for such incidents, the law of that operator's country shall determine whether or not the damage suffered in a State which is not a Party to the Paris Convention is governed by this Act [Section 18(1)].

The King may decide that a State which is not a Party to the Paris Convention may be equated, in whole or in part, with a State Party for the purposes of the Act [Section 19].

The Ministry of Petroleum and Energy may exempt from the types of nuclear installation, nuclear fuel, radioactive products or nuclear substances in relation to which liability may arise under the Act, those which, in its opinion, constitute no significant hazard [Section 2(1)]. If a question arises as to the liability of the operator of a nuclear installation in another State Party to the Paris Convention, any corresponding exemption as well as the scope thereof is governed by the statutory provisions of that State, within the limits of the Paris Convention [Section 2(2)].

Pursuant to this power of exemption and in accordance with Decisions of the OECD Steering Committee for Nuclear Energy pursuant to the Paris Convention, small quantities and certain kinds of nuclear substances are not included in the nuclear substances covered by the Act. These are reprocessed uranium within acceptable limits of residual contamination and with a specified content of uranium 235 and limited quantities of nuclear substances conforming to the quantitative limits and other requirements set out in the International Atomic Energy Agency Regulations for the Safe Transport of Radioactive Materials [Regulation No. 1912 of 15th November 1985, *Norsk Lovtidend* 1985, p. 1189].

* All references are to the Act of 12th May 1972 as amended and in force at the date of publication of this study.

B. NATURE AND ASSIGNMENT OF LIABILITY

a) General – Nuclear Installations

As a general principle, in accordance with the Paris Convention, liability under the Act is vested exclusively and absolutely in the operator of a nuclear installation [Sections 20-28]. The term *nuclear installation* employed in the Norwegian legislation follows the usage of that term in the Paris Convention [Section 1(e)].

Thus, claims for compensation for nuclear damage for which an operator is liable under the Act or the corresponding provisions of the legislation of other States Parties to the Paris Convention may not be brought against any person other than the operator concerned or his insurer or guarantor. This is the case even if the claim against the operator has been extinguished by reason of statutory limitations (see below under "Time Limits for Bringing Claims") [Section 27(1)].

The principle of absolute liability is not applicable, however, insofar as it conflicts with any international Convention in the field of transport to which Norway is a Party [Section 27(4)].

Where two or more operators are liable in respect of the same damage they are jointly and severally liable [Section 31(1)]. In such a case liability is to be shared by the operators with due regard to each installation's share in the damage and to all other relevant circumstances [Section 31(2)].

If two or more operators are liable in respect of the same damage, each operator is liable only up to the limit of liability established under the Act with respect to him. However, if the damage is the result of a nuclear incident during the carriage of nuclear substances, and the substances are located on one and the same means of transport, or under temporary storage in one and the same nuclear installation, the maximum total amount for which such operators are liable is the maximum limit of liability established under the Act with respect to any of them, provided that their nuclear installations are situated in the same State or in States which are Parties to the Paris Convention [Section 31(1)].

With respect to incidents in nuclear installations, the operator – that is anyone having obtained a licence for operating the installation or, in the absence of a licence, anyone in control of the installation or whom the Ministry of Petroleum and Energy has so designated [Section 1(g)] – is liable for nuclear damage caused by a nuclear incident which occurs in his nuclear installation [Section 20]. If the nuclear damage is caused exclusively by nuclear substances merely temporarily stored in the installation incidental to their carriage, however, the operator is not liable provided that another operator is liable for the damage by virtue of a written contract and such liability is compatible with the provisions of the Act relating to liability in the course of carriage [Section 20].

b) Transport

In the case of carriage (including temporary storage incidental to carriage) of nuclear substances from a nuclear installation in Norway or in another State Party to the Paris Convention, the consignor operator is, in the first instance, liable for nuclear damage caused by such substances [Section 21(1)]. The term *nuclear substances* employed in the Norwegian legislation follows the usage of that term in the Paris Convention.

If the consignee operator is an operator of an installation in Norway or another State Party to the Paris Convention, this liability shifts to the consignee operator, if a date for the transfer of liability has been expressly stipulated by written contract between the consignor and the consignee, on that date, and otherwise when the consignee operator takes charge of the nuclear substances [Section 21(2)]. The King is empowered to issue administrative provisions respecting the cases in which, and the conditions subject to which, operators of nuclear installations in Norway shall or may enter into a contract concerning transfer of liability [Section 21(6)].

If nuclear substances are consigned from a State which is not a Party to the Paris Convention to a nuclear installation in Norway or in another State Party with the written consent of the consignee operator, the latter is liable for any nuclear incident which occurs in the course of carriage [Section 21(3)]. In other cases where nuclear substances have come to Norway from a State which is not a Party to the Paris Convention and no operator in a State Party to the Paris Convention had acquired possession thereof prior to the incident, the general law of compensation applies and the operator concerned or any other person on whose behalf the consignment is effected is liable regardless of fault [Section 22]. In case of carriage of nuclear substances between a State Party and a State which is not a Party to the Paris Convention the liability of the consignor or consignee operator in Norway does not extend to nuclear incidents occurring, respectively, either after the nuclear substances have been unloaded from the means of transport in the country of destination or before they have been loaded on the means of transport which is to convey them from that country [Section 28(2)].

If a nuclear incident occurs in Norwegian territory or on the high seas during the carriage of nuclear substances between States neither of which is a Party to the Paris Convention, the general law of compensation applies and the operator concerned or any other person on whose behalf the consignment is effected is liable regardless of fault [Section 21(5)].

If at the time of the incident, the nuclear substances which have caused the damage are neither located in a nuclear installation nor being transported, the operator of a nuclear installation in a State Party to the Paris Convention who had the nuclear substances in his possession at the time of the incident or most recently prior to the incident or who had explicitly assumed liability in a written agreement is liable. If however, the nuclear substances were in the course of carriage and if no operator in a State Party to the Paris Convention had acquired possession thereof between the interruption of the carriage and the incident, the operator liable pursuant to the above-described provisions concerning incidents in the course of carriage is liable [Section 22].

The King may, upon application by a carrier or a similar person who undertakes the carriage, decide that the applicant shall be liable instead of the operator of a nuclear installation in Norway for nuclear incidents occurring in the course of carriage, provided that the operator consents thereto and the carrier is covered by the financial security required pursuant to the Act (see below under "Insurance or other Financial Security"). If such a decision is taken, whatever applies by virtue of the Act to the operator applies instead to the applicant [Section 23].

c) Rights of Recourse

i) Against the operator

Anyone, other than the operator concerned, who is liable to pay compensation in Norway or in a foreign country pursuant to any international Convention in the field of transport to which Norway is a Party or pursuant to the legislation of a State which is not a Party to the Paris Convention may claim recourse against the operator concerned or his guarantor within the limits applicable to compensation under Chapter III of the Act and subject to the exceptions described below [Section 28(1)].

If the nuclear incident occurs or the damage is suffered in a State which is not a Party to the Paris Convention, recourse against the operator who, but for the provisions limiting the territorial scope of the present Act, would have been held liable for the damage may only be claimed by a person having his principal place of business in Norway or in another State Party to the Paris Convention, or by the servant of such a person [Section 28(2)].

ii) By the operator

Any operator who may be held liable under this Act or corresponding provisions in the legislation of another State Party to the Paris Convention may only seek recourse against another person if such person has expressly undertaken by contract to cover the damage, or is an individual who has wilfully caused the damage, or is liable in respect of ionizing radiation which is not covered by this Act, or is a jointly liable operator [Section 33].

iii) By the State

Where the State has paid compensation pursuant to its guarantee (see below), it may claim recourse from:

- a person against whom the operator concerned is entitled to seek recourse under the Act (see above);
- the operator concerned if he failed to take out and maintain the financial security required under the Act; or
- from the guarantor concerned, insofar as he is liable in respect of the damage [Section 39(2)].

In the case of supplementary payments out of Government funds, either pursuant to the Brussels Supplementary Convention or in cases where rights to compensation from the operator had become extinguished by time (see below), the State may claim recourse from an individual who has wilfully caused the damage or from a person who is liable for damage from ionizing radiation, or who has expressly undertaken to cover the damage [Section 44].

d) Exoneration from Liability

The operator of a nuclear installation in Norway is not liable for damage caused by a nuclear incident which is directly due to an act of war or similar act in the course of armed conflict, invasion, civil war or insurrection, or to a grave natural disaster of an exceptional nature [Section 24(2)]. The liability of an operator of a nuclear installation in a foreign State for damage caused in such cases is governed by the law of that State [Sections 1(f) and 24(2)].

C. AMOUNT OF LIABILITY

The liability of an operator in respect of nuclear damage caused by one and the same nuclear incident is, as a rule, limited to 60 million SDRs (Special Drawing Rights of the International Monetary Fund); that is, approximately 500 million Norwegian kroner [Section 30(1)]. However, the King may, having regard to the size and nature of the installation, or to the extent of the carriage involved as well as to other circumstances, prescribe a different limitation of liability, to a lower limit of 5 million SDRs; that is, approximately 42 million Norwegian kroner [Section 30(1].

If a nuclear installation of the liable operator is situated in another State Party to the Paris Convention, the law of such State as concerns limitation of liability applies, even if Norwegian law is otherwise applicable [Section 30(2)].

Liability in respect of nuclear damage caused to the means of transport on which the nuclear substances causing the damage were located at the time of the incident is not to have the effect of limiting liability in respect of other nuclear damage to an amount lower than 5 million SDRs [Section 30(3); see also Section 1(n)].

D. NUCLEAR DAMAGE

a) Damage Covered

The Act covers nuclear damage, that is damage resulting from radioactive properties or a combination of radioactive properties with toxic, explosive or other hazardous properties of nuclear fuel or radioactive products, as well as damage resulting from ionizing radiation emitted by any other source within a nuclear installation [Section 1(h)]. This coverage extends to damage to both persons and property [General Act on Liability, Act No. 26 of 13th June 1969]. Compensation for non-financial damage, however, is payable only if the operator is liable for the damage by virtue of Chapter 3 of the General Act on Liability [Section 24(3)].

When a person has suffered simultaneously both nuclear damage and other damage, the Act applies equally to such other damage to the extent that it is not reasonably possible to separate one type of damage from the other [Section 29(1)].

b) Damage Excluded

Subject to the special case of damage caused wilfully by an individual, the provisions of the Act do not apply to damage caused to the nuclear installation itself, other installations on the same site, including installations under construction, or to any property which at the time of the incident was on the installation site and was being used or was there to be used in connection with that installation [Sections 25(1) and 27(3)]. If the operator of an installation in a State Party to the Paris Convention other than Norway is liable, damage caused in the course of carriage to the means of transport will also be excluded from coverage under the Act if it is excluded under the law of that State [Section 25(2)]. Such exclusion of damage to the means of transport does not affect the operator's liability for this damage under the general law of torts, unless otherwise agreed [Section 27(3)].

II. COVER AND COMPENSATION

A. INSURANCE OR OTHER FINANCIAL SECURITY

In order to cover his liability in respect of nuclear damage, the operator – with the exception of the State itself – of every nuclear installation in Norway has to maintain such insurance or such other security as the Ministry of Petroleum and Industry authorises [Sections 35(1) and 36(1)]. Where the public interest so requires, the King may furnish security in favour of an operator by means of a State guarantee, subject to such conditions as the Parliament (*Stortinget*) may prescribe [Section 36(2)].

The Ministry may approve insurance or other security limited to a fixed amount per installation for a certain term, and which consequently does not fully cover the maximum liability in respect of every possible nuclear incident, provided that the amount is at least 20 per cent greater than the maximum liability for each incident. If, as a result of nuclear damage, the insurance or the security per installation is believed to have fallen below the maximum liability per incident, the Ministry is to revoke this approval until the insurance or security is brought up to the original amount [Section 35(2)].

The Ministry may approve separate insurance or other security to cover liability for nuclear incidents which may occur in the course of carriage [Section 35(3)].

The operator must obtain in good time the Ministry's decision concerning the required date of entry into force of an insurance or security. The period for which the operator shall be required by law to maintain this insurance or security in force is determined by the Ministry [Section 35(4)].

The insurer or the person furnishing security (the guarantor) must submit to the competent authority a declaration of security in the form and containing the particulars prescribed by the Ministry. This declaration of security is subject to the following conditions which it must confirm.

- The injured parties will be entitled to claim directly from the guarantor.
- Except as otherwise authorised by the Ministry in special circumstances, while security for carriage may be limited to the duration of the carriage, all other security will be valid for an unlimited period and irrespective of any change of owner or operator of the nuclear installation concerned.
- The security may not be revoked or terminated without at least two months' prior notice in writing to the competent authority. If carriage is commenced before receipt of such notice, any nuclear incident occurring during such carriage will be covered by the security regardless of the expiration of two months' notice.
- The injured parties may invoke the security even after its termination, if nuclear damage occurred while it was in force [Section 37(1)].

Whenever a nuclear substance is transported to or from a foreign country (including cases merely involving transit through Norway) the operator liable under the Act must furnish the carrier with a certificate of financial security for the carriage issued by or on behalf of the guarantor. The carrier must not commence carriage in Norway before obtaining such certificate [Section 38].

B. STATE INTERVENTION

a) State Guarantee

The State guarantees that the operator of a nuclear installation in Norway will meet the maximum amount of his liability by virtue of the Act or corresponding provisions in another State Party to the Paris Convention; this does not apply if a foreign law provides for the operator's liability in cases in which the Norwegian operator is exonerated by virtue of this Act [Section 39(1)].

b) Supplementary Payments

If claims for compensation against the operator of a nuclear installation used for peaceful purposes situated in Norway or in another State which is a Party to the Brussels Supplementary Convention cannot be satisfied by the maximum amount of the operator's liability, but they are valid under the Act and have been brought within the time limits provided by the Act (see below), the Act provides for the claims, not including interest and litigation costs, to be paid out of Government funds up to a maximum of 300 million SDRs provided that:

i) at the time of the incident the installation of the operator liable was included in the list referred to in Article 13 of the Brussels Supplementary Convention;
ii) actions in respect of the operator's liability come under Norwegian jurisdiction;
iii) the nuclear incident did not occur exclusively in a State which is not a Party to the Brussels Supplementary Convention; and
iv) the claims relate to nuclear damage which has occurred:
   - in Norway or in another State Party to the Brussels Supplementary Convention;
   - on or over the high seas, on board a ship or aircraft registered in a State Party to that Convention; or
   - otherwise on or over the high seas, suffered by a national of such a State Party or a person equated by the State Party with its own nationals, provided that, in the case of damage to a ship or aircraft, such ship or aircraft was registered at the time of the incident in the territory of a Party to the Brussels Supplementary Convention [Sections 40(1) and 41(1)].

The sections of the Act so providing are, however, not yet in force. They will come into force on a date to be decided by the King.

However, irrespective of whether the operator is liable, payment out of Government funds is not available for:

- claims arising out of a nuclear incident directly due to an act of war or similar act in the course of an armed conflict, invasion, civil war or insurrection, or a grave natural disaster of an exceptional nature;
- damage to the nuclear installation itself, other nuclear installations on the same site, including installations that are under construction, or damage to any property on the installation site; or
- damage caused in the course of carriage to the means of transport [Section 40(3)].

Claims pursuant to the Act for recourse against the operator, as described above, may qualify for supplementary government funding, provided that nothing to the contrary is stipulated in a contract entered into with the operator liable or with the State [Section 40(3)].

If 300 million SDRs are not sufficient to ensure full satisfaction of all claims, the amounts of compensation, together with the relevant interest, are to be reduced proportionally. Such proportional reduction is subject to the same provisions as proportional reductions of compensation paid from the 60 million SDRs of the operator's liability (see below under "Compensation") [Section 41(3)].

Special provision is made for compensation for delayed effects of personal injury. Where rights for compensation have become extinguished by reason of the special time-limits under this Act (see below) or under corresponding provisions in another State Party to the Paris Convention, claims relating to personal injury sustained in Norway as a result of a nuclear incident for which the operator of a nuclear installation in Norway was liable, will be compensated by the State provided that there is a valid reason for the claim not having been brought in due time. Actions for such compensation must be directed against the Ministry of Petroleum and Energy within the period of limitation under the general law and in no case later than thirty years after the nuclear incident. The Act Relating to the Limitation Period for Claims [Act No. 18 of 18th May 1979] governs the general law on limitation periods. If other claims arising out of the incident have not been satisfied in full due to the financial limitations provided by the Act, or by corresponding provisions in another State Party to the Paris Convention, compensation under this provision is to be proportionately reduced [Section 42(1)].

In addition, the King may decide that such compensation, subject to specified conditions, is to be paid in relation to nuclear damage suffered outside Norway [Section 42(2)].

C. COMPENSATION

Where an operator is liable under the provisions of this Act or the corresponding provisions of another State Party to the Paris Convention, claims for compensation may only be brought against that operator or his guarantor. The extinction of a claim against the operator by reason of time does not alter this restriction [Section 27(1)].

If the amount of liability of the liable operator is not sufficient to fully satisfy the claims of all injured parties, the compensation and the relevant interest is to be reduced proportionally. Such reduction must be authorised by the Probate Court (*Skifteretten*) [Section 32(1)].

The Ministry of Petroleum and Energy may decide that compensation for personal injuries shall be given preferential liability coverage up to such an amount per person as the Ministry determines [Section 32(2)].

Accordingly, if there is reason to believe that the total damage will exceed the maximum liability of the operator, the operator liable and his guarantor must, as soon as possible, notify the Ministry of Petroleum and Industry in writing of this fact and provide full particulars as to the extent of the damage. In such cases the Ministry may decide that, as a provisional measure, injured persons shall receive payment of a given proportion of their claims, in the light of the claims filed and possible future claims [Section 32(3)].

The King may issue administrative provisions to supplement these provisions [Section 32(4)].

If an injured person has contributed to the damage either wilfully or through gross negligence the compensation to which he would normally have been entitled may be reduced [Section 26].

D. TIME LIMITS FOR BRINGING CLAIMS

Whether or not a claim for compensation or recourse against an operator has become time-barred earlier according to the general rules respecting statutory limitation, it is extinguished if it is not aknowledged or if legal action is not instituted within ten years after the date of the nuclear incident [Section 34(1)]. In addition, if the incident is attributable to nuclear substances which have been stolen, lost or abandoned and have not been recovered at the time of the incident, no claim may be made against the operator after the expiry of twenty years from the date of the theft, loss or abandonment [Section 34(2)].

Special provisions apply if jurisdiction over claims for compensation would lie with the courts of more than one State Party to the Paris Convention. If the victim brings a timely action before any one of these courts and jurisdiction is later assigned to Norwegian Courts by a decision of the European Nuclear Energy Tribunal referred to in Article 17 of the Paris Convention, the claim must be brought before the Norwegian Courts within the period determined by this Tribunal or, in the absence of such determination, within six months after the Tribunal's decision. The same applies if a request is submitted in due time to the appropriate authority in a State Party to the Paris Convention for the institution of proceedings to determine the competent court in accordance with the Paris Convention, and Norwegian Courts are determined as competent [Section 34(3)].

These time limits do not apply to the State's right of recourse against an operator who has failed to discharge his obligation under the Act to take out and maintain insurance or against a person who has wilfully caused the damage or who is liable for damage caused by ionizing radiation not covered by the Act or who has expressly, under the terms of a contract, undertaken to cover the damage [Section 34(4)].

E. COMPETENT COURTS AND PROCEDURE

Norwegian courts have jurisdiction concerning the liability of an operator or his guarantor in respect of nuclear damage in the following cases:

- if the nuclear incident occurred wholly or partly in Norwegian territory;
- if the nuclear incident occurred on or above the high seas outside Norwegian territory and, at the time of the incident, the nuclear substances concerned were being carried between States which are not Parties to the Paris Convention or equated with such States; or
- if the nuclear incident occurred outside the territory of any State Party to the Paris Convention or the place of the incident cannot be determined with certainty and the installation of the liable operator is situated in Norway [Section 45(1)].

In addition, actions concerning claims:

- against an operator or his guarantor in relation to damage caused in the course of carriage to the means of transport;
- in relation to the sharing of liability between two or more operators;

– for recourse by the State for expenditure pursuant to its guarantee; or
– for recourse by the State in respect of supplementary payments

may be brought in Norway if a Norwegian court has jurisdiction under the general rules of procedure [Act No. 6 of 13th August 1915 on procedure in civil cases sets down these rules].

However, actions may not be brought or continued in a Norwegian court if the European Nuclear Energy Tribunal, pursuant to its powers under Article 17 of the Paris Convention, decides that the courts of another State Party to the Paris Convention shall have exclusive jurisdiction as regards such actions or if the King decides, in order to comply with provisions concerning jurisdiction contained in an agreement with a foreign State, that the case shall not come within Norwegian jurisdiction [Section 45(3)].

In addition to the above cases, the King may, if it is necessary in order to comply with provisions concerning jurisdiction in an agreement with a foreign State or to secure the bringing of claims against a Norwegian operator or his guarantor, decide that actions concerning liability for a nuclear incident shall come within Norwegian jurisdiction. Moreover, the competent Ministry may, either on its own initiative or at the request of an interested party, request the European Nuclear Energy Tribunal to decide in which State actions shall be brought [Section 45(4)].

Actions which come under Norwegian jurisdiction may only be brought in the judicial district in Norway in which the nuclear incident occurred [Section 46(1) and (4)].

If the nuclear incident occurred outside Norway but the relevant installation is situated in Norway, actions may only be brought in the judicial district in which that installation is situated [Section 46(2) and (4)]. In the case where the nuclear installation concerned is abroad, actions are to be brought in Oslo although the Ministry of Justice may decide that actions can be brought elsewhere in Norway [Section 46(2) and (4); Section 39 of the Administration of Justice Act (*Domstolloven*) [Act No. 5 of 13th August 1915]].

If actions concerning liability in respect of the same nuclear incident can be brought in more than one judicial district, the Ministry of Justice decides where the case is to be tried. Nevertheless, the actions specified above as able to be brought in Norway if a Norwegian court has jurisdiction under the general rules of procedure may be brought in any judicial district having jurisdiction over the case by virtue of these general rules of procedure. The Ministry may also decide on the question of jurisdiction, on receipt of an application, if it cannot be determined with certainty in which judicial district actions must be brought [Section 46(3)].

A judgment, or a judicial settlement having the force of a court judgment, against an operator or his guarantor in a case concerning liability for nuclear damage by a court of a State Party to the Paris Convention in accordance with that Convention which is enforceable in that State has binding effect and is enforceable in Norway, subject to the financial limit on the liability of the operator under the Act. This does not apply to interim judgments. Enforcements of such foreign judgments or judicial settlements are to be effected in accordance with the provisions of the Compulsory Enforcement Act (*Tvangsfullbyrdelsesloven*) [Act No. 7 of 13th August 1915] and there is to be no review of the merits of the case other than that allowed by the Paris Convention [Section 47(1) and (3)]. Applications for enforcement must be made to the competent court for execution proceedings (*Namsretten*) [Section 47(2)].

PHILIPPINES

INTRODUCTION

In the framework of the Philippines' atomic energy programme the construction of one nuclear reactor has been undertaken. This construction has never been completed. It is owned by the National Power Corporation of the Philippines.

The Philippine Nuclear Research Institute has responsibility for regulating and licensing nuclear activities.

The Philippines is a Party to the Vienna Convention and a Signatory of the Joint Protocol relating to the Application of the Vienna Convention and the Paris Convention. It is also a Signatory of the 1962 Brussels Convention on the Liability of Operators of Nuclear Ships.

The basic legislation on nuclear third party liability in the Philippines is Act No. 5207 of 15th June 1968 and, in particular, Part VII of that Act as amended by Presidential Decree No. 1484 of 11th June 1977 and Executive Order No. 128 of 30th January 1987.

I. THIRD PARTY LIABILITY

A. SCOPE AND DEFINITIONS

Act No. 5207 of 15th June 1968, as amended ("the Act") does not make express provision with respect to its territorial coverage.

The terms *nuclear installation* and *operator* are used in the Philippine legislation in the same sense as they are used in the Vienna Convention.

B. NATURE AND ASSIGNMENT OF LIABILITY

a) General – Nuclear Installations

A nuclear installation operator licensed by the Philippine Nuclear Research Institute is liable for nuclear damage caused by a nuclear incident in his installation, except in cases where the damage is due to nuclear material stored therein incidentally to the carriage of such material and another operator is liable pursuant to the provisions of the Act governing incidents during transport [Section 37(a) and (c)].

This liability is exclusive to the operator and absolute [Section 38(a) and (c)]. The operator is not relieved of this liability even if nuclear damage is caused directly or indirectly by a grave natural disaster of an exceptional character [Section 38(b)].

However, in certain specific cases where the operator is exonerated from liability or the type of damage is covered by the Act, the Act does not prevent a person who caused the damage by an act or omission done with intent to cause damage from being liable [Section 44]. (The particular cases are dealt with below.)

Where more than one operator is liable for nuclear damage and the damage attributable to each is not reasonably separable, the operators are jointly and severally liable [Section 49(a)]. In such a case the liability of any one installation operator is not to exceed the liability ceiling established by the Act [Section 49(c)].

Where several nuclear installations of the same nuclear operator are involved in one nuclear incident, the operator is liable in respect of each installation involved up to the ceiling established for the liability of an operator [Section 50]. However, the Philippine Nuclear Research Institute is empowered to determine that several nuclear installations of the same operator located on the same site are to be considered as a single nuclear installation [Section 58].

b) Transport

A nuclear installation operator licensed by the Philippine Nuclear Research Institute is liable for nuclear damage caused by a nuclear incident involving nuclear material coming from or originating in his installation and occurring before liability with regard to nuclear incidents involving the nuclear material has been assumed, pursuant to the express terms of a contract in writing, by another operator or, in the absence of such express terms, before another operator has taken charge of the nuclear material [Section 37(b)].

The operator is also liable for nuclear damage caused by a nuclear incident involving nuclear material sent to his installation and occurring after liability with regard to nuclear incidents involving the nuclear material has been assumed by him from another operator, pursuant to the express terms of a contract in writing or, in the absence of such express terms, after he has taken charge of the nuclear material [Section 37(c)].

Notwithstanding the above, the operator is liable for nuclear damage caused by a nuclear incident involving nuclear material in the course of carriage to or from his installation from or to, respectively, a nuclear installation located outside the Philippines, unless there are applicable provisions to the contrary in an international agreement to which the Philippines Government and the Government of the country where the other nuclear installation is located are Parties [Section 37(d)]. The exception in the case of alternative provision under an international agreement is intended to cover the case where an operator of another State Party to the Vienna Convention would be liable pursuant to that Convention.

The Philippine Nuclear Research Institute is empowered, subject to such terms and conditions as it may by regulation or order prescribe, to designate a carrier of nuclear material, at his request and with the consent of the operator concerned, as operator and that person thereupon assumes liability in place of the operator [Section 51].

Where under the above-described provisions several operators are jointly and severally liable for nuclear damage caused by an incident occurring in the carriage of nuclear material in one means of transport or, in the case of storage incidental to carriage, occurring in one nuclear installation, the total liability of the operators is not to exceed the ceiling on the liability of an operator established by the Act [Section 49(b)].

c) Rights of Recourse

The operator has a right of recourse if there is such a right pursuant to the express provision of a written contract with another operator [Section 39(a)]. He also has such a right, if the nuclear incident results from an act or omission done with intent to cause damage, against the person who has acted or omitted to act with such intent [Section 39(b)].

d) Exoneration from Liability

An operator is not liable for any nuclear damage caused by a nuclear incident directly due to an act of armed conflict, hostilities, civil war, or insurrection [Section 41]. This does not affect the liability of an individual for damage caused by an act or omission done with intent to cause damage [Section 44].

An operator may also be relieved from his obligation to pay compensation in respect of damage suffered by a person if the damage resulted wholly or partly, either from the gross negligence, or act or omission with intent to cause damage, of that person [Section 40].

As stated above, the fact that the nuclear damage was caused directly or indirectly by a grave natural disaster of an exceptional character does not relieve the operator of liability [Section 38(b)].

C. AMOUNT OF LIABILITY

The liability of an operator under this Act is limited to an amount in Philippine pesos equivalent to $5 million for any single nuclear incident. This amount does not include any interest or costs which may be awarded by a Court [Section 42].

D. NUCLEAR DAMAGE

a) Damage Covered

Liability arises under the Act in the above-described cases for loss of life, any personal injury or any loss of, or damage to, or loss of use of property, which arises out of or results from the radioactive, toxic, explosive or other hazardous properties or any combination thereof, of nuclear fuel or radioactive products or any waste in, or of nuclear materials coming from, originating in, or sent to, a nuclear installation or from the ionizing radiation emitted by any other source of radiation inside a nuclear installation. Personal injury includes any physical or mental injury, sickness or disease whether caused directly by a physical trauma or otherwise [Section 3(f)].

Whenever such nuclear damage and other damage are caused by a nuclear incident or jointly by a nuclear incident and one or more other occurrences, that other damage, to the extent that it is not reasonably separable from the nuclear damage, is to be treated as though it were also nuclear damage. Where, however, damage is caused jointly by a nuclear incident covered by the liability provisions of the Act and an emission of ionizing radiation not so covered, nothing in the liability provisions of the Act is to limit or otherwise affect the liability, either as regards any person suffering nuclear damage or by way of recourse or contribution, of any person who may be held liable in connection with that emission of ionizing radiation [Section 48].

b) Damage Excluded

The operator is not liable under the Act for damage to the nuclear installation itself or to any property on the site of that installation which is used or is to be used in connection with that installation or to any means of transport upon which the nuclear material involved was located at the time of the incident [Section 43]. This provision does not, however, prevent the operator from being liable, outside the Act, for damage to such means of transport [Section 44(b)].

Furthermore, this does not affect the liability for such damage of any individual who caused it by an act or omission done with intent to cause damage [Section 44(a)].

The Philippine Nuclear Research Institute is empowered, if it determines that the small extent of the risks involved so warrants, to make regulations excluding small quantities of nuclear material from the application of the provisions of the Act concerning liability. This is subject to the requirement that maximum limits for the exclusion of such quantities have been established by the Board of Governors of the International Atomic Energy Agency and the quantity to be excluded is within those limits [Section 45].

II. COVER AND COMPENSATION

A. INSURANCE OR OTHER FINANCIAL SECURITY

No licence to operate a nuclear installation is to be issued unless the operator secures and maintains insurance or other financial security covering his liability for nuclear damage under the Act. The type and terms of financial security required is to be prescribed by regulation by the Philippine Nuclear Research Institute. Such security may include private insurance, private contractual indemnity, self-insurance or other proof of financial ability to pay damages under the Act or any combination of such securities. In fixing the type and terms of such financial protection, the Institute is to be guided by the objectives of assuring to potential victims of a nuclear incident adequate and effective compensation without imposing an unreasonable burden on the operator [Section 46].

In the case of carriage, the operator is to provide the carrier with a certificate issued by or on behalf of the insurer or other financial guarantor furnishing the financial security required by the Act. The certificate is to indicate the nuclear material to which the security applies and include verification by the Philippine Nuclear Research Institute that the person designated is an operator under the provisions of the Act. The certificate is to be in such form and contain such information as the Institute prescribes by regulations [Section 47].

It is unlawful for any insurer or other financial guarantor to suspend or cancel the insurance or other financial security provided pursuant to the provisions of this Act with giving such prior notice in writing as may be required by the Philippine Nuclear Research Institute's regulations [Section 60].

Where the Government operates an installation, it is exempted from the requirement of having financial security to cover its liability [Section 59].

B. STATE INTERVENTION

Up to the ceiling of the operator's liability under the Act, the Government indemnifies the operator liable and provides the necessary funds for the payment of claims established against the operator to the extent that the insurance or other financial security is inadequate to satisfy the claims [Section 52].

The Philippines is to enter into agreements with contractors or suppliers of goods or services for an atomic energy facility owned or operated by the Government indemnifying and holding such contractors or suppliers harmless from any loss or liability arising out of or in relation to a nuclear incident occurring in the Philippines in excess of the insurance or other financial security up to a limit of $120 million [Section 52].

C. COMPENSATION

Actions for recovery of compensation for nuclear damage under the Act may be brought against the operator liable or against the insurer or other person furnishing the financial security required by the Act [Section 61].

Where the nuclear damage from an incident will probably exceed the ceiling of the operator's liability, upon petition of the operator liable or the Philippine Nuclear Research Institute, the Court having jurisdiction is to issue orders necessary to assure the equitable distribution of compensation. Such orders may include orders apportioning the payments to be made, orders permitting partial payments to be made before final determination of the total claims and orders setting aside part of the funds available for possible latent injuries not discovered until a later time [Section 53(a)].

In addition, where it appears that the nuclear damage caused by a nuclear incident will exceed the ceiling of the operator's liability, the Philippine Nuclear Research Institute is to furnish a report to Congress with recommendations, including recommendations for the appropriation of additional funds to provide compensation to those suffering nuclear damage [Section 53(b)].

D. TIME LIMITS FOR BRINGING CLAIMS

Rights of compensation under the Act are subject to a limitation period of ten years from the date of the nuclear incident and also of three years from the date on which the person suffering the damage knew or should have known of the damage and the identity of the operator liable therefor. However, once a person has brought a claim, he may amend the claim to take into account any aggravation of the damage even after the expiration of the limitation period, provided that final judgment has not been entered [Section 62].

Where the damage is caused by a nuclear incident involving nuclear material which at the time of the incident was stolen, lost, jettisoned or abandoned, actions are subject to the further limitation period of twenty years from the date of the theft, loss, jettison or abandonment of such material [Section 63].

E. COMPETENT COURTS AND PROCEDURE

The Regional Trial Court situated in the place where the nuclear incident occurs has exclusive jurisdiction over claims for compensation under this Act [Section 54].

POLAND

INTRODUCTION

Since the early 1980s, Poland has been committed to a programme for the production of nuclear power and in 1991, two nuclear power plants, with an estimated capacity of 435 MWe each, will be brought on line. Other units, already ordered, should be operational towards the end of the 1990s. The regulatory authority in this field is the National Atomic Energy Agency (*Panstwowa Agencja Atomistyki*), itself answerable to the Science and Technical Progress Committee of the Council of Ministers.

Poland became a Party to the Vienna Convention in 1990 and acceded to the Joint Protocol on the Application of the Vienna Convention and the Paris Convention also in 1990.

In conjunction with the launching of the above programme, Poland adopted, on 10th April 1986, an Atomic Energy Act. This Act (published on 22nd April 1986 in the Legal Gazette No. 12), entered into force on 1st July 1986. It represents a framework Act regulating all nuclear activities in Poland. Part 8 of the Act contains provisions on third party liability for nuclear damage. It should be noted that this Act predates Poland's accession to the Vienna Convention.

I. THIRD PARTY LIABILITY

A. SCOPE AND DEFINITIONS

Part 1 of the Polish Act (General provisions), contains a definition of the main terms and concepts used in the interpretation of its provisions on third party liability for nuclear damage.

Thus, the *operator* is defined, for purposes of third party liability, as the *organisational unit* carrying on activities in respect of the production, storage, transport, use, etc. of nuclear materials, the construction and operation of nuclear installations (and radioactive waste repositories), or the manufacture and use of devices incorporating radioactive sources or emitting ionizing radiation, etc., under licence from the National Atomic Energy Agency [Sections 3 and 4 of the Act].

More especially, nuclear installations are defined as installations or devices in which nuclear materials are manufactured, processed, stored, transported, etc., in sufficient quantities to allow a spontaneous fission reaction [Section 3.2].

The Act subsequently specifies that the concept of nuclear installation covers nuclear power plants producing electricity and/or heat,establishments using nuclear reactors as a source of energy, establishments for producing, converting and storing nuclear materials, and nuclear reactors used for research and experimentation [Section 14.1].

Nuclear materials are defined as materials containing fissile nuclides or nuclides which could become fissile following nuclear reactions, and in particular, isotopes of uranium, plutonium and thorium [Section 3.1].

The Act does not contain any special provisions with regard to its territorial scope.

In areas not covered by the Act, the provisions of the Polish Civil Code apply to third party liability for nuclear damage [Section 42].

B. NATURE AND ASSIGNMENT OF LIABILITY

a) General – Nuclear Installations

The Act adopts the principle of the absolute and exclusive liability of the operator of a nuclear installation for nuclear damage caused by the operation of that installation [Section 36.1].

When more than one person operates a nuclear installation, they are jointly and severally liable [Section 36.2].

b) Transport

In the event of nuclear damage occurring during the transport of nuclear materials, the operator sending the materials remains exclusively liable until they are handed over to the consignee [Section 37.1].

When nuclear damage occurs during international transport, the moment at which liability is taken over is to be determined in accordance with the agreement between the consignor of the materials and consignee [Section 37.2]. Should, however, no express provision have been made, it is the consignor who remains liable until the materials are handed over to the authorised person at the frontier of the State in which the materials are to be delivered [Section 37.2].

c) Rights of Recourse

The operator of a nuclear installation has a right of recourse against any person intentionally causing nuclear damage [Section 36.3].

Similarly, the operator liable for nuclear damage occurring during transport has a right of recourse against those persons providing transport services if the damage results from intentional fault on their part (Section 37.3).

The Act does not specify whether the nuclear operator may have a right of recourse under contract.

d) Exoneration from Liability

The operator of a nuclear installation is exonerated from liability when nuclear damage is caused by acts of war [Section 38].

Neither is the nuclear operator liable for damage to the victim to the extent that such damage results exclusively from an intentional fault on the part of the victim himself [Section 38].

C. AMOUNT OF LIABILITY

The Polish Act does not, strictly speaking, lay down any limit to the nuclear operator's liability, and provides that liability for all the consequences of an incident leading to nuclear damage lies with the person obliged to pay compensation [Section 39.1]. A ceiling has, on the other hand, been imposed on the financial security which the operator is obliged to provide, thereby constituting at least a financial limitation on his liability (see below).

D. NUCLEAR DAMAGE

The Act defines nuclear damage as damage caused to persons or property, or to the environment by the radioactive, toxic, explosive or other effects of nuclear materials and their fission products [Section 3.9].

II. COVER AND COMPENSATION

A. INSURANCE OR OTHER FINANCIAL SECURITY

The operator of a nuclear installation is required to cover his third party liability for nuclear damage by taking out insurance [Section 40.1]. It is the responsibility of the Minister of Finance to designate the insurance establishment which is to cover the operator's liability. A Regulation of 26th August 1986 of the Minister of Finance stipulates that the third party liability of the operators of nuclear installations is to be insured by the State Insurance Corporation (*Panstwowy Zaklad Ubezpieczen*).

The Act does not specify the amount of financial security nuclear operators are required to provide [Section 40.2], and this has not so far been determined by the Polish authorities.

B. STATE INTERVENTION

When the personal injury suffered as a result of a nuclear incident exceeds the amount of funds available under the insurance contract, the victim may request payment of the excess amount from the Treasury [Section 40.3].

As regards nuclear damage to property and the environment, the Council of Ministers is responsible for establishing procedures to compensate any damage exceeding the amount provided for under insurance [Section 40.4].

C. COMPENSATION

Compensation for nuclear damage covers, for the victim, personal injury or damage to health, and losses resulting from destruction or deterioration of his property, and for other persons (heirs), losses suffered as a result of the death of the victim. It also includes earnings the victim could have made had he not suffered the damage. Lastly, it covers essential expenses which have been or will be incurred following the incident, in order to prevent persons and the environment from being exposed to ionizing radiation [Section 39.2].

In the absence of any special provision, it may be considered that the Act also covers the pain and suffering (solatium) of victims suffering personal injury [Article 445 of the Civil Code].

The Act also establishes the principle that damage to the common property that the environment represents, should be compensated. When nuclear damage to the environment occurs, the Treasury is entitled to claim compensation from the operator; compensation is paid into the Environmental Protection Fund (*Funduz Ochrony Srodowiska*) [Section 39.3].

As stated above (see under "State Intervention"), the Act guarantees full compensation for personal injury, but not for damage to property or the environment.

The provisions of the Act are without prejudice to the regulations on social benefits for industrial accidents and occupational diseases [Section 43].

Lastly, Article 127(2) of Poland's Civil Code provides that a person suffering damage while taking part in a rescue operation involving exposure to ionizing radiation, is entitled to compensation [Section 10].

D. TIME LIMITS FOR BRINGING CLAIMS

In this context also, the Act makes a distinction between personal injury and damage to property or the environment.

There is no prescriptive period for entitlement to compensation for personal injury resulting from a nuclear incident; for damage to property and the environment, on the other hand, the right to compensation is subject to a prescriptive period of ten years from the date of the incident [Section 41.1].

As regards the operator's right of recourse in the event of intentional fault, the prescriptive period is two years from the date on which compensation was paid [Section 41.2].

As between public entities, the right to compensation for nuclear damage to property or the environment is subject to a prescriptive period of ten years from the date of the incident [Section 41.3].

E. COMPETENT COURTS AND PROCEDURE

Since liability for nuclear damage can be considered as similar to liability in tort, claims for compensation can be brought before the civil courts on the basis of the provisions of the Code of Civil Procedure [Articles 27 to 30 and 35]. The competent court may be determined either on the basis of general jurisdiction (the claim is brought before the court of first instance within whose jurisdiction the defender has his residence), or of alternative jurisdiction (since the claim for compensation results from an unlawful act, within the meaning of Polish legislation, it may be brought before the court within whose jurisdiction the incident causing the damage took place).

ROMANIA

INTRODUCTION

The Republic of Romania has as yet no nuclear power reactors in operation but does have research reactors. In 1977, Romania and Canada signed a co-operation agreement on the peaceful uses of nuclear energy. Subsequently, the Romanian Company for External Trade, ROMENERGO, and Atomic Energy of Canada Ltd (AECL) concluded contracts for the construction of Candu reactors in Romania. Construction of the first two reactors of this type (700 MWe gross) started in 1980 and 1981 on the Cernavoda site; their commissioning is scheduled for end 1993-94.

Romania is not a Party to the Nuclear Third Party Liability Conventions. Provisions on civil liability for nuclear damage are to be found in Chapter VI [Sections 35 to 38] of Act No. 61 of 30th October 1974 on Activities in the Field of Nuclear Energy. The Act is published in the Official Gazette (*Buletinul Oficial al Republicii România*), Part I, No. 136 of 2nd November 1974.

The Act provides a comprehensive framework for all peaceful nuclear activities which are exercised, authorised and controlled by the State or State-owned firms. Prior to the events of December 1989, the State Committee for Nuclear Energy was the central organ responsible for the execution and co-ordination of national nuclear policy and in particular, for the licensing of nuclear installations and nuclear activities. By Decree No. 6 of January 1990 of the Council of the Romanian National Salvation Front, responsibility for nuclear power activities was transferred to the Ministry for Electric Power. In addition, by Decree No. 26 of January 1990, this Council created a new regulatory body, the National Commission for the Control of Nuclear Activities. This new body is competent for all regulatory matters previously coming within the domain of the State Committee for Nuclear Energy and has all the powers previously pertaining to that Committee. It is also competent with respect to the licensing and control of nuclear activities. This chapter analyses the 1974 Act taking into account the changes effected by these Decrees.

I. THIRD PARTY LIABILITY

A. SCOPE AND DEFINITIONS

Act No. 61 on Activities in the Field of Nuclear Energy does not define the territorial scope of the third party liability provisions.

The following definitions in the Act [Section 9] are relevant in the context of this study:

- *Nuclear source material* means uranium or thorium or any of their compounds in any physical or chemical form as well as ore deposits containing at least 0.03 per cent by weight of uranium or thorium or any of their mixtures, but excluding special fissionable material.
- *Special fissionable material* means plutonium, uranium 233, uranium enriched in the isotopes 233 and 235 as well as any substances artificially enriched in those isotopes, but excluding nuclear source material.
- *Radioactive substance* means any substance in whatever state showing radioactivity, including radioactive waste.
- *Substance of nuclear use* means other substances which because of certain special nuclear characteristics are of particular interest in the nuclear field and which are determined by the Council of Ministers. Deuterium and heavy water, nuclear-grade graphite, and zirconium tubes have been so determined by the Council of Ministers.
- *Nuclear radiation* includes alpha, beta, gamma, X-ray, laser radiation, neutrons, electrons and higher energy protons or other nuclear particles.
- *Nuclear installation* means devices producing nuclear radiation; installations, apparatus or devices which extract, manufacture, process or contain radioactive substances.
- *Nuclear incident* means an occurrence which damages the installation and causes exposure or contamination of the population or the environment in excess of the applicable norms.

B. NATURE AND ASSIGNMENT OF LIABILITY

Liability for nuclear damage is assigned to the holder of a licence (licensee) under the Act. A licence, to be granted by the National Commission for the Control of Nuclear Activities exclusively to legal persons, is required for the following activities [Sections 6(a), (b), (d), (e) and 10]:

- scientific research, development and application of nuclear technology in economic and social life;
- prospecting, development, mining, manufacture, use, transport and storage of radioactive substances and substances of nuclear use;
- construction, testing and operation of nuclear installations as well as their modifications or important repairs;
- supply, sale, possession, assignment, transfer, import and export of radioactive substances and substances of nuclear use.

The licensee is liable exclusively, irrespective of fault, for damage caused by a nuclear incident occurring in his installation or during carriage ordered by him [Section 33]. It is noted that under the Civil Code [Article 1000] the liability of a person in charge of a thing is absolute; the existence and the proof of fault is not necessary.

If several licensees are liable for nuclear damage, liability is apportioned between them according to the extent of damage caused by one or the other. If such extent cannot be determined, liability for the damage is to be borne in equal parts [Section 35].

The licensee is not liable for damage caused by a nuclear incident directly due to armed conflicts or catastrophes [Section 36].

C. AMOUNT OF LIABILITY

The liability of the licensee may not exceed 80 million lei (approximately 3 million Special Drawing Rights of the International Monetary Fund – SDRs) for each nuclear incident. The Council of Ministers, on proposal by the Ministry or other central organs of the State administration to which the licensee is subordinated and on advice by the National Commission for the Control of Nuclear Activities, fixes the maximum amount of liability for each licensee within the above limit. This amount does not comprise interest or costs of court proceedings [Section 37].

D. NUCLEAR DAMAGE

The liability of the licensee covers loss of life and personal injury as well as the destruction of, or damage to property [Section 33].

Damage caused by a nuclear incident and a non-nuclear incident is deemed to be caused by the former to the extent that the types of damage cannot be separated from each other [Section 34].

II. COVER AND COMPENSATION

A. INSURANCE OR OTHER FINANCIAL SECURITY

The licensee is obliged to take out and maintain insurance or to furnish other financial security to cover his liability under the Act [Section 37(3)].

B. STATE INTERVENTION

The Act is silent on whether the State ensures the payment of claims for compensation should the yield of insurance or other financial security be inadequate to satisfy such claims. Nevertheless, under Romanian law, the obligations of State corporations and other

State bodies having legal personality are not attributable to the State [Decree No. 31 of 1954, Section 37].

Equally, the Act does not specify whether the State has an obligation to provide additional compensation in case the nuclear damage exceeds the licensee's maximum amount of liability. General Romanian law would indicate that there is no such obligation.

C. COMPENSATION

The nature, form and extent of compensation are governed by the provisions of the Civil Code.

D. TIME LIMITS FOR BRINGING CLAIMS

The right to compensation for damage caused by a nuclear incident expires ten years from the date on which the victim had or could have had knowledge of the damage and of the liable licensee.

The victim having received compensation according to the Act may bring a new claim if the damage has been aggravated within or after the expiry of the ten-year period [Section 38].

E. COMPETENT COURTS AND PROCEDURE

The Act is silent on these points. They are governed by the Code of Civil Procedure which provides for jurisdiction to lie with both the court of domicile of the defendant and the court of the place where the incident occurred, it being for the plaintiff to decide in which of these two jurisdictions the action will be brought.

SOUTH AFRICA

INTRODUCTION

At present, electricity is being generated by means of nuclear power in South Africa by two 922 MWe reactors. The nuclear power plants are operated by Eskom, the electricity supply utility in South Africa.

The Minister of Economic Affairs and Technology is the Minister responsible for State actions in the nuclear field, including third party liability aspects.

South Africa is not a Party to the Nuclear Liability Conventions but has enacted legislation covering nuclear third party liability. These provisions are contained in the Nuclear Energy Act, 1982 (Act No. 92 of 1982), as last amended by the Nuclear Energy Amendment Act, 1988 (Act No. 56 of 1988).

I. THIRD PARTY LIABILITY

A. SCOPE AND DEFINITIONS

The Nuclear Energy Act, 1982 applies to nuclear damage caused by an incident occurring in a nuclear installation, on a site, and during transport of nuclear material (*nuclear-hazard material* in the Act) in South Africa and its territorial waters [Section 41(1)(a)].

Several definitions in the Act of particular relevance in the context of nuclear third party liability are reproduced below [Section 1].

... ***licensee*** *means a person to whom a nuclear licence has been granted, whether or not that licence is still in force;* (see Period of Responsibility under "Nature and Assignment of Liability" below);

nuclear accident *means any occurrence or succession of occurrences having the same origin, which causes or is likely to cause nuclear damage;*

nuclear damage *means any injury to or the death or any sickness or disease of a person, or any damage to or any loss of the use of any property, which arises out of, results from, or is attributable to, the radioactive properties of nuclear-hazard material, or the ionizing radiations associated with the generation of nuclear or atomic energy;*

nuclear-hazard material *means any material which consists of or contains isotopes of uranium, thorium or special nuclear material, or any radioactive daughter product thereof, or radioactive waste, which has been declared under sub-section (2)(c) of this Section to be nuclear-hazard material, or any radioactive nuclides produced in the generation of nuclear or atomic energy, or any other radioactive nuclides, but does not include fabricated radioisotopes which are outside a nuclear installation and which are used or intended to be used for medical, scientific, agricultural, commercial or industrial purposes;*

... ***nuclear installation*** *means any installation, plant or structure designed or adapted for or which may involve:*

- *the production, use, processing, reprocessing, storage or disposal of nuclear-hazard material; or*
- *the carrying out of any process involving nuclear-hazard material and which is capable of causing nuclear damage; or*
- *the production of nuclear or atomic energy;*

but shall not include any installation, plant or structure which is situated at any mine or works as defined in Section 1 of the Mines and Works Act, 1956 (Act No. 27 of 1956), and which is used, or is intended to be used, in connection with operations at, and pertaining to, such mine or works, in any manner by means of which source material is produced; ... .

It should be noted that the Act provides that a nuclear licence is that referred to in Section 30(1)(a), namely, a licence granted by the Council for Nuclear Safety (responsible under the Act for licensing matters) for a nuclear installation or use of a site for the purposes of such an installation, or to use, possess, produce, store, transport or dispose of nuclear material which is capable of causing nuclear damage.

For standardisation purposes, the term *incident* and not *accident* will be used in the following paragraphs; however, the term *licensee* will be retained instead of *operator* as it covers both the holder of a licence for a nuclear installation and for nuclear material.

B. NATURE AND ASSIGNMENT OF LIABILITY

a) General – Nuclear Installations

A person to whom a nuclear licence has been granted (the licensee) is absolutely and exclusively liable for any nuclear damage caused during his *period of responsibility* [Section 41(1)].

The Act defines this period as that beginning on the date the relevant licence has been granted and ending on whichever of the following dates is the earliest:

- when the Council for Nuclear Safety gives notice in writing that in its view there is no longer a risk of nuclear damage originating from that nuclear material; or
- when the nuclear licence originally granted to that licensee is transferred to some other person [Section 1].

Liability for nuclear damage is also incurred in the case of a nuclear licence which is not connected with a particular installation or site, but concerns nuclear material in the possession or under the control of the licensee [Section 41(1)(b)].

The licensee of a nuclear installation is liable for any nuclear damage on-site, including damage caused by radioactive waste conveyed or released therefrom in whatever form [Section 41(1)(a)(i)].

b) Transport

A licensee is also liable for any nuclear damage caused by nuclear material in the course of carriage to or from the installation for which he has been granted a licence [Section 41(1)(a)(ii)] while such transport takes place within the borders or territorial waters of South Africa.

c) Rights of Recourse

A licensee has a right of recourse against any person who has deliberately caused or deliberately contributed to causing a damage for which he (the licensee) is liable under the Act [Section 41(3)(b)]. He also has a right of recourse, if stated expressly by contract, against any person regarding damage for which he would normally be liable under the Act [Section 41(3)(c)].

d) Exoneration from Liability

A licensee is not liable to a person for nuclear damage attributable to the presence without permission of that person or that person's property on the site of the nuclear installation or near the nuclear material for which that licensee has been licensed [Section 41(3)(a)(i)]; nor is he liable for nuclear damage to a person deliberately caused or deliberately contributed to by that person [Section 41(3)(a)(ii)].

C. AMOUNT OF LIABILITY

The amount for which a licensee may be liable is not defined or limited in spite of a contribution from the State specially voted by Parliament. Thought is being given to limiting such liability to an appropriate amount retaining the contribution from the State.

D. NUCLEAR DAMAGE

As stated more fully under "Definitions" above, the Act covers any injury to or death or disease of a person, or any damage to or any loss of the use of any property which arises out of or results from the radioactive properties of nuclear-hazard material or the ionizing radiations associated with the generation of nuclear energy [Sections 1 and 41(1)].

II. COVER AND COMPENSATION

A. INSURANCE OR OTHER FINANCIAL SECURITY

The Council for Nuclear Safety will not grant a nuclear licence unless the person concerned has provided security for his liability under the Act as required by the Minister of Economic Affairs and Technology [Section 39(1)]. The amount for which such security is given is determined by that Minister in agreement with the Minister of Finance [Section 39(2)].

The time when security is given and its type are determined by the Minister in agreement with the Minister of Finance [Section 39(1) and (2)].

The Minister may from time to time, in agreement with the Minister of Finance, require the licensee to give additional security, reduce that security or require a different type of security to be given [Section 39(3)].

If a nuclear incident occurs and a claim for compensation is made, or will, in the Minister's view, be made, he may require the licensee to give additional security for that incident or for any subsequent ones to ensure adequate coverage of any claims for compensation [Section 39(4)].

Consideration is being given to legislate for an appropriate maximum for such security.

B. STATE INTERVENTION

If, in the event of a nuclear incident, the aggregate amount of any claims for compensation has exceeded or is likely to exceed the amount of security given by him, the licensee concerned must immediately notify the Minister of Economic Affairs and Technology in writing, giving the particulars of the claims satisfied and an estimate of other claims which may have to be met [Section 43(1)].

If the Minister considers that the aggregate amount of the claims will exceed the amount of security given by the licensee, he submits a report on that nuclear incident to Parliament, recommending that Parliament make an appropriation to provide financial assistance for the sums in excess of the security in question [Section 43(2)(a)]. He will also publish a notice in the Gazette to the effect that the obligation to pay claims in respect of that nuclear incident is suspended until Parliament has decided on the recommendation [Section 43(2)(b)]. If Parliament decides by resolution on an appropriation to satisfy the further claims for compensation, payments will only be made with the approval of the Minister or by court order [Section 43(3)].

The liability of the licensee under the Act is not affected by such appropriation [Section 43(2)(a)]; also, the additional security he may be called upon to provide does not affect the provision of financial assistance by the State [Section 43(4)].

C. COMPENSATION

When, in accordance with the Act, the Council for Nuclear Safety is advised of a nuclear incident by the licensee liable, it despatches an inspector to investigate the incident and report its causes, circumstances and effects. On receipt of this report, the Council defines the period during which and the area within which, in its view, the risk of nuclear damage was or will be such that health and safety are affected [Section 42(1) and (2)].

Furthermore, the Council establishes a record of the names and particulars of persons within that area during that period [Section 42(3)(b)]. In connection with claims for compensation for nuclear damage, the production of such a record by any person in court is admissible in evidence and is prima facie proof of the presence of that person within that area during that period [Section 42(3)(b)].

However, the definition of any area or any period in connection with a nuclear incident or failure to record the name of any person in that respect do not prejudice the right of that person to claim compensation from a licensee liable under the Act [Section 42(4)].

If, during the course of his work, any employee of the Atomic Energy Corporation of South Africa Limited or the Council for Nuclear Safety suffers a personal injury or contracts a disease due to the ionizing radiation of radioactive material or to its other particular properties, or to the ionizing radiation produced by the application of such material or by equipment, the Corporation or the Council, as the case may be, will defray all the medical expenses and pay compensation in the event of disablement or death [Section 73(1)(a) and (b)].

All questions regarding entitlement to any payment, its amount and method are determined by the Workmen's Compensation Commissioner appointed under the Workmen's Compensation Act, 1941 (Act No. 30 of 1941): in making his determination, the Commissioner applies the provisions of that Act [Section 73(2)(a)].

Such employees' entitlement to benefits under the Nuclear Energy Act, 1982, does not affect any rights they may have under their contract of employment or any law to more favourable benefits; however, they may not claim under both counts [Section 73(3)(a) and (b)].

D. TIME LIMITS FOR BRINGING CLAIMS

The time limit for bringing actions for compensation is thirty years from the date of the incident giving rise to the claim, or, in the case of a continual occurrence or a succession of occurrences, the date of the last event in that connection. However, where the damage and the licensee liable have become known to the victim or ought reasonably to have been known, no action may be brought after the expiry of a period of two years from that date or the expiry of thirty years, whichever occurs first [Section 44(a)].

The two-year prescription period may be suspended during negotiations in connection with a settlement; the victim may claim only one such suspension and solely for a five-year duration [Section 44(b)].

E. COMPETENT COURTS AND PROCEDURE

The competent court for claims for compensation of nuclear damage is the Supreme Court of South Africa in its Provincial Division having jurisdiction in the relevant area. For small amounts the Magistrates Court may be used. An appeal against a decision by a Magistrates Court to the Supreme Court may be lodged by a party feeling aggrieved by the decision.

SPAIN

INTRODUCTION

In 1990, Spain's installed nuclear power capacity amounted to some 7 000 MWe (9 reactors). The main nuclear operators, public and private, are grouped within the UNESA (*Unidad Electrica S.A.*), which is responsible for co-ordinating their activities and implementing government policy. The supervisory authority in this field is essentially the Minister of Industry and Energy, with the Nuclear Safety Council having a regulatory role.

Spain is Party to the Paris Convention and the Brussels Supplementary Convention, as amended in 1982, and to the 1971 Brussels Convention relating to Civil Liability in the Field of Maritime Carriage of Nuclear Material. The Spanish Government has also signed the Joint Protocol relating to the Application of the Vienna Convention and the Paris Convention.

The provisions regulating liability for nuclear damage are essentially contained in the Nuclear Energy Act – Act No. 25 of 29th April 1964, published in the Official State Gazette on 4th May 1964. It came into force the following day. Chapters VII to X, inclusive, deal with nuclear third party liability and financial security. The Act of 1964 is a framework Act, intended to be completed by a number of implementing regulations. To this end, implementing Decree No. 2177 of 22nd July 1967 on cover for nuclear hazards was enacted, and published on 18th September 1967 before being itself amended by Decree No. 742 of 28th March 1968.

I. THIRD PARTY LIABILITY

A. SCOPE AND DEFINITIONS

The Spanish Act contains no specific provisions relating to its territorial scope. However, it can be deduced, from the fact that Spain has ratified the Paris Convention, the Brussels Supplementary Convention and the 1971 Brussels Convention, that the Act applies also to nuclear incidents occurring on the high seas and to damage suffered by Spanish nationals on the high seas.

As regards its technical scope, Spanish legislation on nuclear third party liability [1964 Act, Section 2] makes a distinction between *nuclear installations,* which include:

- nuclear power plants and all nuclear reactors;
- factories using nuclear fuel to manufacture or process nuclear materials, including plants for the reprocessing of irradiated fuel;
- facilities for the storage of nuclear materials (other than during transport);

and correspond in substance to the installations covered by the Paris Convention, and *radioactive installations*, which include:

- any installation in which sources of ionizing radiation are kept;
- all equipment producing ionizing radiation;
- any premises, laboratory, factory or other installation in which radioactive materials are produced, handled or stored.

The term *nuclear materials* used in the Act has the same meaning as that given by the Paris Convention to the expression *nuclear substances* [Section 2].

Persons using radioactive materials or equipment which, according to the national standards in force, are incapable of emitting radiation representing a serious hazard, are excluded from the scope of the nuclear liability regime [Decree No. 2177, Section 1].

B. NATURE AND ASSIGNMENT OF LIABILTIY

a) General – Nuclear Installations

The 1964 Act lays down the principle that the operator of a nuclear, or a radioactive installation, bears absolute liability for all nuclear damage [Section 45] up to the maximum amount of his liability.

The term *operator* is defined as the physical or legal person holding the licence required for the operation of such installations [Section 2]. The State is considered as an operator in respect of government funded nuclear installations and activities which are not given to the private sector to operate [Section 54].

This liability is exclusive [Section 51]. However, the Act does not exclude the possibility that third party liability might arise from other, separate causes of nuclear damage and that another person might therefore be held liable for the damage [Section 53].

If more than one operator is liable for damage, the operators concerned are held jointly and severally liable [Section 52].

In respect of any nuclear damage caused by an incident occurring outside a nuclear installation, the person liable will be the operator of the last installation concerned or the operator who last carried out an activity in relation to the materials at the origin of the damage [Section 49].

The Minister of Industry may determine that several nuclear installations located on the same site and for which the same operator is liable, are to be considered as a single installation [Section 2].

Lastly, it should be noted that the third party liability of the operator of a nuclear or radioactive installation for non-nuclear damage or for nuclear damage for which no compensation is payable, is regulated by the rules of the ordinary law, not the provisions of nuclear legislation [Decree No. 2177, Section 19].

b) Transport

The nuclear operator is liable in the same circumstances as in the case of a nuclear or radioactive installation. As concerns the assignment of liability, in the event of a nuclear incident occurring during transport of nuclear materials within Spanish territory or over Spanish territory to another country, the person liable for the damage will be the consigning operator if the nuclear installation concerned is situated in Spanish territory and liability has not been expressly assumed by another operator [Section 47].

If the nuclear materials in question have been imported into Spain, the consignee operator is liable from the time that he takes charge of the materials, save as may be otherwise provided in international Conventions in force in Spain. Such international Conventions also apply in the case of transit across Spanish territory [Section 48].

A carrier of nuclear materials or any person handling radioactive waste may be considered as the operator in relation to such activities in place of the operator who would normally be concerned, provided that such substitution is allowed by the competent authority [Section 50].

c) Rights of Recourse

The operator has a right of recourse whenever the relevant contract expressly so provides [Section 53].

d) Exoneration from Liability

The nuclear operator is not liable for damage caused by a nuclear incident resulting from armed conflict, hostilities, civil war or insurrection, or a grave natural disaster of an exceptional character [1964 Act, Section 45 and Decree No. 2177, Section 4].

Besides this general exception, there may be fault or negligence on the part of the person suffering nuclear damage, which, to the extent that it has contributed wholly or in part to the nuclear damage, can be declared by the competent court to relieve the operator of his obligation to pay compensation to the person in question [1964 Act, Section 45].

C. AMOUNT OF LIABILITY

In the case of nuclear installations, the Act provides that the amount of the operator's liability is the same as the amount of security required to cover his liability, namely 300 million pesetas [Sections 45 and 57]. However, it is also provided that this figure may be increased automatically and at any time so as to reach the level established as a minimum under any international Conventions ratified by Spain. In fact, the amount was subsequently raised to 350 million pesetas by a Decree adopted in 1968, then to 850 million pesetas (approximately 6 million Special Drawing Rights of the International Monetary Fund – SDRs) in 1986, by administrative Decision.

As regards operators of radioactive installations in which radioactive materials are manufactured or handled, it is provided that the limit of their liability for nuclear damage is determined by the amount of financial security required, as laid down by Decree. Decree No. 2177 provides that this amount may not be less than one million pesetas. In practice, the amount is specified in the licensing Decree for the installation concerned and takes account of various factors such as the category of the installation, the quantity and activity of the substances therein, etc. [Decree No. 2177, Section 17].

D. NUCLEAR DAMAGE

a) Damage Covered

Spanish legislation defines nuclear damage as any loss of life, personal injury or damage to property arising out of or resulting from the radioactive properties or a combination of radioactive properties with toxic, explosive or other hazardous properties of nuclear fuel or radioactive products or waste, or from any ionizing radiation emitted by any other source of radiation [1964 Act, Section 2 and Decree No. 2177, Section 3].

This definition covers nuclear damage whether caused by a nuclear incident occurring in a nuclear installation or in the course of any other activity involving radioactive materials or sources of ionizing radiation [1964 Act, Section 46], the distinction lying in the amount of liability.

Section 46 of the Act also makes a distinction between immediate damage and deferred damage, according to whether the damage occurs, appears or is notified to the person liable within ten years of the date of the incident, or after such period (see under "Time Limits for Bringing Claims" below).

b) Damage Excluded

In addition to the above-mentioned cases in which the nuclear operator is exonerated from liability, no compensation is payable under the nuclear liability regime for damage or injury occurring during radiotherapy treatment, or for injury considered under social security legislation as resulting from an industrial accident or occupational disease [Decree No. 2177, Section 4].

Furthermore, no compensation is due for damage to the installation itself or to on-site property, or for damage to any means of transport [Section 4].

II. COVER AND COMPENSATION

A. INSURANCE OR OTHER FINANCIAL SECURITY

The operation of any nuclear or radioactive installation in Spain requires prior licensing, and operators are at the same time required to provide financial security to cover risks of nuclear incidents, as far as immediate damage is concerned [1964 Act, Sections 55 and 56. For deferred damage, see under "Compensation" below].

Such financial security must be provided by taking out an insurance policy or by depositing at the General Deposits Office a sum of money or other security approved by the Ministry of Finance. Whenever such security has been used to pay compensation, it must be reinstated by the operator [1964 Act, Section 56 – Decree No. 2177, Part II].

Third party liability arising out of nuclear activities may be covered by insurance companies authorised to write policies of third party liability insurance subject to such conditions as are specially approved by the Ministry of Finance on the proposal of the Directorate-General of Insurance. Insurance companies may be authorised to form pools for such insurance [1964 Act, Section 58]. Such pools have legal personality and remain under the supervision of the Directorate-General of Insurance. In addition to the customary reserves, nuclear insurance companies must establish a special technical reserve determined by the Minister of Finance [Decree No. 2177, Sections 55 to 58]. If the amount fixed as financial cover cannot be provided by all such Spanish insurance companies together, the Insurance Compensation Consortium, a body under the Directorate-General of Insurance, shares in covering the risks by making up the difference between the amount which can be furnished by the companies and that required by the Act. The Consortium is furthermore represented on the managing committee of the nuclear insurance pool and kept informed of insurance company activities. It possesses a right of veto [1964 Act, Sections 59, 60 and 61].

In view of the special nature of nuclear third party liability risks, it was decided to impose on the insured nuclear operator the obligation to meet personally the first 5 per cent of the amount of compensation awarded in respect of each incident [1964 Act, Section 63 and Decree No. 2177, Section 51].

The operator must take out a separate third party liability insurance policy for each installation for which he is responsible. Any such policy may be taken out for a limited or an unlimited period. The insurer cannot cancel the insurance before its date of expiry without the consent of the Ministry of Finance, and, in the case of carriage, the insurance cannot be terminated before such carriage is completed [Decree No. 2177, Sections 35 to 52].

As far as its own nuclear activities are concerned, the State is not required to take out any insurance to cover its third party liability, but simply undertakes to pay compensation in accordance with the limits laid down in the 1964 Act and in the international Conventions to which Spain is a Party [1964 Act, Section 64].

B. STATE INTERVENTION

The State intervenes with public funds in the cases provided for under the international Conventions ratified by Spain (in particular, the Brussels Supplementary Convention) and under the 1964 Act [Sections 56 and 68].

It also intervenes, through the Ministry of Finance, to organise payment of any compensation due by it and, in certain cases, to pay supplementary compensation (see under "Compensation" below).

C. COMPENSATION

Persons who have suffered damage caused by a nuclear incident are compensated according to an order of priority which ranks personal injury before damage to property [Section 51].

Compensation for personal injury claims (immediate damage) must be at least as high as that provided for under industrial accident insurance scales. The basic principle is that full compensation should be provided and, should the cover available prove insufficient, it is up to the State to take the appropriate measures to make up the difference [Section 51 and Decree No. 2177, Chapter IV of Part I].

Should the funds available be insufficient to provide full compensation for damage to property, on the other hand, payment is to be made on a pro rata basis, in accordance with the amount of damage suffered by each item [Section 51].

Such amounts include neither interest nor costs [Section 51 and Decree No. 2177, Section 27]. Furthermore, they must not exceed the total amount of damage and other injury actually suffered [Decree No. 2177, Section 28].

As regards deferred damage (damage appearing more than ten years after the date of the incident), the State is to adopt appropriate measures to ensure compensation [Section 56].

D. TIME LIMITS FOR BRINGING CLAIMS

Actions for compensation for nuclear damage are barred ten years after the date of the incident in the case of immediate damage, and twenty years after such date in the case of deferred damage. Accordingly, expert reports must be obtained as to the nature and type of damage for which claims are made [Section 67].

In the case of the theft, loss or abandonment of nuclear materials, any liability arising out of damage caused by such materials lapses ten years after the date on which such facts were reported to the competent authorities [Decree No. 2177, Section 9].

Any person who has brought an initial action for compensation within the time prescribed may, after the expiration of such time, make an amended claim, provided however that final judgment has not meanwhile been handed down [1964 Act, Section 67].

E. COMPETENT COURTS AND PROCEDURE

Actions for compensation are to be brought in the ordinary courts, in accordance with the procedure which corresponds to the amount of damages being claimed [Section 65].

Such actions are brought jointly against the operator and the insurance company or companies concerned. Moreover, where financial security has been provided by a deposit of a sum of money or securities, claimants may request the Court to take suitable protective measures [Section 65].

The competent court will be that of the place where the damage occurred, in accordance with the provisions of the Code of Civil Procedure. During the proceedings, a technical report by the Research Centre for Energy, Environment and Technology (formerly the *Junta de Energia Nuclear*) on the nuclear incident, and its causes and effects, may be requested by the Court or by any of the parties [Section 66].

SWEDEN

INTRODUCTION

In 1990, the installed nuclear electricity capacity in Sweden amounted to 9 600 MWe, approximately 28 per cent of the total electricity capacity. The nuclear power plants are operated by the State, local authorities and private undertakings.

Sweden is a Party to the 1960 Paris Convention and the 1963 Brussels Supplementary Convention, as amended by the 1982 Protocols. It is also a Party to the 1971 Brussels Convention relating to Civil Liability in the Field of Maritime Carriage of Nuclear Material and a Signatory of the 1988 Joint Protocol relating to the Application of the Vienna Convention and the Paris Convention.

The basic legislation on nuclear third party liability is contained in the Nuclear Liability Act (SFS 1968:45) of 8th March 1968 published in the Official Gazette (*Svensk Författningssamling* – SFS) of 25th March 1968. This Act implements the provisions of the Paris Convention and the Brussels Supplementary Convention and was amended by an Act of 10th May 1974 (SFS 1974:249) to enable Sweden to ratify the 1971 Brussels Maritime Convention. It was again amended by an Act of 22nd December 1982 (SFS 1982:1275). This latter amendment enabled Sweden to ratify the above-mentioned 1982 Protocols (the text of the Act as amended is reproduced in the Supplement to Nuclear Law Bulletin No. 33). Finally, the Act of 9th June 1988 (SFS 1988:875) further amends the Nuclear Liability Act by raising the operator's liability.

The Ministry of Justice is responsible for all matters regarding third party liability and any amendments to the Nuclear Liability Act required by international agreements or international legislative measures.

I. THIRD PARTY LIABILITY

A. SCOPE AND DEFINITIONS

The liability regime established by the Act applies regardless of whether the installation of the operator liable is situated in Sweden or in the territory of another Contracting State (any State Party to the Paris Convention) [Section 3(b)].

The Act does not apply to nuclear damage resulting from nuclear incidents occurring in the territory of a non-Contracting State [Section 3(a)]. Where liability lies with the operator of an installation situated in Sweden, the Act applies to nuclear damage suffered in a non-Contracting State only if the nuclear incident occurred in Sweden. Where, as mentioned above, liability lies with an operator of a nuclear installation situated outside Sweden, the territorial extent of liability is governed by the law of the Installation State [Section 3(b)]. However, in relation to damage suffered in a non-Contracting State the Government may determine that compensation for nuclear damage suffered in the territory of such States will be payable in Sweden only if and to the extent that compensation for nuclear damage suffered in Sweden would be payable in that State (the principle of reciprocity) [Section 3(c)].

The Government may, having due regard to Sweden's obligations under the Paris Convention, determine that a non-Contracting State shall for the purposes of this Act be deemed to be a Contracting State [Section 4].

For the purposes of this Act, *Installation State*, in relation to a nuclear installation, means the Contracting State within the territory of which that installation is situated or, if it is not situated within the territory of any State, the Contracting State by which the nuclear installation is operated or which has authorised its operation [Section 1(a)(vi)].

The definitions of *nuclear fuel, radioactive products*, *nuclear substances*, *nuclear installation,* and *nuclear incident* are on the whole similar to the definitions in the Paris Convention [Section 1(a)].

Isotopes for industrial, commercial, agricultural, scientific and educational purposes are excluded from the scope of the Act [Section 1(a)]. Also, the Government may prescribe, if warranted by the small extent of the risks involved, the exclusion of any nuclear installation, nuclear fuel or radioactive products from the scope of the Act [Section 1(b)].

B. NATURE AND ASSIGNMENT OF LIABILITY

a) General – Nuclear Installations

The operator is absolutely and exclusively liable for nuclear damage caused by a nuclear incident which occurs in his installation [Sections 5 and 11(a)].

The Government or an authority appointed by it may determine that two or more nuclear installations in Sweden having the same operator and which are situated on the same site will be considered as a single installation for the purposes of this Act [Section 2].

In the event of more than one operator being liable for the same incident, the operators concerned are jointly and severally liable, provided that the liability of each operator is limited to the amount established with respect to him under the Act [Section 18(a)]. In this case, the apportionment of the aggregate liability as between the operators liable is determined with due regard to each installation's share in the cause of the damage and any other relevant circumstances [Section 18(b)].

The provisions of this Act on claims for compensation [Section 14] will not apply to the extent their application would be incompatible with obligations undertaken by Sweden in an international agreement notably in the field of transport [Section 14a].

b) Transport

i) Operator's liability

Where nuclear substances from a nuclear installation situated in Sweden or in the territory of another Contracting State are carried to a nuclear installation situated in Sweden or in another Contracting State, the consignor operator remains liable for nuclear damage caused by such substances until the time of transfer of liability as fixed by a written contract between himself and the consignee. In the absence of such a contract, liability is transferred to the consignee when the nuclear substances are taken in charge by him [Section 6(a) and (b)].

Where nuclear substances are sent from a non-Contracting State to a nuclear installation situated in Sweden or in the territory of another Contracting State with the written consent of the operator of that installation, the latter will be liable for damage caused by any nuclear incident occurring in the course of carriage [Section 7(a)].

If a nuclear incident occurs in Sweden in the course of carriage of nuclear substances between non-Contracting States, the person authorised under the Swedish Atomic Energy Act (SFS 1956:306) to perform the carriage will be liable [Section 7(c)].

The operator's liability for nuclear damage caused by a nuclear incident in the course of carriage of nuclear substances includes nuclear incidents occurring while the substances are stored incidentally to their carriage to or from another nuclear installation situated in the territory of another Contracting State, except where the substances have been stored in a nuclear installation and the operator of that installation is liable pursuant to a contract in writing [Sections 5 and 8].

If damage occurs during the carriage of more than one consignment of nuclear substances, involving the liability of more than one operator, and the substances are carried on one and the same means of transport, the aggregate amount of liability of the operators will not exceed the highest amount established with respect to any one of them. The same applies where damage occurs when more than one consignment has been stored in one and the same installation incidentally to carriage [Section 18(a)].

Where nuclear substances are carried to a nuclear reactor with which a ship or any other means of transport is equipped for use as a source of power, the consignor operator ceases to be liable when the substances have been taken in charge by the person authorised to operate that reactor [Section 6(c)].

Where nuclear substances are carried from a nuclear reactor, with which a ship or any other means of transport is equipped for use as a source of power, to a nuclear installation in Sweden or in the territory of another Contracting State, the operator of that installation will be liable from the time he takes charge of the nuclear substances [Section 7(b)].

Where nuclear damage is caused by nuclear substances which are not in the possession of any operator at the time of the incident, liability lies with the operator who last had the substances in his possession; however, if an operator has accepted liability for nuclear damage by written contract, it will lie with that operator [Section 9].

If prior to the nuclear incident the nuclear substances had been in the course of carriage, and no operator had taken charge of the substances after the carriage was interrupted, liability lies with the operator who, at the time when the carriage was ended, was liable, pursuant to the Act, for nuclear damage caused by a nuclear incident occurring in the course of carriage [Section 9].

The Act further provides that the principle of channelling of liability onto the operator should be applied also with regard to such nuclear damage not covered by the Act or corresponding legislation in another Contracting State which is caused in the course of maritime carriage of nuclear substances, as soon as there is an operator liable under the Vienna Convention or under national law which is in all respects as favourable to victims as either the Paris or Vienna Conventions [Section 14(c)].

ii) Carrier's liability

The Government or an authority appointed by the Government, namely the Nuclear Power Inspectorate (*Statens Kärnkraftinspektion* – SKI) may, upon the request of the carrier who undertakes the carriage, determine that this carrier shall be liable, instead of the operator of a nuclear installation in Sweden, for nuclear damage caused by a nuclear incident occurring in the course of or in connection with the carriage. Such decision can only be taken with the consent of the operator concerned, and subject to proof that the carrier has taken out insurance or furnished other financial security required under the Act [Section 10(a)].

If such decision has been taken, any provision of the Act relating to the operator will apply instead to the carrier in respect of nuclear incidents occurring in the course of or in connection with the carriage [Section 10(a)]. This is also the case if, by a corresponding decision under the law of another Contracting State, the liability of an operator of a nuclear installation situated in that State has been transferred to a carrier [Section 10(b)].

c) Rights of Recourse

Any person other than the operator liable under this Act who has been held liable for damage caused by a nuclear incident shall acquire by subrogation the rights of the person suffering the damage against the operator liable [Section 15(a)].

Legislation was adopted by Parliament in 1986 (SFS 1986:620) to ratify the Montreal Protocols No. 3 and 4 to amend the Warsaw Convention relating to International Carriage by Air. The Nuclear Liability Act was amended to give the air carrier a right of recourse against the operator liable under the nuclear legislation in case of a nuclear incident in course of carriage. However, this legislation is not yet in force.

Any operator who may be held liable under the Act or under the corresponding legislation of another Contracting State may only seek recourse against an individual who has caused the damage by an act or omission done with intent to cause damage or against a person who has assumed liability under the express terms of a contract in writing with the operator [Section 20].

The rights of recourse granted to the State are described under "State Intervention" below.

d) Exoneration from Liability

The operator of a nuclear installation situated in Sweden is not liable for nuclear damage caused by a nuclear incident directly due to an act of war, armed conflict, civil war or insurrection or a grave natural disaster of an exceptional character [Section 11(b)].

In addition, if the person suffering damage has contributed to the damage either by acting or omitting to act with intent to cause damage or through gross negligence, the operator may be exonerated, wholly or in part, from his liability [Section 13(b)].

C. AMOUNT OF LIABILITY

The liability of the operator of a nuclear installation in Sweden is limited to 800 million Swedish kronor (approximately 100 million Special Drawing Rights of the International Monetary Fund – SDRs) for nuclear damage caused by any one incident. However, the operator's liability for installations solely for the production, treatment or storage of irradiated uranium and for nuclear incidents occurring during carriage of such uranium is limited to 100 million kronor. As regards a nuclear incident occurring during carriage of nuclear substances, the operator's liability for damage other than that to the means of transport shall in no case be less than 100 million kronor [Section 17(a)].

The liability of an operator of a nuclear installation situated outside Sweden will be determined by the law of the Installation State [Section 17(a)].

The amounts referred to above do not include any interest or costs awarded by a court [Section 17(b)].

D. NUCLEAR DAMAGE

a) Damage Covered

The Act covers any damage to persons or property resulting from the radioactive properties of nuclear fuel or radioactive products or a combination of radioactive properties with toxic, explosive or other hazardous properties of such fuel or products, as well as damage resulting from ionizing radiation emitted by any source of radiation inside a nuclear installation other than nuclear fuel or radioactive products [Section 1(a)(viii)].

The provisions of the Act are applicable to damage suffered simultaneously with nuclear damage for which the claimant is entitled to compensation under the Act, if such damage is not reasonably separable from the nuclear damage. However, this shall not affect the liability of a person other than the operator liable under this Act, as regards damage caused by an emission of ionizing radiation not covered by the Act [Section 16].

The Act also covers damage to the means of transport of nuclear substances involved in an incident having occurred during carriage [Section 17(a)]. However, where the operator of a nuclear installation situated in the territory of another Contracting State is liable for such damage, the question whether compensation will be awarded is governed by the law of that State [Section 12(b)].

b) Damage Excluded

The Act does not apply to damage caused to the nuclear installation itself or to another installation in its immediate vicinity, including an installation under construction; nor does it apply to any property which at the time of the nuclear incident was on the site of the installation and was used or intended to be used in connection with that installation [Section 12(a)].

In addition, in accordance with the already mentioned powers granted by the Act [Section 1(b)], the Government has excluded certain kinds and certain small quantities of nuclear substances from the scope of the Act [Decree of 29th April 1981 – SFS 1981:32]. This followed the adoption in 1977 of two Decisions by the OECD Steering Committee for Nuclear Energy excluding such nuclear substances from the application of the Paris Convention.

II. COVER AND COMPENSATION

A. INSURANCE OR OTHER FINANCIAL SECURITY

The operator of a nuclear installation situated in Sweden must take out and maintain insurance to cover his liability for nuclear damage under the Act, namely eight hundred million kronor; the insurance must be approved by the Government or an authority appointed by the Government [Section 22(a)].

Insurance may be taken out to cover either:

- liability for each nuclear incident up to the maximum amount of liability for the operator concerned; or
- the nuclear installation, at any time, by an agreed amount after deduction of any sum of compensation paid or to be paid out by the insurer under the insurance policy [Section 22(b)].

When insurance is taken out to cover liability for each nuclear incident, it will not be less than the amount of liability established for the operator concerned, i.e. 800 million kronor. When insurance is taken out to cover the nuclear installation, the amount must be at least 120 per cent of that latter amount [Section 23(a)]; this provision was laid down so as to ensure that the maximum amount of compensation available is not used up as a result of a first incident.

When as a result of compensation paid or to be paid, the amount of remaining insurance cover has fallen below the amount of maximum liability, the operator is required to take out forthwith such supplementary insurance as will bring the reduced amount up to at least 120 per cent of the amount of maximum liability [Section 23(b)].

Separate insurance may be taken out for nuclear damage occurring in the course of carriage [Section 22(c)].

If the insurance is cancelled or otherwise becomes invalid without a new insurance contract having entered into effect, the insurer will remain liable to pay compensation for damage caused by a nuclear incident occurring within two months from the date when the authority appointed by the Government for this purpose has been notified in writing of the time of expiry of the contract. Where the insurance concerns carriage of nuclear substances and where such carriage has started before expiry of this period, the insurer will remain liable for any damage until the carriage has come to an end [Section 25(c)].

The Government or an authority appointed by the Government may exempt the operator from the obligation to take out insurance if he furnishes adequate security for his obligations under the Act and produces evidence that he has taken satisfactory measures to ensure the settlement of any claim for compensation [Section 27(b)].

The State is not required to take out and maintain insurance [Section 27(a)].

In case of international carriage to or from a nuclear installation situated in Sweden, the operator provides the carrier with a transport certificate issued by the insurer and corresponding to the model certificate issued by the OECD Steering Committee for Nuclear Energy [Section 39 and Decree of 24th April 1981].

B. STATE INTERVENTION

The State intervenes to compensate victims when the operator's financial coverage fails or when the victim's rights to compensation have been extinguished, and also provides compensation in the framework of the Brussels Supplementary Convention. Furthermore, the State grants an additional tier of compensation, beyond that provided under the Conventions.

If a person who, under the Act or the corresponding legislation of another Contracting State, is entitled to obtain compensation for nuclear damage from the operator of a nuclear installation situated in Sweden has been unable to obtain compensation from the operator's insurer, the State will pay such compensation up to the maximum amount of liability fixed for the operator [Section 28(a) and (b)].

In such case, the State will have a right of recourse only against an individual who has caused the damage by an act or omission done with intent to cause damage, or against the operator liable and his financial guarantor [Section 35(a)].

In case of a nuclear incident involving the liability of the operator of a Swedish nuclear installation, compensation for nuclear damage suffered in Sweden which comes to light only after the right to obtain compensation from the operator liable has been extinguished, pursuant to the Act or to corresponding provisions of the national law of another Contracting State, but within a period of thirty years from the nuclear incident, compensation will be paid out of public funds. Compensation for damage having come to light before the rights to compensation have been so extinguished will also be paid out of public funds if the victim had reasonable grounds for failing to bring an action against the operator [Section 32(a)].

Furthermore, the Government may decide that such compensation shall be payable also in respect of nuclear damage suffered outside Sweden [Section 32(c)].

If a claim for compensation against an operator of a nuclear installation used for peaceful purposes situated in Sweden or in another State which is a Party to the Brussels Supplementary Convention cannot be satisfied by the maximum amount of the operator's liability, the claims shall be paid out of public funds up to an amount equivalent to 300 million SDRs, provided that:

- at the time of the incident the installation of the operator liable was included in the list referred to in Article 13 of the Supplementary Convention [Section 29(a)];
- jurisdiction over actions for compensation lies with Swedish courts [Section 29(a)];
- the claims relate to nuclear damage which occurred [Section 31a(a) and (b):
  - in Sweden or in the territory of another State Party to the Supplementary Convention, or
  - on or over the high seas on board a ship or aircraft registered in Sweden or in the territory of another State Party to the Supplementary Convention, or
  - in any other case on or over the high seas by a State Party to the Supplementary Convention, or by a national of such State; provided however, that compensation shall be payable for damage to a ship or an aircraft only if such ship or aircraft was registered at the time of the nuclear incident in the territory of a State Party to the Supplementary Convention.

In addition, there is provision for State intervention over and above the compensation available under the Paris Convention and the Brussels Supplementary Convention. If, in the case of a nuclear incident for which the operator of a nuclear installation located in Sweden is liable, the amounts available under the two Conventions are insufficient to allow compensation in full, the State will indemnify the victims up to a ceiling of 3 000 million Swedish kronor (approximately 375 million SDRs) per incident. This extra State indemnification will apply to nuclear damage sustained in Sweden, Denmark, Finland or Norway and also to damage within the territory of any other Contracting Party to the Brussels Supplementary Convention to the same extent that such State provides compensation for damage caused in Sweden [Section 31a(a) and (c)].

The amounts referred to above do not include any interest or costs awarded by a court [Section 31(a) and 31a(c)].

C. COMPENSATION

Claims for compensation of nuclear damage may only be brought against the operator or directly against the person providing insurance or other security for his liability, unless this is incompatible with obligations entered into by Sweden in an international agreement [Sections 14(a), 14a and 24].

When the operator is not liable under the Act (namely in case of damage due to war, natural disaster or caused to the installation itself ...) or the corresponding provisions of the law of another Contracting State, claims for compensation can be brought only against an individual who has caused the damage by an act or omission done with intent to cause damage [Section 14(b)].

If the maximum amount of liability applicable to an operator is not sufficient to satisfy in full the claims, the compensation for each claimant will be reduced proportionally [Section 19(a)]. If, following a nuclear incident, there are reasons to believe that such reduction will prove necessary, the Government or an authority appointed by the Government may decide that until further notice the compensation payable will be provisionally reduced by such percentage of the full amount of compensation as it will determine [Section 19(b)].

Similarly, when compensation has been paid in the framework of the Brussels Supplementary Convention and the amount available out of public funds proves to be or is likely to be insufficient, the amount of compensation for each claimant will be reduced proportionally [Section 31(c)].

D. TIME LIMITS FOR BRINGING CLAIMS

As a general rule, the right to compensation for nuclear damage is extinguished if no action has been brought within ten years from the date of the nuclear incident concerned; if, however, the incident is attributable to nuclear substances which have been stolen, lost or abandoned and have not yet been recovered at the time of the incident, the limitation period will run twenty years from the date of theft, loss or abandonment [Section 21(b)].

Furthermore, the right to compensation for nuclear damage from the operator or his insurer will be extinguished if the person suffering damage has not notified the operator of his claim within three years from the date on which he had knowledge or ought reasonably to have known of the damage caused and the person liable [Section 21(a)].

E. COMPETENT COURTS AND PROCEDURE

With regard to actions for compensation against the operator or his insurer, Swedish courts are competent in the following cases [Section 36(a)]:

- when the nuclear incident has occurred wholly or partly in Sweden;
- when the nuclear installation concerned is situated in Sweden and either the nuclear incident has occurred wholly outside the territory of any Contracting State or the place of the incident cannot be determined with certainty.

In these cases, jurisdictional competence is conferred upon the court which has jurisdiction over the place where the nuclear incident occurred. If two or more courts are competent, actions may be brought before either of them. Where the nuclear incident occurs outside Sweden, actions shall be brought before the District Court of Stockholm [Section 37(a) and (b)].

However, notwithstanding the above, the Government shall restrict the jurisdictional competence conferred upon Swedish courts if necessary, in order to comply with the provisions of the Paris Convention providing for the possibility of submitting a dispute between Contracting Parties to the European Nuclear Energy Tribunal [Section 36(b)].

SWITZERLAND

INTRODUCTION

In 1990, Switzerland had five nuclear power plants with a capacity of some 3 000 MWe. The main nuclear operators are electricity companies governed by private law and local authorities. The supervisory authority in the field of nuclear energy is the Federal Energy Office.

Switzerland has signed the Paris Convention and the Brussels Supplementary Convention, but has ratified neither. It has also signed the Joint Protocol relating to the application of the Vienna and the Paris Conventions.

The provisions regulating third party liability are contained in the Act of 18th March 1983 on Nuclear Third Party Liability, which entered into force on 1st January 1984 by Order of the Federal Council. (The text of the Act is reproduced in the Supplement to Nuclear Law Bulletin No. 32.) The rules introduced by this Act have been completed by an Ordinance of 5th December 1983, amended on 2nd December 1985, on nuclear third party liability, which specifies the procedures to be followed in providing financial cover for liability.

I. THIRD PARTY LIABILITY

A. SCOPE AND DEFINITIONS

The Swiss Act on Nuclear Third Party Liability ("the Act") applies to nuclear damage caused by nuclear installations or by the carriage of nuclear substances [Section 1.1].

When the operator of a nuclear installation in Switzerland or the holder of a transport licence issued by Switzerland is responsible for nuclear damage suffered abroad, compensation is due to the victims resident in the countries concerned, to the extent that the foreign State in question has made provision for at least equivalent treatment with regard to Switzerland. The maximum cover must not in such a case be lower than SF 50 million, even if the foreign State concerned provides for a lower limit for third party liability [Section 34].

The Act defines various terms, including *nuclear operator*, *nuclear installation* and *nuclear damage*. These terms will all be analysed in the following paragraphs.

B. NATURE AND ASSIGNMENT OF LIABILITY

a) Nature of Liability

The operator of a nuclear installation, i.e. the person who builds or possesses it [Section 2.7], or the holder of a transport licence issued by the Swiss authorities for the transit, through Switzerland, of nuclear substances, is liable for nuclear damage occurring during operation or in the course of carriage. This liability is unlimited [Section 3.1] and absolute: it does not require any fault (intentional or negligent) on the part of the person liable.

Liability is also exclusive: no other person may be held liable towards injured parties [Section 3.6].

b) General – Nuclear Installations

Within the meaning of the Act, a nuclear installation is used to produce, use, store or reprocess nuclear substances [Section 2.5]. The operator of a nuclear installation is liable for nuclear damage caused by nuclear substances in his installation [Section 3.1]. If the installation does not belong to the operator, the owner is jointly liable with the operator [Section 3.4].

c) Transport

The operator of a nuclear installation is also liable for damage caused by nuclear substances from his installation if the damage occurs before the substances have been taken over by the operator of another nuclear installation. In the case of transport within Switzerland, the nuclear substances are taken over at the moment when they cross the boundary of the other installation. In the case of a consignment sent abroad, on the other hand, the substances are taken over at the moment when they cross an agreed boundary fixed by contract outside Swiss territory [Section 3.2].

If the operator of a nuclear installation receives substances from abroad, he is liable for nuclear damage in Switzerland caused by those substances in the course of carriage, without prejudice to his right of recourse against the foreign shipper [Section 3.3].

In the case of the transit of nuclear substances, the holder of the transport licence is liable for any damage suffered in Switzerland. If he has no domicile in Switzerland, he must, by a declaration in writing, submit himself to the jurisdiction of the Swiss courts and elect a domicile in Switzerland for the purposes of any claims under the Act [Section 3.5].

d) Rights of Recourse

Persons who have compensated nuclear damage in accordance with international Conventions have a right of recourse against the operator or other person liable under the Act [Section 3.6].

Moreover, the operator (or holder of a transport licence) has a right of recourse against certain persons [Section 6], namely those:

- who caused the damage intentionally;
- who stole or unlawfully received the nuclear substances which caused the damage;
- who have granted such a right by contract, unless they are employed by the operator liable.

An operator has a right of recourse against the foreign shipper of nuclear substances causing nuclear damage in Switzerland [Section 3.3].

Private insurers and the Confederation also have a right of recourse against the policy-holder or the insured party (when different) to the extent that they are entitled to refuse or reduce payment under the contract of insurance or the Federal Act on insurance contracts [Section 20.1]. However, they are not entitled to exercise their right of recourse except insofar as the interests of the injured parties are not prejudiced thereby. Similarly, when the person liable has a right of recourse pursuant to Sections 3.3 or 3.6, the private insurer and the Confederation (in its capacity as insurer under Section 12) may not exercise the rights of recourse of the person liable except insofar as the interests of the injured parties are not prejudiced thereby [Section 20.2].

e) Exoneration from Liability

The operator of a nuclear installation is relieved of liability to an injured party if he proves that the latter has caused the damage intentionally or by gross negligence [Section 5]. However, for the purposes of the Act, agreements concluded by the operator excluding or restricting third party liability under the Act are considered as null and void [Section 8.1].

It may be noted that there is no exoneration from liability if the accident is caused by armed conflict, natural disasters or unlawful acts by third parties (see in this respect "Insurance or Other Financial Security" and "State Intervention" below).

C. AMOUNT OF LIABILITY

The liability of the operator is unlimited [Section 3.1]. This liability is covered as follows:

- by private insurance up to SF 400 million;
- by the Confederation up to SF 1 billion above the amount covered by private insurance;
- by all the assets of the person liable.

All these aspects are developed further under "Cover and Compensation".

D. NUCLEAR DAMAGE

a) Damage Covered

The Act defines nuclear damage as damage caused by the hazardous properties of nuclear substances during the operation of a nuclear installation or in the course of carriage [Section 2.1.a].

Nuclear damage, except for loss of profits, can also result from measures ordered or recommended by the authorities to avert or mitigate an immediately threatening nuclear danger [Section 2.1.b]. In such a case, the cost of any measures taken by the competent authorities to avert or mitigate any such danger may be charged to the operator of the nuclear installation in question or the holder of the relevant transport licence [Section 4].

The Act also takes account of deferred damage which, appearing only after the thirty-year extinction period, is no longer covered by the nuclear third party liability regime. Section 13 provides that the Confederation shall compensate such damage, a procedure studied under the heading "State Intervention" below.

b) Damage Excluded

Damage caused by radioisotopes used or intended to be used outside a nuclear installation for industrial, commercial, agricultural, medical or scientific purposes, is not covered [Section 1.2].

Furthermore, since damage caused to the nuclear installation itself constitutes damage caused to the operator liable, it cannot give rise to compensation on grounds of third party liability within the meaning of the Act. The same applies to damage caused to a means of transport belonging to the operator. It is not, on the other hand, the case for damage caused to means of transport belonging to third parties.

II. COVER AND COMPENSATION

A. INSURANCE OR OTHER FINANCIAL SECURITY

At the present time, all operators of nuclear installations must take out insurance with a Swiss insurer for at least SF 400 million for each nuclear installation, plus at least SF 40 million for interest payable and procedural costs. The same cover applies to transport operations for which the operator is liable. In the special case of the transit of nuclear substances through Switzerland, insurance must amount to at least SF 50 million, plus at least SF 5 million for interest payable and procedural costs [Section 11.1].

The amount of financial security is to be reviewed by Order of the Federal Council when the insurance market offers higher cover on acceptable terms [Section 11.2]. Thus, by an amendment of 2nd December 1985 of the Nuclear Third Party Liability Ordinance, the amount initially established at SF 300 million (plus SF 30 million for interest payments and procedural costs) by the Act on Nuclear Third Party Liability, was increased to SF 400 million (plus SF 40 million for interest payments and costs).

When, following an incident, the making of payments or setting up of reserves reduces the cover by more than 10 per cent, the insurer is obliged to notify the competent Federal authority and the operator [Section 18.1]. The operator must then take out additional insurance to reinstate the full initial cover. However, this additional insurance only covers damage caused after it was taken out. In case of doubt, the competent authority decides as to the obligation of the policy-holder to increase his cover, taking into account the size of the reserves [Section 18.2].

However, if an amount set aside to compensate damage occurring before the additional insurance was taken out has not been used, it may not be used to cover damage caused after that date [Section 18.3].

The suspension or cancellation of insurance is effective only six months after the competent authority received notification from the insurer, unless the insurance in question is replaced earlier by another insurance [Section 21].

The Federal Council defines the risks that private insurers may exclude from cover in respect of injured parties [Section 11.3]. The 1985 Ordinance on Nuclear Third Party Liability defines these risks as:

- nuclear risks arising from natural disasters or armed conflict;
- rights of action which have not been exercised in the ten years following the incident or cessation of *prolonged effects* (see under "Time Limits for Bringing Claims", below);
- rights of action which have not been exercised within twenty years following the loss, theft, abandonment or cessation of possession of nuclear substances.

In such circumstances, victims may no longer take direct action against the private insurer [Section 4 of the Ordinance].

The Federal Council may exempt the operator from the obligation to take out insurance if he offers equivalent financial security for the injured parties [Section 17.1 of the Act]. Lastly, the Confederation is not obliged to take out insurance for the nuclear installations which it operates itself [Section 17.2].

B. STATE INTERVENTION

The Confederation intervenes in various capacities in the compensation of nuclear damage:

- it manages the Nuclear Damage Fund [Section 15];
- it compensates victims in certain special cases listed in the Act [Section 16];
- it compensates victims of *major occurrences* [Section 29].

The Nuclear Damage Fund was set up by the Federal Council [Section 15]. Financially independent, it does not have its own legal personality. The Federal Energy Office is responsible for managing the Fund [Section 8 of the Ordinance on Nuclear Third Party Liability, as amended in 1985].

The task of the Fund is to cover nuclear operators, up to SF 1 billion for each nuclear installation or transport operation (plus SF 100 million for interest payments and procedural costs), in as much as the damage involved exceeds the amount covered by private insurance or if it is excluded from such cover [Sections 11.3 and 12 of the Act]. On this last point, see under "Insurance or Other Financial Security" above.

The Fund is also used to cover, up to the above-mentioned total, deferred damage for which compensation can no longer be claimed from the person liable because the thirty-year extension period for bringing actions has expired [Section 13].

Operators (and holders of transport licences) pay contributions into the Fund. The Federal Council calculates, in this respect, how much is required to ensure as far as possible that costs are covered. It is then left to the authority designated by the Federal Council to calculate and levy the contributions. Its decisions may be challenged in the Federal Court by way of proceedings under administrative law [Section 14].

Nuclear power plants pay contributions amounting to twice the premium they pay for private third party liability insurance. Contributions are established once a year for nuclear installations and on a case-by-case basis for transport operations. They are payable 30 days after the decision determining their amount becomes enforceable [Sections 5 and 6 of the Ordinance, as amended in 1985].

In certain special cases, the Confederation covers nuclear damage, but out of its own resources, up to SF 1 billion provided that the injured party did not cause the damage intentionally [Section 16.1 of the Act]. These special cases are as follows:

- where the person liable cannot be identified;
- where the damage is caused by an uninsured nuclear installation or an uninsured transport operation;
- where the insurer and the person liable are insolvent;
- where a person who has suffered nuclear damage in Switzerland as a result of an occurrence abroad cannot, in the country concerned, obtain compensation equivalent to that available under the Act.

In the case of *major occurrences*, the seriousness of which gives reason to believe that insurance cover will be insufficient to satisfy all claims, the Confederation establishes a special indemnity scheme by Order. This Order may cancel the right of recourse of all public and private insurers against the person liable. It determines the principles for the equitable distribution of available funds among the injured parties. The Federal Assembly may set up a special body to ensure that the Order is strictly implemented; appeals to the Federal Court are allowed against decisions taken by this body. The Confederation may also pay additional contributions in respect of damage not otherwise covered [Section 29].

Where a state of emergency is created by a major occurrence, the Federal Council is empowered to issue regulations on private insurance, relating to:

- modification of the insurers' liability;
- the levying of retrospective premiums on policy-holders;
- the deduction of such premiums from insurance payments.

However, this power does not extend to insurance which has to be taken out to cover nuclear third party liability by virtue of the Act. The Federal Council is empowered to take corresponding measures in relation to social insurance and public law insurance [Section 30].

C. COMPENSATION

After the occurrence of an incident of a serious nature, the Federal Council orders an inquiry in order to determine the injured parties and invite them, by published notice, to make themselves known within three months of the date of publication, with a note of the date and place of damage involved [Section 22.1]. Should a victim fail to make himself known, this does not compromise his right to compensation but can nevertheless make its exercise more complicated since it will then be more difficult to establish proof of a causal link between the damage and the incident [Section 22.2].

The victim of nuclear damage may proceed directly against the private insurer and the Confederation within the limits of the amount covered by insurance, and exceptions under the contract of insurance may not be invoked against him [Section 19].

Injured parties who are insured under the Federal Industrial Accident Insurance Act retain, subject to the provisions of Section 44 of that Act, their rights under the Nuclear Third Party Liability Act*. Benefits paid to the victim of a nuclear incident under a non-compulsory accident insurance, the premiums for which have been paid by the operator, are deducted from the amount of compensation to be paid by him in proportion to his share of the premium payment [Section 9].

It should be noted that (private law) agreements establishing manifestly inadequate compensation may be challenged within three years of the date of their conclusion [Section 8.2].

The nature and extent of damages together with the granting of solatium are governed by the principles of the Code of Obligations relating to liability in tort. However, Article 44.2 of the Code is not applicable. Where the victim of damage receives an unusually high income, the Court may reduce compensation on a fair basis [Section 7].

If legal proceedings are likely to last a considerable time, the competent Court may award provisional payments on account without, however, prejudice to its final judgment [Section 28].

When the Confederation pays out benefits in respect of cover for special cases (see "State Intervention" above), it may reduce or refuse payment where the injured party has caused the damage through gross negligence [Section 16.2].

D. TIME LIMITS FOR BRINGING CLAIMS

The right to compensation is time-barred three years from the date on which the injured party became aware of the damage and of the identity of the person liable. It is extinguished, except for claims relating to deferred damage, if no proceedings are brought within a period of thirty years following the incident. If the damage is due to prolonged effects, this period runs from the moment when these effects cease [Section 10.1]. The term *prolonged effects* covers cases in which persons were exposed to radiation over a certain period without necessarily being aware of the fact.

Where the state of health of the injured party deteriorates after the judgment or if new evidence or facts come to light, application may be made for revision of the judgment within

* Section 44 of the Industrial Accident Insurance Act specifies that:

1. Persons who have taken out compulsory insurance and their heirs are entitled to pursue their civil claims against the policy-holder's spouse, ascendants or descendants or the persons living in his household, only if they caused the incident intentionally or through gross negligence.
2. Civil claims arising from an industrial accident against the employer, members of his family or workers in his enterprise, are limited in the same way. Special third party liability provisions in Federal and Cantonal legislation are not applicable.

This means that for the employees in a nuclear installation, the provisions of the Act on Nuclear Third Party Liability are not applicable against the operator of the installation, but are replaced by the benefits provided for under the Industrial Accident Insurance Act.

three years of the date on which the injured party became aware thereof, but in no case later than thirty years from the date of the incident [Section 10.3].

E. COMPETENT COURTS AND PROCEDURE

The Act incorporates the principle of single court jurisdiction at Cantonal level, and each Canton is required to designate a court competent to hear claims for compensation for nuclear damage [Section 23].

If damage is caused by a nuclear installation, the competent court is that of the Canton in which the installation is situated [Section 24.1].

When damage is caused during the carriage of nuclear substances, jurisdiction lies with the court of the Canton in which the incident took place; however, if the place of the incident cannot be determined, the competent court is that of the Canton in which the nuclear installation is situated or of the place where the person liable resides or has elected domicile [Section 24.2].

In any case in which the above-mentioned conditions do not apply, an action brought against the Confederation for the compensation of deferred damage [Section 13], or occurring in the context of a *special case* [Section 16], must be brought before the highest court of the Canton of Bern [Section 24.3].

The Cantonal Court hands down its decision on the basis of the facts as established by it and the evidence it receives. All the parties concerned are heard by the Court, which is not bound by their submissions [Section 26.1].

When a claim is brought against the person liable, the private insurer or the Confederation, the Court gives the other parties concerned an opportunity to defend their interests in the proceedings [Section 26.2].

In determining legal and other costs, the Court may take into consideration the financial circumstances of the party liable therefor [Section 27].

In accordance with the provisions of the Federal Act on the Organisation of the Courts, an appeal against a judgment of the Cantonal Court may be brought before the Federal Court (a single Court at national level, constituting the last Court of Appeal) [Section 25].

*

* *

The Federal Republic of Germany and the Swiss Confederation concluded an Agreement on Third Party Liability in the Nuclear Field on 22nd October 1986. The Agreement, which entered into force on 21st September 1988, declares the principle of equal treatment for the nationals of both States and is intended, in particular, to facilitate the settlement of disputes if they are due to an event which occurs on the territory of either State, causing damage on the territory of the other. A translation of the Agreement is reproduced in Nuclear Law Bulletin No. 39.

TAIWAN

INTRODUCTION

Taiwan has four nuclear power plants in operation totalling 5 144 MWe. The Atomic Energy Council is responsible for administering and regulating nuclear activities and also deals with nuclear third party liability matters. The Council (AEC) is the top and independent administrative authority for nuclear energy within the Executive (*Yuan*) (the Cabinet).

Taiwan is not a Party to the Paris or the Vienna Conventions but applies their principles in its domestic legislation, namely, the channelling of liability onto the operator, and its limitation in amount and in time.

The basic legislation on nuclear third party liability is contained in the Act of 26th July 1971 on Compensation for Nuclear Damage; the Act entered into force and was published on the same date in the Gazette of the Presidential Office. It was last amended on 6th May 1977.

I. THIRD PARTY LIABILITY

A. SCOPE AND DEFINITIONS

The Act provides that it applies to compensation for nuclear damage resulting from the peaceful uses of nuclear energy; where it is silent, the provisions of the Civil law and other laws are applicable [Section 1]. The law applying to incidents occurring outside the country is determined by the Law Governing the Application of Laws to Civil Matters Involving Foreign Elements of 6th June 1953.

The manufacture, use and storage of nuclear material in quantities which are not sufficient to be hazardous are outside the scope of this Act. Such quantities are defined by the Atomic Energy Council [Section 10]. Radioisotopes manufactured for scientific, medical, agricultural, commercial and individual uses are also excluded from the Act [Section 11].

The definitions of *nuclear installation, nuclear incident, nuclear fuel, nuclear material, radioactive products or waste*, etc., are similar to those provided by the Vienna Convention [Sections 2, 3, 5, 6 and 9 of the Act].

B. NATURE AND ASSIGNMENT OF LIABILITY

a) General – Nuclear Installations

The *operator* in relation to a nuclear installation means the person designated or approved by the Government as being responsible for the operation of that installation [Section 7]. The Act provides that no person other than the operator of a nuclear installation is liable for nuclear damage caused by a nuclear incident occurring in his nuclear installation [Sections 11 and 22]. The operator is also liable for such nuclear damage regardless of whether it is caused intentionally or through negligence [Section 17].

Where nuclear damage involves the liability of more than one operator and the damage attributable to each is not reasonably separable, they are jointly and severally liable; however, each operator's liability will not exceed the limit laid down in the Act [Section 14] (see below under "Amount of Liability").

Where several nuclear installations of one and the same operator are involved in one nuclear incident, he will be liable in respect of each nuclear installation involved up to the amount applicable to him under the Act [Section 16]; the Act provides, however, that several nuclear installations belonging to one operator which are located on the same site are to be considered as a single nuclear installation [Section 6].

Where nuclear material which has been stolen, lost or abandoned causes a nuclear incident, the operator who last had it in his possession, is liable for any damage caused by such material [Section 12].

b) Transport

When a nuclear incident occurs in the course of carriage of nuclear material within Taiwan, the sending nuclear operator is liable therefor unless such liability has been assumed by written agreement by another nuclear operator; and in the absence of a written agreement, when the material has been taken in charge by another nuclear operator [Section 13(a) and (b)].

The sending nuclear operator is also liable for nuclear damage in course of carriage of nuclear material intended for a reactor comprised in a means of transport, unless the material has been taken in charge by the person duly authorised to operate that reactor [Section 13(c)].

Also, the operator of a nuclear installation is liable for nuclear damage caused in Taiwan by nuclear material being carried from his installation to a foreign country or from a foreign country to his installation [Section 13(d)].

The operator of a nuclear installation is not liable for nuclear damage involving nuclear material in storage incidental to transport where another operator has assumed liability therefor [Section 13].

Where a nuclear incident occurs during the carriage of nuclear material on the same means of transport, or in the case of storage incidental to the carriage in the same nuclear installation, and several operators are liable for the damage caused, the total amount of compensation should not exceed the limit laid down by the Act [Section 15] (see below under "Amount of Liability").

c) Rights of Recourse

The operator of a nuclear installation has a right of recourse where this has expressly been stipulated in an agreement in writing; he also has such a right where the nuclear incident results from an act or omission with intent to cause damage against the person having acted or omitted to act with such intent [Section 21].

d) Exoneration from Liability

The operator of a nuclear installation is not liable for nuclear damage caused by a nuclear incident due to an international conflict, civil war, a riot or a major natural disaster [Section 17].

Where the operator proves that the nuclear damage was caused by a victim's action or omission to act, the court may exonerate him from liability to that victim or reduce the compensation due [Section 18].

C. AMOUNT OF LIABILITY

Liability for damage arising from each single nuclear incident is limited to 70 million silver dollars (approximately 6 million Special Drawing Rights of the International Monetary Fund – SDRs). This amount is exclusive of any interest or costs [Section 23].

D. NUCLEAR DAMAGE

a) Damage Covered

The Act defines *nuclear damage* as: loss of life, personal injury or damage to property which arises out of or results from:

a) the radioactive, toxic, explosive or other hazardous properties of nuclear fuel or radioactive products or waste in, or of nuclear material coming from or sent to a nuclear installation; and

b) other ionizing radiation emitted by any other source of radiation inside a nuclear installation [Section 8].

All damage caused by a nuclear incident alone or in combination with other (non-nuclear) incidents will be considered as nuclear damage to the extent that the damage other than nuclear damage cannot be reasonably separated from the latter [Section 19].

b) Damage Excluded

The operator of a nuclear installation is not liable under the Act for damage to the installation itself or to property on the site of the installation which is used or intended to be used in connection with that installation [Section 20]. In such case his liability is governed by general tort law.

Also, the operator is not liable for damage to the means of transport on which the nuclear material was involved at the time of the nuclear incident [Section 20].

II. COVER AND COMPENSATION

A. INSURANCE OR OTHER FINANCIAL SECURITY

The operator of a nuclear installation must take out insurance or some other financial security to cover his liability to a maximum amount, as decided by the competent authorities, namely, the Atomic Energy Council [Section 24].

The Central Government as well as provincial or municipal governments and their academic research organisations are exempted from the above obligation [Section 24].

Operators of privately operated nuclear installations may, within certain limits, ask the competent authorities to reduce the insurance for their liability; such limits are determined by the authorities [Section 24].

Termination of the insurance or financial security only becomes effective when approved by the authorities following a request in writing from the insurer or guarantor, two months prior to the expiry of such insurance or guarantee [Section 25].

In the case of transport of nuclear material, the insurance or financial security cannot be terminated during the transport [Section 25].

B. STATE INTERVENTION

If the amount provided by the insurance or financial security is insufficient to compensate the nuclear damage, the Government will loan the balance remaining to the operator to cover his liability, up to the limit set by the Act; the operator must reimburse this loan [Section 26].

Following a nuclear incident, the Atomic Energy Council is empowered to set up a committee to investigate the occurrence. The Council decides the organisation of the committee [Section 32].

The Act specifies that following a nuclear incident, the Government will take the necessary relief and rehabilitation measures, beyond the limit of liability where necessary [Section 33].

C. COMPENSATION

Where the nuclear operator is unable to compensate nuclear damage, actions for compensation may be brought directly against the insurer or financial guarantor.

Where the amount of compensation exceeds or may exceed the operator's limit of liability, the court may distribute the compensation available at its discretion, allotting a higher proportion to loss of life and personal injury than to property damage and may reserve no more than one-tenth of the amount for deferred damage [Section 31].

D. TIME LIMITS FOR BRINGING CLAIMS

Claims for compensation of nuclear damage are extinguished if no action is brought within three years from the date on which the person entitled to compensation knew of the damage and the operator liable and, in any event, ten years from the date of the nuclear incident [Section 27].

Where nuclear damage is caused by a nuclear incident involving nuclear material which has been stolen, lost or abandoned, the period for bringing claims will in no case exceed twenty years from the date of such theft, loss or abandonment [Section 28].

Persons who have brought claims for compensation within the requisite period may amend their claims to take account of any aggravation of the damage after expiry of that period provided final judgment has not been entered [Section 29].

E. COMPETENT COURTS AND PROCEDURE

The Act is silent in this respect. However, under the general law, the competent court is the court of the area where the legal person's headquarters are located or that of the area where the nuclear incident occurs.

UNITED KINGDOM

INTRODUCTION

At present, the nuclear electricity capacity in the United Kingdom amounts to approximately 10 900 MWe. The nuclear power plants are operated by Nuclear Electric plc, for England and Wales, Scottish Nuclear Ltd for Scotland, and the United Kingdom Atomic Energy Authority (UKAEA). There are also a number of facilities in the nuclear fuel cycle, including reactors and fuel reprocessing plants, operated by British Nuclear Fuels plc (BNFL).

Under the Atomic Energy Act 1946, the Secretary of State for Energy has the general duty to promote and control the development of atomic energy.

The United Kingdom is a Party to the 1960 Paris Convention and the 1963 Brussels Supplementary Convention, both as amended in 1982. The United Kingdom has also signed but not ratified the 1963 Vienna Convention and the 1971 Brussels Convention. It is also a Signatory of the Joint Protocol of 1988 relating to the application of the Vienna and Paris Conventions.

The basic legislation on nuclear third party liability in the United Kingdom is contained in the Nuclear Installations Act, 1965, as amended. The Act, which came into force on 1st December 1965, implements the provisions of the Paris Convention and the Brussels Supplementary Convention. The provisions of the 1965 Act have been amended on several occasions. In particular, the Nuclear Installations Act, 1969 made minor amendments for the purposes of conformity with international agreements on nuclear liability, particularly the Paris Convention and the Brussels Supplementary Convention. The 1965 Act was further amended by the Energy Act, 1983. Part II of that Act amends the provisions of the 1965 Act to give effect to the two 1982 Protocols to amend the Paris Convention and the Brussels Supplementary Convention respectively.

I. THIRD PARTY LIABILITY

A. SCOPE AND DEFINITIONS

The liability, which under the Nuclear Installations Act 1965 (all references are to this Act unless otherwise specified) is imposed on operators of nuclear installations in the United Kingdom, arises whenever a nuclear incident occurs either on the site of the installation or, as a general rule, in the course of carriage of nuclear material to or from that installation [Section 7].

No compensation is payable under the 1965 Act for damage caused by a nuclear incident which occurs wholly within the territory of one of the Parties (other than the United Kingdom) to the Paris Convention because in such case the right to compensation will depend on the law of the country where the incident took place [Section 13(1)].

The Act does not cover compensation in respect of a breach of duty of the kind imposed by Section 7(1) (see under "Nature and Assignment of Liability" below) occurring in a country not Party to the Paris Convention except in relation to persons or property on a ship or aircraft registered in the United Kingdom or in relation to such a ship or aircraft itself [Section 13(2)].

A number of orders in Council have been made under the Act extending, with the appropriate adaptations, the relevant Sections of the Act to, for example, the Channel Islands, the Isle of Man and certain dependent territories* [Section 28(1)].

The Act does not apply to incidents occurring off-site which involve nuclear material defined as *excepted matter* and consisting of one or more of the following:

- isotopes prepared for industrial, commercial, agricultural, medical, scientific or educational purposes;
- natural uranium;
- any uranium of which the isotope 235 forms not more than 0.72 per cent;
- such other nuclear material as prescribed by regulations; the Nuclear Installations (Excepted Matter) Regulations 1978 (S.I. 1978/1979) exempt certain forms and quantities of nuclear material from the application of the Act in accordance with the OECD Steering Committee for Nuclear Energy's decision of 27th October 1977 pursuant to Article 1(b) of the Paris Convention;
- nuclear material excluded by a State Party to a nuclear Convention from the operation of that Convention (such as under Article 1(b) of the Paris Convention) [Sections 7(2) and 26(1)].

The 1965 Act [Section 26] provides for the interpretation of terms used throughout the Act. In particular, when the term *relevant* is applied to *international agreement*, it refers to any international agreement about third party liability in the field of nuclear energy to which the United Kingdom is Party, and so includes the Paris Convention, the Brussels

* Several Nuclear Installations Orders made under Section 28: British Solomon Islands (Statutory Instrument 1972/12); Cayman Islands (S.I. 1972/123); Falkland Islands and Dependencies (S.I. 1972/124); Gibraltar (S.I. 1970/1116); Gilbert and Ellice Islands (S.I. 1972/125); Guernsey (S.I. 1978/1528, as amended by S.I. 1985/1640); Hong Kong (S.I. 1972/126); Isle of Man (S.I. 1977/429, as amended by S.I. 1987/668); Jersey (S.I. 1980/1527); Montserrat (S.I. 1972/127); St. Helena (S.I. 1972/128); Virgin Islands (S.I. 1973/235).

Supplementary Convention and covers the States Parties thereto. *Relevant* is similarly applied in relation to *foreign operator*, *foreign contribution* and *foreign judgment*. For standardisation purposes this terminology will not be used in this Chapter. Instead, the Conventions will be referred to explicitly where applicable.

B. NATURE AND ASSIGNMENT OF LIABILITY

a) Nature of Liability

The Nuclear Installations Act 1965 provides that it is the duty of the licensee of a nuclear site (the nuclear operator) to secure that no occurrence or incident involving nuclear material or the emission of ionizing radiation (the latter being on-site) for which he is responsible causes personal injury or damage to property other than his own [Section 7].

The operator is exclusively (and absolutely) liable for breach of that duty [Section 12(1) and (2)]. This liability is limited in amount and in time, but must be covered by insurance or by some other means approved by the Secretary of State for Energy [Sections 16(1), 15(1) and 19(1)].

If two or more persons are liable for the same damage by virtue of the provisions of the 1965 Act and the law of another country Party to the Paris Convention, their liability shall be joint and several [Section 17(3)].

The operator's liability for any breach of this duty to avoid damage runs for a *period of responsibility* starting either on the date a nuclear site licence comes into force or on some other date fixed by the Health and Safety Executive with the consent of the Secretary of State, being the date when nuclear material first comes onto the site. The Health and Safety Executive is the authority for licensing nuclear installations [Section 5(3)].

No liability under the 1965 Act is placed on an operator from a country which is not Party to the Paris Convention. However, in respect of a nuclear incident occurring in the course of carriage of nuclear material on behalf of such an operator in the United Kingdom, a similar duty to that placed upon a Paris Convention operator is placed upon the Party responsible for that carriage.

b) General – Nuclear Installations

As already mentioned, an operator is under a duty to secure that any occurrence (i.e. a nuclear incident) within the scope of the Act does not cause injury to persons or damage to property, and he is liable for breach of this duty [Section 7(1)].

Damage to the nuclear installation itself or to on-site property in connection with the construction or operation of the installation does not give rise to the liability of the operator [Section 7(3)]. However, the person responsible for the damage may be held liable if this has been expressly provided for by written agreement or if the damage was caused intentionally [Section 12(3A)(a) and (b)].

c) Transport

The operator is also under duty to avoid all damage in the course of carriage of nuclear material effected on his behalf, including such carriage with his agreement from a country which is not a Party to the Paris Convention [Section 7(2)].

It is also provided that a foreign operator from a country Party to the Paris Convention shall be liable under the Act for damage caused by a nuclear incident in the course of carriage of nuclear material on his behalf, if the incident takes place wholly or partly within the United Kingdom (or in certain circumstances outside the United Kingdom or other Convention territories where a duty falls on a Convention operator, for example on the high seas) [Section 10]. However, this operator cannot be made liable under the Act for damage to a means of transport if he is not liable under his own national law for such damage, but he is not exempt from common law liability for such damage if any [Section 21(2)].

Any question arising as to whether a person comes under the designation of an operator as above shall be referred to and determined by the Secretary of State for Energy [Section 26(3)].

In addition, if any person other than a United Kingdom operator or a foreign operator from a country Party to the Paris Convention is responsible for nuclear material in the course of carriage within the United Kingdom's territorial limits he is made liable for any damage which might be caused within the United Kingdom [Section 11].

Where liability has been incurred by the operator no other person can be held liable for the injury or damage, but the operation of certain international transport conventions which may involve other persons in liability is not affected [Section 12(1)(b) and (4)].

d) Rights of Recourse

Where, in the case of a nuclear incident, a person other than the operator has paid compensation under certain international transport conventions, he shall acquire the same rights of compensation under the Act as if he himself has suffered the damage, up to the amount of his payment [Section 13(5)(a)].

The same rule applies, if the incident occurred or the damage was suffered within the territory of a non-Contracting State to the relevant nuclear international agreements and the payment is made under the law of that State and by a person who has his principal place of business in a Contracting State or is acting on behalf of such a person.

e) Exoneration

Where a nuclear incident, or the damage caused thereby, is attributable to hostile action in the course of armed conflict (whether within or outside the United Kingdom) it does not give rise to liability under the Act [Section 13(4)](see under "Nuclear Damage" below).

C. AMOUNT OF LIABILITY

The liability of an operator to pay compensation under the 1965 Act by virtue of a breach of duty as specified therein shall not exceed £20 million (approximately 26 million Special Drawing Rights of the International Monetary Fund – SDRs) apart from payments in respect of interest or costs; in the case of sites specified as *Prescribed Sites* by the Nuclear Installations (Prescribed Sites) Regulations 1983 (S.I. 1983/919), whose licensees are subject to a lower limit of liability, the amount is limited to £5 million (approximately 6 million SDRs) [Section 16(1)]. The Secretary of State for Energy may, with the approval of the Treasury, by order increase either or both of the above amounts [Section 16(1A)].

Where damage to the means of transport is incurred, the claim will be satisfied provided that the equivalent in sterling of 5 million SDRs is available to meet other claims [Section 21(1)]. The Secretary of State for Energy may, with the approval of the Treasury, by order increase that amount [Section 21(1A)].

Where a foreign operator from a country Party to the Paris Convention is liable for damage caused by a nuclear incident in the course of carriage on his behalf, he will only be required to pay compensation to the extent that his own national law provides for this and only up to an amount equal to that established by his own law [Section 16(2)].

For further compensation see under "State Intervention" below.

D. NUCLEAR DAMAGE

a) Damage Covered

The operator is liable for an injury to persons or damage to property caused by the radioactive properties or a combination of those properties and any toxic, explosive or other hazardous properties, of nuclear material involved in a nuclear incident. In addition, such a liability covers injury to persons or damage to property caused by ionizing radiations emitted from other sources of radiation on the site of the nuclear installation and from any waste discharged (in whatever form) on or from the site [Section 7(1)].

Liability arises where damage has been caused by an incident which occurred on the site of the nuclear installation or in the course of carriage on behalf or with the agreement of the operator of the nuclear installation. In certain circumstances liability also arises where the incident took place off the site but not during carriage, for example, in relation to waste discharged or where the nuclear material has been stolen, lost, jettisoned or abandoned [Section 7(2)].

Where damage which would not normally come within the Act is not reasonably separable from damage which is covered by the Act, such damage is deemed to be covered by the Act [Section 12(2)].

Where a child is born disabled as a result of an injury to either of its parents within the meaning of the 1965 Act, the child's disabilities are to be regarded as injuries caused on the same occasion and by the same breach of duty as the parent's injury [Congenital Disabilities (Civil Liability) Act 1976, Section 3(3)].

Furthermore, the operator is liable for injury or damage attributable to a natural disaster even if it is of such an exceptional character that it could not have been foreseen [Section 13(4)].

b) Damage Excluded

When the operator of a nuclear installation is held liable for a nuclear incident on the site of his nuclear installation, as already mentioned, no account shall be taken of damage to the installation itself or to any other property which is on the site for the purposes of the construction or operation of the installation. Such property, whether or not it belongs to the operator, is deemed to be his property and therefore cannot be the subject matter of a claim by him for damages, as he cannot claim against himself [Section 7(3)].

II. COVER AND COMPENSATION

A. INSURANCE OR OTHER FINANCIAL SECURITY

The operator must provide financial security either by insurance or some other means, approved by the Secretary of State with the consent of the Treasury so as to ensure that claims against him (in respect of damage occurring in the United Kingdom or in a country Party to the Paris Convention) can be met up to the required amount (£20 million or £5 million as prescribed) in respect of each period of liability (*cover period*) [Section 19(1) and (1A)].

Where financial security is provided otherwise than by insurance, and the same person guarantees two or more sites for the same operator, the security will be considered sufficient if it covers the total of the two largest sites, unless the Secretary of State for Energy requires the provision of a larger amount, which may be any amount up to the full cover for all the sites concerned [Section 19(3)].

By reason of the gravity of any nuclear incident which has resulted or may result in claims against the operator, or having regard to any previous occurrences, the Secretary of State may, if he thinks it proper, by notice in writing, direct the operator that a new cover period shall begin on a specified date at least two months after the date of the notice [Section 19(4)].

No new cover period begins on the grant of a new nuclear site licence to the same licensee in respect of a site which consists of or includes the existing site.

Any person on whose behalf carriage of nuclear material is undertaken outside the territorial limits of the United Kingdom must deliver to the carrier, before the carriage is begun, a certificate of insurance, containing various prescribed particulars of the carriage, the nuclear material and the financial cover [Section 21(3) as amended by the Energy Act 1983; Nuclear Installations (Insurance Certificate) Regulations 1965, S.I. 1965/1823 as amended by S.I. 1969/64].

The operator, whenever claims against him in respect of a nuclear incident have reached three-fifths of the amount under Section 19(1) – i.e. £20 million or £5 million as the case may be, must give notice to the Secretary of State of Energy. Thereafter claims may not be settled between the operator and the claimant except with the agreement of the Secretary of State [Section 20(1)].

B. STATE INTERVENTION

All established claims under the Act, whether arising in the United Kingdom or elsewhere, will be met in full, subject to the limit of 300 million SDRs specified in Section 18 given the commitments of the United Kingdom as a Party to the Brussels Supplementary Convention. If the limit of liability of the operator is exceeded, provision is made for a procedure whereby claims are made to the appropriate Government authority instead of against the operator. The same applies if claims are made after the expiry of the applicable period of limitation or the claims relate to damage to the means of transport in those cases where the operator is not liable [Section 16(3)].

The Act provides that, where liability is incurred by a United Kingdom operator, or by a foreign operator in respect of carriage, funds will be made available to meet compensation claims up to a maximum of 300 million SDRs after taking account of amounts available from United Kingdom operators or foreign operators (under their insurance arrangements) and any relevant foreign contributions under the third tier of the Brussels Convention [Section 18(1) and (1A)]. This provision applies also to claims made against a United Kingdom operator under the law of a State Party to the Paris/Brussels Conventions, except that:

a) if the claim is made under the law of a country Party only to the Paris Convention, the total amount to be made available will not exceed the sums specified as the liability of the operator (£20 million); and

b) if the claim is made under the law of a country Party to the Brussels Supplementary Convention, the total amount to be made available will not exceed the sums made available pursuant to this latter Convention in that country (on the basis of reciprocity).

Interests and costs in connection with claims for which public funds are made available are also met out of public funds [Section 18(3)].

If a claim is made against an operator later than ten years after the nuclear incident (or in the case of theft, loss, jettison or abandonment after twenty years from the date of the theft, etc.) it will fall to the State to satisfy it out of moneys to be provided by Parliament and not by the operator or his insurance [Section 16(3), (4) (5)].

C. COMPENSATION

Compensation is payable by a nuclear operator when any injury or damage has been caused by a breach of his duty within the meaning of the Act [Section 12].

When a person is entitled to claim compensation on two different bases, for example under the Act and under common law, he is not entitled to recover compensation in respect of the same injury or damage both under the Act and otherwise than under the Act [Section 12(3)].

When the damage suffered by a victim is attributable to an act committed by him with the intention of causing harm or with reckless disregard of the consequences, the amount of compensation payable to him may be reduced [Section 13(6)].

D. TIME LIMITS FOR BRINGING CLAIMS

A claim will not be entertained after the expiration of thirty years from the date of the incident which gave rise to the claim [Section 15(1)].

However, in the event of theft, loss, jettison or abandonment of nuclear material the claim will only be entertained if the nuclear incident occurred within a period of twenty years from the date of such event [Section 15(2)].

E. COMPETENT COURTS AND PROCEDURE

Each of the High Courts in England and Wales, the Court of Session in Scotland and the High Court in the Province of Northern Ireland have concurrent jurisdiction throughout the United Kingdom. Where the Secretary of State certifies that any claim or question should be determined by a court in a particular part of the United Kingdom, his certificate shall be conclusive evidence of the jurisdiction of that court [Section 17(2)].

Where the Secretary of State for Energy certifies that a claim or question under the 1965 Act should be determined by a court of another country Party to the Paris Convention, no court in the United Kingdom may have jurisdiction therefor. Any proceedings to enforce such a claim in a court of the United Kingdom will be set aside [Section 17(1)].

Any judgment given in a court of a country Party to the Paris Convention, which is certified by the Secretary of State to be a judgment rendered in accordance with the Paris Convention or the Brussels Supplementary Convention, may be enforced in the United Kingdom under the Foreign Judgments (Reciprocal Enforcement) Act 1933 [Section 17(4)].

However, a judgment given by the courts of any non-Contracting State to the Paris Convention and the Brussels Supplementary Convention will not be enforceable in the United Kingdom, except where it is enforceable in pursuance of an international agreement [Section 17(5) and (5A)].

Where the Government of a country Party to the Paris Convention is the operator involved in a claim, that Government will be deemed to have submitted to the jurisdiction of the United Kingdom courts, but no judgment of the court may be enforced by levying execution against the property of that Government [Section 17(6), Rules of the Supreme Court 1981, Order 11, Rule 1].

UNITED STATES

INTRODUCTION

There are 111 nuclear power plants licensed to operate in the United States in 1990, producing approximately 17 per cent of the total electricity generation in the country. The Federal Government assumes primary responsibility for nuclear energy questions. The United States Nuclear Regulatory Commission (NRC) and the United States Department of Energy (DOE) share most authority over nuclear affairs. The NRC is responsible for licensing and regulating nuclear materials and facilities while the DOE exercises central responsibility for co-ordination and management of research and development of all energy sources, including nuclear energy.

The federal legislation on nuclear indemnity and limitation of liability in the United States of America, the Price-Anderson Act, forms part of the Atomic Energy Act of 1954 (Public Law 83-703, 42 United States Code 2011), as amended. Originally enacted in 1957 for a ten-year term, the Price-Anderson Act was amended several times; its duration was extended to 1st August 1977 in 1965, to 1st August 1987 in 1975 and currently by the Price-Anderson Amendments Act of 1988, to 1st August 2002. The Price-Anderson Act governs liability and compensation in the event of a nuclear incident arising from the activities of NRC licensees and DOE contractors. The NRC has issued Regulations for determining the financial protection required of licensees for the indemnification and limitation of liability of licensees [Code of Federal Regulations (CFR), Title 10, Chapter 1, Part 140]. The NRC has modified these Regulations in order to implement changes made by the Price-Anderson Amendments Act of 1988. The present study is based on those modifications effective 1st July 1989.

The DOE has the authority under the Atomic Energy Act to enter into indemnification agreements with its contractors [ERDA Procurement Regulations, subpart 9-4.50 and Code of Federal Regulations (CFR), Title 10, Chapter 2, Part 840]. DOE published on 21st September 1989 a notice of inquiry on its plans to implement the Price-Anderson Amendments Act of 1988.

The United States is not a Party to the Paris and Vienna Conventions. However, the Price-Anderson Act achieves the same objectives as the Conventions within the framework of the existing legal system of the individual states without creating, in most cases, a special regime of substantive federal law providing, for example, for absolute and exclusive liability.

I. THIRD PARTY LIABILITY

A. SCOPE AND DEFINITIONS

Generally, the Price-Anderson Act applies to nuclear incidents, including an *extraordinary nuclear occurrence*, occurring within the United States and causing damage within or outside the United States. It also applies, in part, to *precautionary evacuations* (see below for an explanation of the terminology).

The Act also applies to nuclear incidents occurring outside the United States if they involve source, special nuclear, or by-product material owned by and used by or under contract with the United States. The Act applies furthermore to nuclear incidents occurring outside both the United States and any other nation (i.e. on the high seas), if they involve nuclear material licensed by the NRC which is used in connection with a licensed stationary production or utilisation facility or shipments between NRC licensees in the United States routed beyond territorial limits [Section 11q].

When used in a geographical sense, the term *United States* includes all territories and possessions of the United States, the Panama Canal Zone and Puerto Rico.

Definitions particularly pertinent to the Price-Anderson Act are included in Section 11 of the Atomic Energy Act of 1954, as amended, as follows:

The term ***nuclear incident*** *means any occurrence, including an extraordinary nuclear occurrence, within the United States causing, within or outside the United States, bodily injury, sickness, disease, or death, or loss of or damage to property, or loss of use of property, arising out of or resulting from the radioactive, toxic, explosive, or other hazardous properties of source, special nuclear, or by-product material ...* [Section 11q].

The term ***extraordinary nuclear occurrence*** *means any event causing a discharge or dispersal of source, special nuclear, or by-product material from its intended place of confinement in amounts offsite, or causing radiation levels offsite, which the NRC or the Secretary of Energy, as appropriate, determines to be substantial, and which the NRC or the Secretary of Energy, as appropriate, determines has resulted or will probably result in substantial damages to persons offsite or property offsite. Any determination by the NRC or the Secretary of Energy, as appropriate, that such an event has, or has not, occurred shall be final and conclusive and no official shall have power or jurisdiction to review any such determination. The NRC or the Secretary of Energy, as appropriate, shall establish criteria in writing setting forth the basis upon which such determination shall be made. As used in this subsection,* ***offsite*** *means away from* **the location** *or* **the contract location** *as defined in the applicable indemnity agreement entered into pursuant to Section 170* [Section 11j].

The term ***person*** *means (1) any individual, corporation, partnership, firm, association, trust, estate, public or private institution, group, Government agency other than the NRC, any state or any political subdivision of, or any political entity within a state, any foreign government or nation or any political subdivision of any such government or nation, or other entity; and (2) any legal successor, representative, agent, or agency of the foregoing* [Section 11s].

The term ***person indemnified*** *means (1) with respect to a nuclear incident occurring within the United States or outside the United States as the term is used in Section 170c, ... the person with whom an indemnity agreement is executed* (see below under "State

Intervention") *or who is required to maintain financial protection, and any other person who may be liable for public liability or (2) with respect to any other nuclear incident occurring outside the United States, the person with whom an indemnity agreement is executed and any other person who may be liable for public liability by reason of his activities under any contract with the Secretary of Energy or any project to which indemnification under the provisions of Section 170d has been extended or under any subcontract, purchase order, or other agreement, of any tier, under any such contract or project* [Section 11t].

The term ***public liability*** *means any legal liability arising out of or resulting from a nuclear incident or precautionary evacuation (including all reasonable additional costs incurred by a state ... in the course of responding to a nuclear incident or precautionary evacuation) ...* [Section 11w].

The term ***public liability action****, as used in Section 170, means any suit asserting public liability. A public liability action shall be deemed to be an action arising under Section 170, and the substantive rules for decision in such action shall be derived from the law of the state in which the nuclear incident involved occurs, unless such law is inconsistent with the provisions of such Section* [Section 11hh].

The term ***financial protection*** *means the ability to respond in damages for public liability and to meet the costs of investigating and defending claims and settling suits for such damages* [Section 11k].

The term ***indemnitor*** *means (1) any insurer with respect to his obligations under a policy of insurance furnished as proof of financial protection; (2) any licensee, contractor or other person who is obligated under any other form of financial protection, with respect to such obligations; and (3) the NRC or the Secretary of Energy, as appropriate, with respect to any obligation undertaken by it in an indemnity agreement entered into pursuant to Section 170 of the Price-Anderson Act* [Section 11m].

As used in Section 170, the term ***legal costs*** *means the costs incurred by a plaintiff or a defendant in initiating, prosecuting, investigating, settling, or defending claims or suits for damage arising under such Section* [Section 11jj].

The term ***precautionary evacuation*** *means an evacuation of the public within a specified area near a nuclear facility, or the transportation route in the case of an accident involving transportation of source material, special nuclear material, by-product material, high-level radioactive waste, spent nuclear fuel, or transuranic waste to or from a production or utilisation facility, if the evacuation is:*

1. *the result of any event that is not classified as a nuclear incident but that poses imminent danger of bodily injury or property damage from the radiological properties of source material, special nuclear material, by-product material, high-level radioactive waste, spent nuclear fuel, or transuranic waste, and causes an evacuation; and*

2. *initiated by an official of a state or a political subdivision of a state, who is authorised by state law to initiate such an evacuation and who reasonably determined that such an evacuation was necessary to protect the public health and safety* [Section 11gg].

B. NATURE AND ASSIGNMENT OF LIABILITY

a) General – Nuclear Installations

Liability under the Price-Anderson Act is assigned to persons who cause bodily injury, death or loss of or damage to property. It also includes, as already mentioned, legal liability arising out of or resulting from a precautionary evacuation.

The Price-Anderson Act does not itself establish a legal basis for liability in the event of a nuclear incident at a licensed facility. Rather, the matter is left to the tort laws of the individual states, including whether or not an operator's liability will be strict. Under these laws not only the operator of a nuclear installation may be held liable, but also other persons such as the supplier of a reactor component or the carrier of nuclear materials.

However, with respect to extraordinary nuclear occurrences, the NRC and DOE are authorised to incorporate provisions in indemnity agreements (see below under "State Intervention"), or may require their incorporation in insurance policies, which waive certain defences which may be available to the defendant in a tort action under state law, e.g. any issue or defence as to conduct of the claimant or fault of persons indemnified, or any issue or defence as to charitable or governmental immunity. The waivers authorised by the Act shall, as to indemnitors, be effective only with respect to those obligations set forth in the insurance policies or the contracts furnished as proof of financial protection and in the indemnity agreements. Such waivers do not apply to, or prejudice the prosecution or defence of, any claim or portion of claim which is not within the protection afforded under (a) the terms of insurance policies or contracts furnished as proof of financial protection, or indemnity agreements and (b) the limit of liability provisions of the Price-Anderson Act.

These waiver provisions apply to any extraordinary nuclear occurrence which:

i) arises out of, results from, or occurs in the course of the construction, possession, or operation of a production or utilisation facility,

ii) arises out of, results from, or occurs in the course of transportation of source material, by-product material, or special nuclear material to or from a production or utilisation facility,

iii) during the course of the contract activity, arises out of or results from the possession, operation, or use by a DOE contractor or subcontractor of a device utilising special nuclear material or by-product material,

iv) arises out of, results from, or occurs in the course of, the construction, possession, or operation of any plant licensed to possess and use special nuclear material, source material or by-product material under Sections 53, 63, or 81 of the Act for which the NRC has imposed as a condition of the licence a requirement that the licensee have and maintain financial protection,

v) arises out of, results from, or occurs in the course of, transportation of source material, by-product material, or special nuclear material to or from any plant licensed to possess and use such material under Sections 53, 63, or 81 of the Act, for which the NRC has imposed as a condition of the licence a requirement that the licensee have and maintain financial protection, or,

vi) arises out of, results from, or occurs in the course of nuclear waste activities.

The NRC has determined that a utilisation facility is any nuclear reactor other than one designed or used primarily for the formation of plutonium or uranium 233, thus subjecting to licensing requirements nuclear reactors used for power production and other peaceful purposes. Also, a production facility is any nuclear reactor designed or used primarily for the formation of plutonium or uranium 233, any facility designed or used for separation of uranium and plutonium (except for laboratory scale facilities), and any facility designed or used for processing of irradiated materials (except laboratory scale facilities) [Title 10 CFR, Section 50.2(a) and (b)].

Also, a DOE contractor with whom the Secretary of Energy has concluded an indemnity agreement, and whose work involves underground detonation of a nuclear explosive device will be liable, to the extent indemnified, for injuries or damage similarly to a private person as defined by the Act and no immunity or defence, based upon the federal, state or municipal character of the contractor or the work to be performed, may be invoked to bar such liability [Section 170(d)(7)].

b) Transport

As explained, the tort laws of the individual states may provide that carriers of nuclear materials may be held liable for a nuclear incident. Furthermore, the effect of the definitions of the Price-Anderson Act is also to assign liability for injuries caused by a nuclear incident to carriers of source, special nuclear, or by-product material.

c) Rights of Recourse

As noted above, the Act does not establish a legal basis for liability in the event of a nuclear incident; this matter is left to the laws of the individual states of the United States. However, the Act defines *person indemnified* as the person with whom an indemnity agreement (see below under "State Intervention") is executed by the NRC (normally the nuclear operator) or DOE as well as any other person who may be held legally liable (see supra "Definitions"). Accordingly, *public liability* is defined to include any legal liability arising out of or resulting from a nuclear incident (including precautionary evacuation). Thus, the combined insurance/indemnity system protects not only the licensee but also other persons, such as the manufacturer of a component part, who could conceivably be held liable for a nuclear incident under state law.

The operator of a nuclear installation is therefore not exclusively liable as not all liability is legally channelled to him as under the Paris and Vienna Conventions. The practical effect, however, is very much the same because regardless of who actually caused the nuclear damage, the action is likely to be brought against the operator (de facto or economic channelling). Whether the operator has a right of recourse against persons who have caused the damage intentionally or under the express terms of a contract depends upon the state law.

d) Exoneration from Liability

The Price-Anderson Act provides for exoneration from liability as permitted by the laws of the several states, except claims under state or federal workmen's compensation laws of employees of persons indemnified who are employed at the site of and in connection with the activity where the nuclear incident occurs, or claims arising out of an act of war or for loss of or damage to property which is located on the site of and used in connection with the licensed activity where the nuclear incident occurs [Section 11w].

In the case of a non-profit educational institution licensed by the NRC, the licensee may waive any exemption to which it is entitled, except that in the case of a facility for which a construction permit was issued between 30th August 1954 and 1st August 2002, the licensee may waive any exemption for an operating licence issued after 1st August 2002 [Section 170k.*]

C. AMOUNT OF LIABILITY

The Price-Anderson Act imposes a limitation of liability for a nuclear incident of approximately $7 billion. In the case of all operating NRC-licensed power plants, the amount is made up of a primary layer of $200 million from private sources (insurance, private contractual indemnities ...) and of a retrospective premium of $63 million per nuclear reactor to be paid over a period of seven or more years, depending on the claims, so as to alleviate the burden on the operators, but no more than $10 million per incident in any one year [Section 170b(1)(C)]. In addition, subsection 170t requires the NRC to adjust the amount of the maximum standard deferred premium at least once every five years in accordance with the average percentage change in the Consumer Price Index published by the US Secretary of Labour.

For DOE contractors with whom the Secretary of Energy has entered into an agreement of indemnification, the limitation on liability is the same as that for large power plants (see preceding paragraph) [Section 170d(3)(C)]. Costs caused by accidents resulting from DOE activities conducted under the Nuclear Waste Policy Act of 1982, as amended, would be covered by funds from the Nuclear Waste Fund [Section 170d(1)(B)(ii)]; Section 302(c) and (d) of the Nuclear Waste Policy Act].

In the case of all other licensees of the NRC required to maintain financial protection, the limit of liability is (a) $500 million together with the amount of financial protection required of the licensee or (b) if the amount of the financial protection required of the licensee exceeds $60 million, $560 million or the amount of financial protection required of the licensee, whichever is more [subsection 170e(1)(C)].

With respect to any nuclear incident occurring outside the United States to which an agreement of indemnification with DOE is applicable, the aggregate public liability shall not exceed the amount of $100 million, together with the amount of financial protection required of the contractor [Section 170e(4)].

* Section 170k was added to the Act by Public Law85-744 in 1958 because numerous state-owned educational institutions were, by state law, immune from tort liability and forbidden to pay for liability insurance protection. The purpose of adding Section 170k was to authorise the then Atomic Energy Commission (AEC) to exempt such non-profit institutions from the requirements of obtaining financial protection in order to entitle them to receive the benefits from the Price-Anderson Act. Thus, it is left to those institutions, on the basis of their own state laws or their own decisions, to determine what type of protection, if any, they will provide for the first $250 000 liability, before the NRC indemnity comes into play. This division of responsibility is made applicable to those licensees having immunity from public liability because they are state agencies. It is provided that the NRC will make payments under the contract in the same manner and to the same extent as it would be required to do so if they were not state-owned.

D. NUCLEAR DAMAGE

a) Damage Covered

Nuclear damage covered by the Price-Anderson Act includes bodily injury, sickness, disease, death or loss of or damage to property, or loss of use of property arising out of or resulting from the radioactive, toxic, explosive or other hazardous properties of source, special nuclear or by-product material [Section 11q].

The Act also covers damage caused by a precautionary evacuation of the public within a specified area near a nuclear facility or a transportation route in case of an accident involving nuclear materials [Section 11gg]. The *specified area* is determined by the state or local government official who is authorised to initiate a precautionary evacuation.

b) Damage Excluded

As discussed above, the Price-Anderson Act excludes from coverage, by reason of the definition of *public liability* in Section 11w, (i) claims under state or federal workmen's compensation laws, (ii) claims arising out of an act of war; and (iii) with respect to NRC licensees, claims for loss of, or damage to, or loss of use of property located at the site of and used in connection with the licensed activity where the nuclear incident occurs. Also excepted is damage to the property of persons indemnified covered under the terms of the financial protection required, if such property is located at the site of and used in connection with the activity where the nuclear incident occurs.

II. COVER AND COMPENSATION

A. INSURANCE OR OTHER FINANCIAL SECURITY

a) Price-Anderson Act, Section 170

Section 170a of the amended Price-Anderson Act [42 USC 2210(a)] provides that each licence to construct or operate a production or utilisation facility shall, and each licence to possess and use special nuclear material, source material or by-product material may have as a condition that the licensee have and maintain financial protection of such type and in such amounts as the NRC shall require in accordance with subsection b to cover public liability claims. To the extent that a precautionary evacuation constitutes a *public liability*, insurance or other financial protection are also required under this subsection. Whenever such financial protection is required, it may be a further condition of the licence that the licensee execute and maintain an indemnification agreement in accordance with subsection c.

Section 170b of the Price-Anderson Act specifies that the amount of primary financial protection required shall be the amount of liability insurance available from private sources. However, the NRC may establish a lesser amount on the basis of criteria set forth in writing, which it may revise from time to time, taking into consideration such factors as the cost and terms of private insurance, the type, size and location of the licensed activity and other factors pertaining to the hazard involved, and also the nature and purpose of the licensed activity.

For large power reactors, the amount of primary financial protection required is the maximum amount available at reasonable cost and on reasonable terms from private sources, excluding the amount of private liability insurance available under the required industry retrospective rating plan [see under (b) below]. Such primary financial protection may include private insurance, private contractual indemnities, self insurance, other proof of financial responsibility, or a combination of such measures and is subject to such terms and conditions as the NRC may prescribe.

The NRC must require large power reactor licensees to maintain private liability insurance available under an industry retrospective rating plan providing for premium charges deferred in whole or major part until public liability from a nuclear incident exceeds or appears likely to exceed the level of the primary financial protection required of the licensee involved in the nuclear incident. Provided it is required of the licensee and is available, such insurance must be maintained regardless of how the primary layer of financial protection is obtained, e.g. by self-insurance, private contractual indemnities or other proof of financial responsibility. As noted, the maximum amount of the standard deferred premium that may be charged a licensee following any nuclear incident under such a plan shall not be more than $63 million (subject to adjustment for inflation), but not more than $10 million in any one year, for each large power reactor. The amount which may be charged a licensee following any nuclear incident must not exceed the licensee's pro rata share of the aggregate public liability claims and costs [excluding payment of legal costs which have not been authorised under Section 170o(1)(D)] arising out of the nuclear incident. Payment of any state premium taxes which may be applicable to any deferred premium is the responsibility of the licensee and may not be included in the retrospective premium established by the NRC.

The NRC may, however, on a case by case basis, assess annual deferred premium amounts less than the standard annual deferred premium amount:

i) for any facility, if more than one nuclear incident occurs in any one calendar year; or

ii) for any licensee licensed to operate more than one facility, if the NRC determines that the financial impact of assessing the standard annual deferred premium amount would result in undue financial hardship to such licensee or its ratepayers [Section 170b(2)(A)].

In the event that the NRC assesses a lesser annual deferred premium amount, the NRC must require payment of the difference between the standard annual deferred premium and any such lesser annual deferred premium within a reasonable period of time, to be fixed by the NRC, taking into consideration the factors set out in the preceding pararaph with interest at a rate determined by the Secretary of the Treasury on the basis of the current average market yield on outstanding marketable obligations of the United States of comparable maturities during the month preceding the date that the standard annual deferred premium would become due [Section 170b(2)(B)].

The NRC must establish requirements necessary to assure availability of funds to meet any assessment of deferred premiums within a reasonable time when due, and may provide reinsurance or otherwise guarantee the payment of such premiums in the event it appears that the amount of such premiums will not be available on a timely basis through the resources of private industry and insurance. Any agreement by the NRC with a licensee or indemnitor to guarantee the payment of deferred premiums may contain such terms as the NRC deems appropriate to carry out the purposes of subsection 170b. They may also include provisions to assure reimbursement to the NRC for its payments made due to the failure of such licensee or indemnitor to meet any of its obligations arising under or in connection with financial protection required including, without limitation, terms creating liens upon the licensed facility and the revenues derived therefrom or any other property or revenues of such licensee to secure such reimbursement and consent to the automatic revocation of any licence [Section 170b(3)].

In the event that the funds available to pay claims in any year are insufficient as a result of the limitation on the amount of deferred premiums that may be required of a licensee in any year, or the NRC is required to make reinsurance or guaranteed payments, the NRC shall, in order to advance the necessary funds:

i) request the Congress to appropriate sufficient funds to satisfy such payments; or

ii) to the extent approved in appropriation statutes, issue to the Secretary of the Treasury obligations in such forms and denominations, bearing such maturities, and subject to such terms and conditions as may be agreed to by the NRC and the Secretary [Section 170b(4)(A)].

Except for the funds appropriated for reinsurance or guaranteed payments, any funds appropriated by the Congress must be repaid to the general fund of the United States Treasury from amounts made available by standard deferred premium assessments, with interest at a rate determined by the Secretary of the Treasury on the basis of the current average market yield on outstanding marketable obligations of the United States of comparable maturities during the month preceding the date that the appropriate funds are made available [Section 170b(4)(B)].

Except for the funds appropriated for reinsurance or guaranteed payments, redemption of obligations to the Treasury shall be made by the NRC from amounts made available by standard deferred premium assessments. The obligations shall bear interest at a rate determined by the Secretary of the Treasury by taking into consideration the average market yield on outstanding marketable obligations to the United States of comparable maturities during the month preceding the issuance of the obligations. The Secretary shall purchase any issued obligations, and for such purpose he may use as a public debt transaction the proceeds from the sale of any securities issued by him; the purposes for which securities may be issued are extended to include any purchase of such obligations. The Secretary of the Treasury may at any time sell any of the obligations so acquired by him. All redemptions, purchases, and sales by the Secretary of obligations under this authority shall be treated as public debt transactions of the United States [Section 170b(4)(C)].

b) Regulation 10 CFR Part 140

The NRC has implemented subsections 170a and b of the Price-Anderson Act in its Regulation 10 CFR Part 140, Financial Protection Requirements and Indemnity Agreements.

Section 140.11(a) requires each reactor licensee to have and maintain financial protection:

1. in the amount of $1 million for each nuclear reactor he is authorised to operate at a thermal power level not exceeding ten kilowatts;

2. in the amount of $1.5 million for each nuclear reactor he is authorised to operate at a thermal power level in excess of ten kilowatts but not in excess of one megawatt;
3. in the amount of $2.5 million for each nuclear reactor other than a testing reactor or a reactor licensed under Section 104b of the Atomic Energy Act which he is authorised to operate at a thermal power level exceeding one megawatt but not in excess of ten megawatts; and
4. in an amount equal to the sum of $200 million and the amount available as secondary financial protection (as already mentioned, in the form of private liability insurance available under an industry retrospective rating plan) for each large power reactor, except that under a plan for deferred premium charges for each nuclear reactor which is licensed to operate, no more than $63 million with respect to any nuclear incident (plus any surcharge assessed under Section 170o(1)(E) of the Act) and as specified, no more than $10 million per incident within one calendar year shall be charged.

If a person is authorised to operate two or more nuclear reactors at the same location, the total primary financial protection he is required to maintain for all such reactors is the highest amount which would otherwise be required for any one of those reactors if the primary financial protection covers all reactors at the location.

Section 140.12 requires a reactor licensee to have and maintain financial protection for each nuclear reactor for which the amount of financial protection is not determined in Section 140.11, in an amount determined pursuant to a specified formula except that in no event shall the amount of financial protection required for any nuclear reactor under that Section be less than $4.5 million or more than $74 million.

In any case where a person is authorised to operate two or more nuclear reactors at the same location, the total financial protection required of the licensee for all such reactors is the highest amount which would otherwise be required for any one of those reactors, provided that such financial protection covers all reactors at the location.

Section 140.13 pertains to certain holders of construction permits. Each holder of a construction permit for a nuclear reactor, who is also the holder of a licence authorising ownership, possession and storage only of special nuclear material at the site of the nuclear reactor for use as fuel in operation of the nuclear reactor after issuance of an operating licence must (during the period prior to issuance of the operating licence) have and maintain financial protection in the amount of $1 million. Proof of financial protection shall be filed with the NRC in the manner specified in Section 140.15 prior to issuance of the fuel licence.

Section 140.13a requires each holder of a licence issued to possess and use plutonium at a plutonium processing and fuel fabrication plant to have and maintain financial protection in the form specified in Section 140.14 in the amount of $200 million. Proof of financial protection must be filed with the NRC in the manner in Section 140.15 prior to issuance of that licence.

A person authorised to possess and use plutonium at two or more plutonium processing and fuel fabrication plants at the same location, must maintain a total financial protection for all such plants in the highest amount which would otherwise be required for any one of them, provided that the financial protection covers all the plants at the location.

Section 140.14 permits the required amounts of financial protection to be furnished and maintained in the form of:

1. an effective policy of liability insurance from private sources; or
2. adequate resources to provide the financial protection required by Sections 140.11, 140.12, 140.13 or 140.13a; or
3. such other type of financial protection as the NRC may approve; or
4. any combination of the foregoing.

Where the NRC has approved proof of financial protection filed by a licensee, the licensee must not substitute one type of financial protection for another type without first obtaining the written approval of NRC.

Section 140.15, proof of financial protection, provides that licensees who maintain financial protection in whole or in part in the form of liability insurance must provide proof of financial protection that consists of a copy of the liability policy (or policies) together with a certificate by the insurers issuing the policy stating that the copy is a true copy of the currently effective policy issued to the licensee.

Such proof may, alternatively, consist of a copy of the declarations page of a nuclear energy liability policy issued to the licensee.

The NRC will accept any other form of nuclear energy liability insurance as proof of financial protection if it is satisfied that it meets the requirements of the NRC's Regulations and the Act regarding financial protection.

Proof of financial protection in the case of licensees who maintain financial protection through other resources consists of a showing that the licensee clearly has adequate resources to provide the financial protection required.

The licensee must promptly notify the NRC of any material change in proof of financial protection or in other financial information filed with the NRC.

Where a licensee undertakes to maintain financial protection through resources other than liability insurance for all or part of the required financial protection, the NRC may require such licensee to file with it such financial information as it decides is appropriate for the purpose of determining whether the licensee is maintaining the required financial protection.

Neither federal agencies nor non-profit education institutions are required to furnish financial protection [10 CFR Sections 140.51 and 140.71]. However, the NRC must enter into agreements of indemnification with such agencies and institutions (for further details see below under "State Intervention"). Section 170d(3)(A) of the Price-Anderson Act provides that when the maximum amount of financial protection required of NRC licensees is increased by the NRC, the amount of indemnity, together with any financial protection required of a DOE contractor, must at all times remain equal to or greater than the maximum amount of financial protection required of NRC licensees.

Under Section 170d(3)(C) all agreements of indemnification under which the DOE (or its predecessor agencies) may be required to indemnify any person, are deemed to have been amended on 20th August 1988 to reflect the amount of indemnity for public liability and any applicable financial protection required of the contractor under that Section on that date.

B. STATE INTERVENTION (INDEMNITY)

Section 170c provides that the NRC shall, with respect to licences issued between 30th August 1954 and 1st August 2002, for which it requires financial protection of less that $560 million, agree to indemnify and hold harmless the licensee and other persons indemnified, as their interest may appear, from public liability arising from nuclear incidents which is in excess of the level of financial protection required of the licensee. This Section does not apply to large power reactors since, as a result of the 1975 amendments to the Price-Anderson Act, government indemnity for large power reactor licensees was phased out.

The aggregate indemnity for all persons indemnified in connection with each nuclear incident shall not exceed $500 million, excluding costs of investigating and settling claims and defending suits for damage. If the financial protection required exceeds $60 million, the indemnity provided by the NRC will be reduced accordingly. The contract of indemnification shall cover public liability arising out of or in connection with the licensed activity. With respect to any production or utilisation facility for which a construction permit is issued between 30th August 1954 and 1st August 2002, such requirements apply to any licence issued for that facility subsequent to 1st August 2002.

The NRC no longer has legal authority to indemnify any of its contractors under the Price-Anderson Act as amended [Section 170d]. However, as noted above, DOE continues to have authority to indemnify its contractors, and its authority is extended to cover contractor activities under the Nuclear Waste Policy Act of 1982, activities relating to the Waste Isolation Pilot Project, and DOE demonstration reactors licensed by NRC under Section 202 of the Energy Reorganisation Act of 1974 [Section 170d].

The NRC must agree to indemnify holders of licences issued to non-profit educational institutions, for public liability in excess of $250 000 arising from a nuclear incident; the aggregate indemnity for all such persons indemnified for each nuclear incident may not exceed $500 million. The NRC indemnifies federal agencies other than DOE in an amount not to exceed $500 million for any nuclear incident or, with respect to a common occurrence, $560 million less the amounts of financial protection established under all applicable indemnity agreements.

Where a nuclear incident is considered an *extraordinary nuclear occurrence* (see supra "Definitions"), the NRC or the Secretary of Energy may require provisions to be incorporated in indemnity agreements and insurance policies constituting waivers of defence by the licensee concerned (for further details on waiver provisions see supra "Nature and Assignment of Liability").

If the aggregate liability of persons indemnified is likely to exceed the limit of approximately $7 billion, the Congress will thoroughly review the particular incident and take whatever action is determined to be necessary (including approval of appropriate compensation plans and appropriation of funds) to provide full and prompt compensation to the public for all public liability claims resulting from a disaster of such magnitude. The Congress is not precluded from enacting a revenue measure (tax), applicable to licensees of the NRC required to maintain financial protection to fund any such action [Section 170e(2) and (3)].

In effect, a Presidential Commission on Catastrophic Accidents has been established under the Atomic Energy Act, as amended by the Price-Anderson Amendments Act of 1988, to study the means of fully compensating victims of a catastrophic nuclear accident that exceeds the amount of aggregate public liability [Section 170(l)(1)]. This Commission, appointed by the President of the United States, represents a broad range of interests and was required to submit to Congress by 20th August 1990 a final report containing recommendations on this question [Section 170(l)(1) and (3)].

C. COMPENSATION

As explained above, the nature, form and extent of compensation for nuclear damage, within the maximum limits of liability, depend on the applicable state law. It is to be noted that the waiver of defences under indemnity agreements does not preclude a defence which may be available under the applicable state law to take reasonable steps to mitigate the damage; furthermore, such waivers do not apply to injury or damage intentionally sustained or resulting from a nuclear incident intentionally or wrongfully caused by the claimant.

D. TIME LIMITS FOR BRINGING CLAIMS

The Price-Anderson Act does not contain substantive rules on prescription or extinction periods; this is a matter left to the applicable state law.

However, as regards extraordinary nuclear occurrences, the indemnity agreements may provide for the waiver of any defence based on any statute of limitations if action is brought within three years from the date on which the claimant first knew, or reasonably should have known, of his injury or damage and the cause thereof.

E. COMPETENT COURTS AND PROCEDURE

In the case of any public liability action arising out of or resulting from a nuclear incident, the United States District Court in the district where the nuclear incident takes place, or in the case of a nuclear incident taking place outside the United States, the United States District Court for the District of Columbia, has original jurisdiction without regard to the citizenship of any party or the amount in controversy. Upon motion of the defendant or of the NRC or the Secretary of Energy as appropriate, any such action pending in any state court (including any such action pending on 20th August 1988) or any United States District Court should be removed to the United States District Court having venue as indicated. Process of such district court shall be effective throughout the United States. In any action that is or becomes removable, a petition for removal must be filed within thirty days after receipt of the defendant of a copy of the initial pleading (or within the thirty-day period beginning on 20th August 1988, whichever occurs later) [Section 170n(2)].

Following any nuclear incident, the chief judge of the United States District Court having jurisdiction (or the judicial council of the judicial circuit in which the nuclear incident occurs) may appoint a special caseload management panel (the *management panel*) to co-ordinate and assign (but not necessarily hear themselves) cases arising out of the nuclear incident if:

i) a United States District Court determines that the aggregate amount of public liability is likely to exceed the amount of primary financial protection available; or

ii) the chief judge of the United States District Court (or the judicial council of the judicial circuit) determines that cases arising out of the nuclear incident will have an unusual impact on the work of the court.

Each management panel shall consist only of members who are United States district judges or circuit judges. Members of a management panel may include any United States district judge or circuit judge of such other District Court or Court of Appeals if the chief judge of such other court consents to such assignment.

Each management panel shall:

i) consolidate related or similar claims for hearing or trial;

ii) establish priorities for the handling of different classes of cases;

iii) assign cases to a particular judge or special master;

iv) appoint masters to hear particular types of cases, or particular elements or procedural steps of cases;

v) promulgate special rules of court, not inconsistent with the Federal Rules of Civil Procedure, to expedite cases or allow more equitable considerations of claims;

vi) implement such other measures, consistent with existing law and the Federal Rules of Civil Procedure, as will encourage the equitable, prompt, and efficient resolution of cases arising out of the nuclear incident; and

vii) assemble and submit to the President such data, available to the court, as may be useful in estimating the aggregate damages from the nuclear incident [Section 170n(3)].

YUGOSLAVIA

INTRODUCTION

The Socialist Federative Republic of Yugoslavia operates a 632 MWe nuclear power plant situated at Krsko in the Socialist Republic of Slovenia and is also engaged in nuclear research and activities such as radioisotope production. Yugoslavia is made up of six Republics and two Autonomous Provinces, and nuclear activities are administered and regulated both at Federal level and at Republic or Autonomous Province level, as defined in the national Constitution.

The Federal authority in the nuclear field, also for nuclear third party liability questions, is the Federal Secretariat of Energy and Industry in Belgrade. Since the only Yugoslav nuclear power plant is situated in Slovenia, the corresponding authority of this Republic in that field is the Republic Administration for Nuclear Safety in Ljubljana.

Yugoslavia is a Party to the Vienna Convention on Civil Liability for Nuclear Damage (published in the Official Gazette – SFRY International Agreements No. 5/77) and has enacted legislation in that field: the Act of 19th April 1978 on Liability for Nuclear Damage (published in the Official Gazette of the SFRY No. 22/78 of 28th April 1978) and amended on 17th July 1979 (Official Gazette of the SFRY No. 34/79), henceforth referred to as the Act.

I. THIRD PARTY LIABILITY

A. SCOPE AND DEFINITIONS

The 1978 Act applies to liability for any nuclear damage arising from peaceful nuclear activities in Yugoslavia [Section 1]. The Act has no provisions on its application outside the country. This question is left to the general regime of Yugoslav private international law. If there are no special provisions in international agreements to which Yugoslavia is a Party, the conflict-of-law rules of the 1982 Act on conflict of laws with regulations of other countries (Official Gazette of the SFRY Nos. 43/82, 72/82) are applicable.

The Act defines the operator of a nuclear installation as "an organisation of associated labour" (*organizacija udruzenog rada*) which has received approval for the site, commissioning and operation of a nuclear installation from the authority designated by the regulations of the Republic or Autonomous Province concerned; or a foreign person recognized as the operator pursuant to the regulations of the State where the nuclear installation is situated [Section 2(3)].

It should be noted that the terms *nuclear incident, nuclear installation, nuclear fuel, nuclear material* and *radioactive products or waste* have the same meanings as in the Vienna Convention [Section 2].

Radioisotopes which have reached the final stages of fabrication so as to be usable for scientific, medical or commercial purposes are excluded from the scope of the Act [Section 2(7)].

B. NATURE AND ASSIGNMENT OF LIABILITY

a) General – Nuclear Installations

The operator of a nuclear installation is liable for nuclear damage regardless of fault if such damage has been caused by a nuclear incident in his nuclear installation [Sections 3 and 4].

Where liability for nuclear damage is incurred by more than one operator, the operators involved insofar as the damage attributable to each one is not separable, will be jointly and severally liable; in such case, the liability of each operator whose nuclear installation is located on the territory of Yugoslavia will not exceed the limit for each operator applicable under the Act [Section 14].

The Act provides furthermore that several nuclear installations of one operator located on the same site are considered as one nuclear installation [Section 2(4)].

b) Transport

The operator of a nuclear installation is liable for nuclear damage caused by a nuclear incident occurring in course of carriage of nuclear material from his nuclear installation or during storage incidental thereto, if the nuclear incident caused by the nuclear material occurs before the operator of another nuclear installation has assumed liability with regard to nuclear incidents pursuant to the express terms of a contract in writing; or, in the absence of such express terms, before the operator of another nuclear installation has taken charge of this nuclear material [Section 5(1)].

The operator of a nuclear installation is liable for nuclear damage caused by a nuclear incident occurring in course of carriage of nuclear material to his nuclear installation or during storage incidental thereto if he has assumed liability for nuclear incidents caused by the nuclear material of the operator of another installation, pursuant to the express terms of a contract in writing; or, in the absence of such express terms, from the moment he has taken charge of this nuclear material [Section 5(2)].

Where a nuclear incident occurs in course of carriage of nuclear material on the same means of transport or in case of storage incidental thereto, and such material belongs to more than one operator, the operators concerned will be jointly and severally liable for the nuclear damage up to the limit of liability of that operator whose limit is the highest [Section 14].

A carrier of nuclear material may, in agreement with the competent authority designated by the regulations of a Republic or Autonomous Province, assume liability in place of the operator concerned, with the latter's written consent [Section 8].

c) Rights of Recourse

The operator of a nuclear installation has a right of recourse only against an individual who has caused nuclear damage intentionally or against a contracting party if this has been expressly provided for in writing [Section 7].

If an organisation of associated labour, a self-managed organisation or any other such association pays part of the compensation for nuclear damage for which an operator is liable, the body concerned has a right of recourse against that operator up to the amount which it has paid [Section 19].

d) Exoneration from Liability

The operator of a nuclear installation is not liable for nuclear damage if it is caused by a nuclear incident directly due to an aggression, war or to an act of armed conflict, or to a grave natural disaster upon proof that damage caused by the latter could not have been anticipated and avoided [Section 6].

Also, the operator of a nuclear installation is exonerated from his liability for nuclear damage suffered by a person upon proof that such person has caused the damage intentionally [Section 6].

C. AMOUNT OF LIABILITY

The operator of a nuclear installation is liable for up to 40 billion dinars for each nuclear incident [Section 13]. This amount does not include any interest or costs awarded by a court [Section 13].

The Act provides that in case of a change of parity of the dinar, the Federal Executive Council may determine a new amount for the liability limit of a nuclear operator [Section 24]. This provision was applied by decrees in 1987 (Official Gazette of the SFRY No. 49/87) and in 1988 (Official Gazette of the SFRY No. 76/88). This latter Decree raised the previous limit of 450 million dinars to the present amount. A new Decree, further raising the liability limit is in preparation.

D. NUCLEAR DAMAGE

a) Damage Covered

The Act defines nuclear damage as:

- *damage resulting in death, personal injury or any other damage to a person's health, any loss of, or damage to, property or any contamination of the environment, which arises out of or results from the radioactive properties or a combination of radioactive properties with toxic, explosive or other hazardous properties of nuclear fuel or radioactive products or waste in, or of nuclear material coming from, processed in or sent to a nuclear installation;*

- *damage resulting in death, personal injury or any other damage to a person's health, any loss of, or damage to, property or contamination of the environment which arises out of or results from other ionizing radiation emitted by any other source of radiation inside a nuclear installation* [Section 2(1)].

Whenever nuclear damage and damage other than nuclear damage have been caused by a nuclear incident or jointly by a nuclear incident and another occurrence, such other damage, to the extent that it cannot be separated from the nuclear damage, will be considered as nuclear damage caused by that nuclear incident [Section 11].

b) Damage Excluded

The operator of a nuclear installation is not liable for nuclear damage caused to the installation or to property on the site of that installation, used or to be used in connection therewith. Also, the operator is not liable for nuclear damage caused to the means of transport carrying nuclear material for which he was liable at the time of the nuclear incident [Section 6].

II. COVER AND COMPENSATION

A. INSURANCE OR OTHER FINANCIAL SECURITY

a) General Regime

The operator of a nuclear installation is required to take out and maintain insurance or other financial security to cover his liability for nuclear damage to an amount specified by regulations made by the Republic or Autonomous Province concerned. This amount may not be less than 150 million dinars [Section 15]. Since the only Yugoslav nuclear power plant is situated in Slovenia, only this Republic has adopted the necessary regulations, namely, the Act of 25th April 1980 on insurance for liability for nuclear damage (Official Gazette of the SRS No. 12/80) referred to as the 1980 Slovene Act. In the case of nuclear reactors whose power exceeds 1 kWe the amount of insurance is equal to the amount of liability.

A lower amount of insurance or financial security may be specified in respect of nuclear reactors with low power which are used for scientific purposes [Section 15].

The insurer or financial guarantor may not suspend or cancel his coverage without giving six months' notice in writing to the operator and to the designated authority in the Republic or the Autonomous Province concerned [Section 16].

b) Transport

The operator of a nuclear installation must furnish the carrier of his nuclear material with a certificate related to the insurance or financial security provided by the insurer or financial guarantor in accordance with the Act. The certificate must include a statement by the authority designated by the Republic or Autonomous Province concerned that the person named in the certificate is the operator of a nuclear installation [Section 9]. According to the 1980 Slovene Act [Section 5] and the 1987 Act on the Organisation and Sphere of Activity of the Republic Administrative Organs and Organisations [Section 33a], in Slovenia this authority is the Republic Administration for Nuclear Safety.

Nuclear material may be imported into or transit through Yugoslavia only if the carrier has obtained such a certificate, including the statement referred to above [Section 10].

Where insurance or financial security relates to the carriage of nuclear material, the insurer or financial guarantor cannot suspend or cancel his coverage during the period of the carriage in question [Section 16].

B. STATE INTERVENTION

Where the amount of insurance or financial security provided is insufficient for compensating nuclear damage the State intervenes to provide the difference. The financial resources and the procedure for settling the difference between that amount and the compensation required, up to a maximum of 40 billion dinars, will be specified by regulations issued by the Republic or Autonomous Province concerned [Section 17]. According to the 1980 Slovene Act [Section 4], the Socialist Republic of Slovenia ensures the payment of the above mentioned difference.

Where serious contamination of the environment occurs due to a nuclear incident and the nuclear damage caused exceeds the maximum amount of 40 billion dinars, the Federal Executive Council and the Executive Councils of the Republics and the Autonomous Provinces are to propose to the Assembly of the Socialist Federative Republic of Yugoslavia the measures to provide the resources required for decontamination [Section 18].

C. COMPENSATION

Actions for compensation of nuclear damage may be brought directly against the insurer or financial guarantor [Section 21].

If it is justifiably assumed that nuclear damage caused by a nuclear incident exceeds the amount of liability specified by the Act, the procedure for establishing such damage and its compensation will be implemented in accordance with Sections 397-423 of the Act on Maritime and Inland Navigation – Official Gazette of the SFRY Nos. 22/77, 13/82, 30/85 [Section 23].

Under the Act on Maritime and Inland Navigation, the procedure for limiting the liability is initiated on the operator's proposal to the competent court [Section 398]. If the operator's financial means are put at the disposal of the court and if other conditions are met, the court makes a ruling on the establishment of the fund of limited liability [Section 400]. The ruling is published in the Official Gazette of the SFRY and handed to all creditors (persons, who have suffered nuclear damage), whose addresses are known to the court.

The creditors must announce their claims to the court ninety days after publication of the ruling in the Official Gazette. These claims are put to proof on the court's hearing. If they are disputed, the question must be resolved in a special lawsuit in Civil Court [Sections 404 to 412].

Having proved the announced claims, the court establishes with a ruling, which claims are recognized and to what extent [Section 413]. The fund of limited liability is then distributed. The court prepares a draft distribution, discussed at a special hearing.

D. TIME LIMITS FOR BRINGING CLAIMS

Actions for compensation of nuclear damage must be brought within ten years from the date of the nuclear incident; where nuclear damage is caused by a nuclear incident involving nuclear material which at the time of the nuclear incident was stolen, lost, jettisoned or abandoned, the period for bringing such actions is twenty years from the date of theft, loss, jettison or abandonment [Section 20].

A claim for compensation may be brought within a period of three years from the date on which the person suffering the nuclear damage had knowledge of such damage and of the operator liable, provided that either of the above-mentioned time limits, as the case may be, is not exceeded [Section 20].

Any person who has brought an action for compensation of nuclear damage within the period applicable may amend his claim to take account of any aggravation of the damage even after expiry of that period, provided that final judgment has not yet been entered [Section 20].

E. COMPETENT COURTS AND PROCEDURE

Jurisdiction for compensation for nuclear damage lies only with the local court within whose territory the nuclear installation is located [Section 22].

Where nuclear damage occurs during carriage of nuclear material, products or waste, jurisdiction for such compensation lies with the local court of the territory where the nuclear incident has occurred or the court of the territory in which the operator liable has his residence [Section 22].

Part III

LIABILITY REGIME OF OPERATORS OF NUCLEAR SHIPS

BELGIUM

I. APPLICABLE LEGISLATION

The Belgian legislation applicable to nuclear ships is provisional in nature, pending the possible adoption of rules based on the Brussels Convention of 1962 on the liability of operators of nuclear ships. The Act of 9th August 1963 relating to the liability of operators of nuclear ships (published in the *Moniteur Belge* of 8th October 1963) was, in fact, drafted with a view to the coming visit of the NS Savannah. It was completed by a Royal Order of 17th September 1965, published in the *Moniteur Belge* of 22nd September 1965.

II. LIABILITY REGIME

The operator of a nuclear ship bears absolute and exclusive liability for all damage proved to have resulted from a nuclear incident caused by his ship [Act of 9th August 1963, Section 1].

III. AMOUNT OF LIABILITY AND COVER

The Belgian Act provides that the liability of the operator is, for any given ship, limited to BF 5 billion for each nuclear incident, including legal costs. On the considered opinion of the Council of Ministers, the King may increase this limit to a higher amount [Section 2]. Use was in fact made of this last provision when, in the framework of the 1963 Agreement governing the visit of the NS Savannah to Belgian ports, the maximum amount of the liability of the ship's operator was established by Royal Order at BF 25 billion per nuclear incident [Royal Order of 17th September 1965, Section 1].

IV. COMPENSATION FOR NUCLEAR DAMAGE

Bodies which, pursuant to the legislation applicable, make financial payments or pay out benefits, are entitled, by subrogation, to the rights of the victims of a nuclear incident or their heirs, against the operator of a nuclear ship, up the amounts which have been paid out or which represent the outstanding costs [Act of 9th August 1963, Section 3].

The Antwerp Civil Court has sole jurisdiction at first instance to hear actions based on the provisions of the Act or on international agreements in this sphere [Section 4].

V. VISITS BY NUCLEAR SHIPS

As indicated above, Belgium and the United States concluded an Agreement, on 3rd April 1963, relating to the visit of NS Savannah to Belgian ports.

CANADA

At present, there is no special legislation on the liability of operators of nuclear ships. However, the definition of nuclear installations covered by the Act of 19th June 1970 Respecting Civil Liability for Nuclear Damage (Nuclear Liability Act) includes nuclear reactors forming part of the equipment of a ship or other means of transportation [Section 2(f)]. It is therefore reasonable to conclude that the liability regime for operators of land-based nuclear installations would also apply to the operators of nuclear ships. It should be noted that where a nuclear incident caused by such a vessel causes damage in places in respect of which more than one court may have jurisdiction, the court having jurisdiction will be the one of the home port of the nuclear ship as stated in its operating licence [Section 14].

Canada has not concluded any agreements relating to the visit of foreign nuclear-powered ships in its territorial waters or ports.

DENMARK

The provisions of the Act of 19th June 1974 on Compensation for Nuclear Damage do not cover reactors used as a source of power in a ship or any other means of transport [Section 4]. However, the Act provides that the Minister of Justice may make regulations as to the rules governing compensation for nuclear damage caused by a nuclear-powered means of transport [Section 39].

Denmark and the United States concluded an Agreement on 2nd July 1964 relating to the visit of the NS Savannah to Danish ports.

FRANCE

I. APPLICABLE LEGISLATION

The legislation applicable is Act No. 65-956 of 12th November 1965 on the third party liability of operators of nuclear ships (published in the Official Gazette – *Journal officiel de la République française* – JORF of 13th November 1965). This Act was amended by Act No. 68-1045 of 29th November 1968 (published in the JORF of 30th November 1968), and Act No. 88-1093 of 1st December 1988 (published in the JORF of 3rd December 1988). The Act of 12th November 1965, as amended, was the subject of an implementing Decree No. 82-5 of 5th January 1982 (published in the JORF of 7th January 1982). French legislation in this field closely follows the provisions of the 1962 Brussels Convention on the Liability of Operators of Nuclear Ships. It applies both to French nuclear vessels and to nuclear ships the operation of which is authorised by a foreign State.

II. LIABILITY REGIME

The operator of a nuclear ship is absolutely liable, to the exclusion of any other person, for nuclear damage caused by a nuclear incident [Act of 12th November 1965, as amended, Section 1, paragraph 1].

Under the Act:

- the operator is the person authorised by the Flag State to operate a nuclear ship, or the State which operates such a ship [Section 1, paragraph 2];
- nuclear ship means any ship equipped with a nuclear reactor as a source of power, whether for propulsion of the ship or for any other purpose [Section 1, paragraph 3];
- any occurrence or series of occurrences having the same origin and causing nuclear damage is considered as a single nuclear incident [Section 9, paragraph 4];
- nuclear damage means any damage which arises, in whole or in part, from the radioactive properties of the nuclear fuel or of radioactive products or waste of the ship [Section 1, paragraph 4].

The operator is not liable for nuclear incidents occurring before the nuclear fuel has been taken in charge by him, or after the nuclear fuel or radioactive products or waste have been taken in charge by another duly authorised person [Section 4]. The operator's liability does not extend to nuclear damage suffered by the nuclear ship itself or its apparel and tackle, fuel or stores [Section 5].

Neither is the operator liable under the Act for nuclear damage caused by an act of war, civil war, hostilities or insurrection [Section 6], nor does he bear any liability in relation to a victim who wilfully caused the damage [Section 7].

Where the origin of the damage is both nuclear and non-nuclear and it is not possible to determine the separate effects of each of the causes of the incident, the provisions of the Act are applicable to the entire damage which is consequently the liability of the operator of the ship concerned [Section 2].

Where nuclear damage involves the liability of more than one operator, and the damage attributable to each operator is not reasonably separable, the operators involved are jointly and severally liable for the damage. Each operator is liable for the entire damage, but has a right of recourse against the other operators in proportion to their respective faults. If the degree of fault attaching to each of them cannot be determined, all the operators involved must contribute in equal parts. However, in no case may the liability of any one operator exceed the limit of liability provided for in the Act [Section 11].

The operator has a right of recourse against any person who wilfully caused or provoked the incident, and against any person who has carried out wreck-raising operations without proper authorisation, as well as by virtue of any express contractual stipulation [Section 8].

The owner of a nuclear ship is deemed to be the operator as defined in the Act, between the date of launching the vessel and the date on which authorisation is granted for its operation [Section 3].

Moreover, in the event of damage resulting from the nuclear fuel or radioactive products or waste of a nuclear ship the operation of which was not duly authorised by a State at the time of the incident, the owner of the ship is deemed to have been the operator thereof, save that he may not benefit from the limit to the liability of an operator of a nuclear ship under the Act [Section 20].

III. AMOUNT OF LIABILITY AND COVER

The liability of the operator as regards any one nuclear ship is limited to FF 500 million per nuclear incident, even where such incident was attributable to the personal fault of the operator. This amount includes neither interest nor costs awarded by a court [Section 9, paragraph 1].

However, the maximum limit of liability of the operator of a foreign nuclear ship is, in the absence of any agreement to the contrary with the Flag State, the limit fixed by the law of such State, although this figure may in no case be less than FF 500 million [Section 9, paragraph 2].

In addition, in the event of nuclear damage caused on the territory or in waters subject to the sovereignty of a foreign State by a French nuclear ship in the public service, the maximum amount of the operator's liability is, in the absence of any agreement concluded with the State concerned, determined by the law of that State. If there is no limit fixed by law, liability is unlimited [Section 9, paragraph 3].

The operator is, subject to penalties [Section 23], required to maintain insurance or furnish other financial security covering his liability for nuclear damage [Section 10]. The sums provided by this insurance or financial security are to be used exclusively for the payment of compensation for nuclear damage [Section 18].

The Central Reinsurance Fund is authorised, with State guarantee, to cover the risks for which operators of French nuclear ships are liable and regarding which provision is made for State intervention in a subsidiary capacity [Decree No. 73-322 of 15th March 1973 on the insurance and reinsurance by the Central Reinsurance Fund of nuclear risks and other risks of an exceptional nature].

IV. COMPENSATION FOR NUCLEAR DAMAGE

A person who has suffered nuclear damage may bring proceedings directly against the insurer of the operator liable or against any person who has provided financial security [Section 12].

The provisions of the Act regarding the payment of compensation for nuclear damage do not affect the rules laid down by the legislation on social insurance and on the compensation of industrial accidents and occupational diseases or by legislation of the same kind applicable to certain professional categories [Section 21, paragraph 1]. If the person suffering damage was employed by the operator at the time of a nuclear incident and has received compensation for an industrial injury (or occupational disease), and if such incident was caused by a person other than the operator or his agents, then the victim and the organisation which paid him social benefits may exercise directly against the operator their right of recourse against the person who caused the damage, within the limits of the operator's liability [Section 21, paragraph 3].

When the person injured was not employed by the operator and did not receive any compensation for an industrial injury (or occupational disease), proceedings are to be brought against the operator or the person providing him with insurance or financial security [Section 21, paragraph 2].

If a nuclear incident causes bodily injury, a non-restrictive list of the disorders which will be presumed to have been caused by the incident will be established by decree, having regard to the amount of irradiation and to the length of time that elapsed before the damage became apparent [Section 11-1].

No repayment of compensation paid to victims, whether on a provisional or final basis, may be claimed on the ground of the limit of liability provided under the Act [Section 11-2].

The State intervenes in the payment of compensation for damage when, following a nuclear incident, it appears that the total damage is likely to exceed the maximum liability of the operator. In this event, a decree made in the Council of Ministers is to confirm this situation no later than six months from the date of the incident. This decree may lay down the method of identifying the victims and the extent of provisional compensation, which may not be reduced. A subsequent decree may increase such compensation if new facts have emerged [Section 15].

Where the insurance or other financial security maintained by the operator of a French nuclear ship is insufficient for the payment in full of the claims established against him, up to the limit of his liability, such compensation will, in the last resort, be paid by the State. If such intervention is rendered necessary by the operator's failure to take out insurance or other financial security, the State may require the operator to reimburse it for compensation so paid. The State may also intervene in any proceedings against the operator, his insurer or guarantor, to challenge the principle and amount of compensation awarded [Section 19].

Actions for compensation of nuclear damage must be brought within fifteen years from the date of the incident. However, if the law of the Flag State provides that the operator's liability must be covered by insurance or financial security for a period exceeding fifteen years, legal action may be brought during the whole of such period, without prejudice to the rights of persons who have instituted proceedings against the operator in respect of bodily injuries before the end of the fifteen-year period [Section 16, paragraph 1].

Without prejudice to the fifteen-year period mentioned above, actions for compensation must be brought within three years from the date the claimant was informed that the damage was caused by a given nuclear incident [Section 17].

Where nuclear damage is caused by nuclear fuel or radioactive products or waste which were stolen, lost, jettisoned or abandoned, the fifteen-year time limit begins to run from the date of the nuclear incident which caused the damage, but such period may not exceed twenty years from the year of the theft, loss, jettison or abandonment [Section 16, paragraph 2].

The civil courts have jurisdiction to hear all cases brought under the Act. In no case may a criminal court in which proceedings have been instituted entertain a civil claim [Section 14].

Any person having paid compensation to victims is entitled to the same rights of recourse as the operator [Section 13].

Lastly, the liability regime for operators of nuclear ships prevails over the special rules concerning the prescription of claims against the State, départements, communes and public bodies [Section 23-1].

V. VISITS BY NUCLEAR SHIPS

The entry of any foreign nuclear ship into French waters is subject to authorisation by the French authorities which must be obtained by the Flag State from the Minister of Foreign Affairs. The application must be accompanied by all necessary information on the nature and amount of security supplied by the Flag State and the nuclear operator, with a view to the conclusion of an agreement between the governments concerned [Decree of 5th January 1982, Section 1].

Under the terms of the Act, any foreign vessel may be refused access to territorial waters, internal waterways and French ports unless the operator and the Flag State agree to supply security at least equivalent to that required under the Act [Section 22].

France has not entered into any agreements concerning visits by nuclear ships.

FEDERAL REPUBLIC OF GERMANY

I. APPLICABLE LEGISLATION

The third party liability of operators of nuclear ships is in principle governed by the liability provisions of the 1959 Atomic Energy Act, as amended, applicable to land-based installations (see Part II of this study). There are, however, a number of modifications, the most important being that the liability of the operator of a nuclear ship is governed by the directly applicable provisions of the 1962 Brussels Convention on the Liability of Operators of Nuclear Ships in conjunction with the provisions of the Atomic Energy Act. As this Convention is not yet in force, it is provided that it shall be applied as domestic law of the Federal Republic of Germany irrespective of its binding force under international law, unless such application requires reciprocity effected by its entry into force [Section 25a(1), No. 1].

Mandatory provisions of international agreements on the liability of nuclear ships take precedence over the provisions of the Atomic Energy Act to the extent that they derogate from its provisions [Section 25a(2)].

II. TERRITORIAL SCOPE

The liability provisions of the Atomic Energy Act apply to nuclear ships entitled to sail under the flag of the Federal Republic of Germany, wherever the incident occurred and the damage was suffered [Section 25a(1), No. 4]. If the damage was suffered in another State, the operator's maximum amount of liability is subject to reciprocity [Section 25a(1), No. 2].

As regards foreign nuclear ships, the liability provisions of the Act apply if the nuclear damage caused by the ship was suffered in the Federal Republic of Germany [Section 25a(1), No. 4].

III. AMOUNT OF LIABILITY AND COVER

The liability of the operator is unlimited. However, if the damage is suffered in another State, compensation exceeding the maximum amount under the 1962 Brussels Convention (1 500 million Poincaré francs) will be payable only to the extent that such State has provided, at the time of the nuclear incident, an equivalent third party liability regime for operators of nuclear ships which is applicable in relation to the Federal Republic of Germany [Section 25a(1), No. 2]. According to Section 6 of the Act of 9th June 1980 on conversion of the gold franc (BGBl. Part II, p. 721) 15 Poincaré francs equal one Special Drawing Right of the International Monetary Fund.

The operator of a nuclear ship must take out and maintain financial security which is in due proportion to the hazards of his ship [Section 13(1) and (2)].

The provisions of the 1977 Nuclear Financial Security Ordinance apply as to the type of financial security (see Part II of this study).

As to the amount, the standard coverage for ship reactors is fixed at DM 1 million per MWth up to a maximum of DM 400 million [Financial Security Ordinance, Section 10].

The licensing authority may reduce the coverage to up to one half of the standard coverage in order to further the development of nuclear ships [Financial Security Ordinance, Section 17].

IV. STATE INTERVENTION

With respect to nuclear ships authorised to sail under the flag of the Federal Republic of Germany, the operator is indemnified against claims for compensation to the extent that his liability is not covered by or cannot be satisfied out of his financial security. The maximum amount of indemnification is twice the amount of the maximum financial security and is to be borne as to 75 per cent by the *Bund* and 25 per cent by the *Land* competent for the licensing of the nuclear ship.

If, within the Federal Republic of Germany, a nuclear ship is built or equipped with a reactor for another State or for the national of another State, the operator will be equally indemnified until the nuclear ship is registered in the other State or acquires the right to sail under its flag [Section 25a(1), No. 3].

As in the case of land-based installations, the *Bund* will grant additional compensation up to twice the maximum amount of financial security, whenever nuclear damage is suffered within the Federal Republic of Germany, and the applicable foreign law or international agreement provides for compensation falling considerably short of the compensation which would have been available under the Atomic Energy Act. With respect to foreign nationals who do not have their habitual residence in the Federal Republic of Germany, such compensation is subject to reciprocity [Sections 25a(1), No. 1, 38(2) and (3)].

V. COMPENSATION FOR NUCLEAR DAMAGE

The provisions on compensation, time limits and apportionment of claims are the same as for land-based installations [Section 25a(1)].

Jurisdiction over actions for compensation lies with the courts of the State under whose flag the nuclear ship is entitled to sail. If nuclear damage caused by a foreign nuclear ship was suffered within the Federal Republic of Germany, the court of the place where the damage was suffered also has jurisdiction [Section 25a(5)].

VI. VISITS BY NUCLEAR SHIPS

Between 1968 and 1974, the Federal Republic of Germany concluded a number of visiting agreements for the NS *Otto Hahn* which are no longer relevant, as the ship has since been transformed into a freighter with conventional propulsion. The liability of the operator of the Otto Hahn was in all cases limited to DM 400 million, guaranteed by the Federal Republic of Germany. The following table lists those agreements.

VISITING AGREEMENTS FOR THE NS OTTO HAHN CONCLUDED BY THE FEDERAL REPUBLIC OF GERMANY

Country	Date of signature	Date of entry into force
Argentina	21st May 1971	3rd Nov. 1972
Brazil	7th June 1972	4th Sept. 1974
Liberia	27th May 1970	....
Netherlands	28th Oct. 1968	18th Mar. 1871
Portugal	29th Jan. 1971	15th June 1972

Section 2 of the Act of 8th July 1975 relating to the Paris and Brussels Nuclear Conventions (BGBl. 1975, Part II, p. 957) authorises the Federal Government to put into force, by statutory ordinance, international agreements concerning the use of foreign territorial waters and ports by German nuclear ships and the use of German territorial waters and harbours by foreign nuclear ships. Such ordinances must meet the following requirements:

- the safety requirements must correspond in substance to the Regulations of Chapter VIII of the International Convention for the Safety of Life at Sea (Solas Convention, 1960) and the Recommendations contained in Annex C of the Final Act of the 1960 International Conference on the Safety of Life at Sea in their then current form;
- the third party liability provisions must correspond in substance to Articles I, paragraphs 4 to 8, II, III paragraph 2, IV, V paragraph 1, first sentence and paragraphs 2 to 4, VIII, X paragraphs 1 and 2, XI paragraph 4 of the 1962 Brussels Convention, and must provide for a limitation of liability at least equal to the amount referred to in Article III paragraphs 1 and 4, but not exceeding DM 500 million;
- the liability provisions of the international visiting agreements mentioned above must expressly exclude the application of national or international law on the limitation of the shipowner's liability.

No such ordinance has so far been promulgated.

The Federal Republic of Germany and the United States concluded an Agreement on 29th November 1962 relating to the visit of the NS Savannah to German ports.

JAPAN

I. APPLICABLE LEGISLATION

The Japanese nuclear third party liability regime for nuclear ships is contained in the Compensation Law (Law No. 147, 1961) and the Indemnity Agreement Law (Law No. 148, 1961), and is the same as that for the operator of a land-based nuclear installation while a Japanese nuclear ship remains in Japanese territorial waters. There are, however, special provisions concerning a Japanese nuclear ship entering foreign territorial waters and a foreign nuclear ship entering Japanese territorial waters.

II. AMOUNT OF LIABILITY AND COVER

Where a foreign nuclear ship enters Japanese territorial waters, the foreign operator's financial security must be approved by the Director-General of the Science and Technology Agency and not be less than 36 billion yen, as agreed between the Government of Japan and the foreign Government concerned. This amount constitutes the foreign operator's maximum amount of liability for nuclear damage [Compensation Law, Section 7.2(2)].

Where a Japanese nuclear ship enters the territorial waters of a foreign country, the financial security required is to be provided by means of a liability insurance and an indemnity agreement or other financial security. The amount of financial security is to be agreed between the Japanese Government and the foreign Government and constitutes the maximum amount of the operator's liability for nuclear damage [Compensation Law, Section 7.2(1); Indemnity Agreement Law, Sections 3(4) and 4(2)].

The period of an indemnity agreement relating to nuclear damage caused by a Japanese nuclear ship outside Japan runs from the time when the ship leaves the territorial waters of Japan until it returns to them [Indemnity Agreement Law, Section 5(2)].

III. STATE INTERVENTION AND COMPENSATION FOR NUCLEAR DAMAGE

As already mentioned, the State intervenes, in the case of a Japanese nuclear ship, by concluding an indemnity agreement with the operator if this is necessary to provide adequate financial security [Indemnity Agreement Law, Sections 3(4) and 4(2)].

Where nuclear damage is caused by a Japanese nuclear ship, the Government shall assist the operator in compensating the damage exceeding his financial security, if it considers this necessary to fulfil the purposes of the Law. Such assistance is subject to authorisation by the Diet [Compensation Law, Section 16].

In the case of nuclear damage caused by a foreign nuclear ship which exceeds the operator's maximum amount of liability, the Government shall take the necessary measures to relieve victims and to prevent an increase of the damage [Compensation Law, Section 17].

IV. VISITS BY NUCLEAR SHIPS

No foreign nuclear ship may enter the Japanese water basin without a permit from the Japanese authorities [The Law for the Regulation of Nuclear Source Material, Nuclear Fuel Material and Reactors (Law No. 166, 1957 – Regulation Law), Section 23.2].

Japan has constructed a civilian nuclear ship *Mutsu* which was first launched in 1969. In 1990, the Japan Atomic Energy Research Institute (JAERI) began to carry out various inspections and tests for purposes of experimental navigation for approximately one year.

NETHERLANDS

I. APPLICABLE LEGISLATION

The legal provisions applicable in this field are contained in the Act of 24th October 1973 concerning the Liability of Operators of Nuclear Ships (Stb. 1973, No. 536). This Act is based on the provisions of the 1962 Brussels Convention on the Liability of Operators of Nuclear Ships which was approved by an Act of the same date (Stb. 1973, No. 535). It should be noted that the Convention is not in force.

II. TERRITORIAL SCOPE

The Act applies to nuclear damage caused by a nuclear incident occurring in any part of the world and involving the nuclear fuel or radioactive products or waste of a nuclear ship flying the Netherlands flag [Section 28(1)].

As regards a nuclear ship flying a foreign flag, the Act applies if either the nuclear incident occurred or the nuclear damage was suffered on Netherlands territory [Section 28(2)].

III. LIABILITY REGIME

a) Person Liable

The operator is defined as the person authorised by a State to operate a nuclear ship under its flag or as the State that operates a nuclear ship [Section 1(b)]. He is absolutely and exclusively liable for any nuclear damage caused by a nuclear incident involving the nuclear fuel of, or the radioactive products or waste produced in, such a ship [Section 2(1) and (2)].

The operator's liability does not cover damage to the nuclear ship itself, its equipment, fuel or stores [Section 2(3)].

The Government may conclude with States not a party to the 1962 Brussels Convention agreements concerning the liability of those States for nuclear warships and nuclear government ships used in public service, which deviate from the provisions of the Act, provided the Government is satisfied that such States guarantee at least an equivalent security [Section 26].

b) Rights of Recourse

The operator has a right of recourse if the nuclear incident results from a personal act or omission with intent to cause damage against the individual concerned; if the incident occurred as a consequence of a wreck-raising operation, against whoever has carried the operation out without his authority or that of the State having licensed that ship or in whose waters the wreck is situated and, finally, if recourse is expressly provided by contract [Section 2(6)].

c) Exoneration from Liability

The operator may be exonerated wholly or partially from his liability if he proves that the nuclear damage resulted from an act or omission done with intent to cause damage by the individual who suffered the damage [Section 2(5)]. He is further exonerated in respect of nuclear damage caused by a nuclear incident directly due to an act of war, hostilities, civil war or insurrection [Section 12].

IV. AMOUNT OF LIABILITY AND COVER

The operator's liability is limited to the equivalent in guilders of 1 500 million gold francs (one franc corresponding to 65.6 milligrammes of gold of millesimal fineness 900) [Section 3].

The operator of a nuclear ship flying the Netherlands flag is required to cover his liability by insurance or other financial security on terms to be specified by the Minister of Finance [Section 5(1)].

The Minister is authorised to conclude an insurance contract with the operator, or may provide other guarantees on behalf of the State, if the operator cannot obtain adequate financial security or may only obtain it under unreasonable conditions [Section 5(2)].

In the case of an operator of a foreign nuclear ship, the Minister of Finance determines whether the financial security provided is sufficient [Section 7].

V. COMPENSATION FOR NUCLEAR DAMAGE

Actions for compensation must be instituted at the District Court of The Hague [Section 15].

The operator of a nuclear ship flying the Netherlands flag must inform the Minister of Finance of any nuclear incident for which he is liable and any claims for compensation against him [Section 16]. He may meet claims and make settlements only with the approval of the Minister.

The court may order insurers or guarantors to pay compensation directly to the victims [Section 18].

To the extent that the insurance or financial guarantee prove insufficient to compensate the nuclear damage, the State shall make public funds available to the operator up to the maximum amount of his liability. If the lack of financial security is due to the operator's fault, the State has right of recourse against him [Section 6].

If the aggregate amount of compensation exceeds the operator's maximum amount of liability, claims for compensation are to be reduced proportionally [Section 20].

If such a contingency is likely to occur, the court may, upon application by an interested person, enjoin the operator, insurer or guarantor from making any payments until the exact amounts of compensation have been fixed [Section 21].

In the meantime, the Minister of Finance may grant advance payments to the victims or may order the operator, insurer or guarantor to make such payments [Sections 23 and 24].

The 1962 Brussels Convention not being applicable, an operator, before he is granted a licence to operate his nuclear ship in the Netherlands, must undertake to compensate damage for which he may be held liable under the Act without any restrictions other than those expressly mentioned in the Act [Section 25].

VI. VISITS BY NUCLEAR SHIPS

The Netherlands concluded Agreements with the Federal Republic of Germany and the United States on 28th October 1968 and 6th November 1963 respectively relating to the visits of the NS Otto Hahn and the NS Savannah to Netherlands ports.

SOUTH AFRICA

I. APPLICABLE LEGISLATION

The liability of operators (*licensees*) of nuclear ships is governed by the Nuclear Energy Act, 1982.

II. LIABILITY REGIME

Nuclear ships may not operate in the territorial waters of South Africa or enter its ports without a licence granted by the Council for Nuclear Safety [Section 32(1)].

Licences granted for nuclear ships are subject to conditions determined by the Minister of Economic Affairs and Technology, in agreement with the Minister of Finance; these conditions relate, inter alia, to liability for nuclear damage and security therefor [Section 35(1)(a)].

These conditions, in particular, contain provisions determining, limiting or precluding the liability of the operator concerned for nuclear damage caused (with or without his fault) by anything or any action on the ship while it is in the territorial waters or in a port of South Africa, notwithstanding any provisions to the contrary in any law or rules of common law [Section 35(2)(a)].

In the case of a nuclear ship flying a foreign flag, the licence granted is subject to the terms of an agreement concluded between the Government of South Africa and the Government of the country concerned [Section 35(1)(c)].

III. COMPENSATION FOR NUCLEAR DAMAGE

The provisions in respect of claims and compensation for nuclear damage are the same as those for licensees of land-based nuclear installations [Section 32(4)]. A detailed description of these provisions is provided under "State Intervention" [Section 43] and "Compensation" [Section 42] in the Chapter on South Africa in Part II of this study.

SPAIN

I. APPLICABLE LEGISLATION

The third party liability of operators of nuclear ships (i.e. ships designed to use nuclear fuel) is also governed by the provisions of the Act of 29th April 1964 on Nuclear Energy and by Decree No. 2177 of 22nd July 1967 on cover for nuclear hazards (see Part II of this study). The 1964 Act also applies to nuclear warships.

II. LIABILITY REGIME

The operator of a nuclear ship is considered as the operator of a nuclear installation and as such, the provisions in force with regard to nuclear third party liability apply to him [1964 Act, Section 79].

The operator of a nuclear ship, whether Spanish or foreign, is liable for any nuclear damage caused by such ship while in Spanish territorial waters [Decree No. 2177, Section 17].

III. AMOUNT OF LIABILITY AND COVER

The provisions governing the furnishing of financial security by operators of nuclear installations also apply to operators of nuclear ships if the latter are registered in Spain [1964 Act, Section 79].

The amount of liability of the operator of a nuclear ship, whether national or foreign, is to be determined by a Decree made on the proposal of the Ministry of Finance in the light of the international Conventions ratified by Spain [Decree No. 2177, Section 17].

The financial cover required will be fixed accordingly.

IV. COMPENSATION FOR NUCLEAR DAMAGE

Under the 1964 Act, the conditions governing compensation for nuclear damage caused by a nuclear ship are the same as those applying in the case of nuclear installations [Section 79].

The obligations of the State with regard to compensation when it is operating a nuclear ship itself are the same as those of a private operator [Decree No. 2177, Section 65].

V. VISITS BY NUCLEAR SHIPS

The passage of nuclear ships through its territorial waters is regarded by Spain as an exception to the right of innocent passage [1964 Act, Section 70].

Apart from the guarantees it must provide with regard to safety, the Government of the country in which a nuclear ship is registered and which has granted the corresponding licence to the operator thereof is required to provide a guarantee of adequate financial cover for any third party liability that might arise from any nuclear damage caused by the ship concerned. This guarantee is based on acceptance by the Government concerned of all liability arising from nuclear incidents or damage caused by the ship and on provision of cover for nuclear hazards, the amount of which must not be lower than that established in international Conventions ratified by Spain, or may even be greater where so provided by mutual agreement between the Government of Spain and that of the country in which the nuclear ship is registered. Lastly, the guarantee must include the assurance that the country in which the ship is registered has adopted measures to ensure effective payment of compensation [Section 71].

The liability of the operator of any such foreign nuclear ship is automatically incurred upon proof that the damage was due to a nuclear incident involving the nuclear fuel or the radioactive products or waste of the ship. This provision extends to cases where nuclear missiles or nuclear fuel are being carried, even when the latter is not being used as a source of power [Section 72].

Where the conditions as to the guarantee mentioned above are not fulfilled satisfactorily, the maritime authorities may refuse a nuclear ship permission to visit a port. Furthermore, such authorities are empowered to specify which ports nuclear ships are allowed to visit.

Nuclear ships must also comply with the international rules on passage through territorial waters and zones contiguous to national territory [Section 80].

Spain and the United States concluded an Agreement on 16th July 1964 relating to the visit of the NS Savannah to Spanish ports.

UNITED STATES

Originally, Section 170(l) of the Price-Anderson Act provided for indemnification agreements regarding the nuclear-powered ship *Savannah*, now no longer in operation. [The Price-Anderson Amendments Act 1988 replaced this provision by one creating the Presidential Commission on Catastrophic Nuclear Accidents – see US Chapter in Part II of this study.]

Prior to enactment of the above-mentioned Price-Anderson Amendments Act of 1988, the Nuclear Regulatory Commission (NRC) was authorised, until 1st August 1977, to enter into an agreement of indemnification with any person engaged in the design, development, construction, operation, repair, maintenancc or use of the NS Savannah authorised by Section 716 of the Merchant Marine Act of 1936 [Atomic Energy Act of 1954, subsection 170e]. The NRC could require that person to provide and maintain financial protection of such a type and in such amounts as the NRC considered appropriate to cover public liability arising from a nuclear incident in connection with such activities. The indemnification agreement covered claims exceeding the financial protection and up to $500 million, excluding costs of investigating and settling claims and defending suits for damage.

The following table lists several agreements concluded by the United States for visits of the Savannah to foreign ports.

VISITING AGREEMENTS FOR THE NS SAVANNAH
CONCLUDED BY THE UNITED STATES

Country	Date of signature	Date of entry into force	Citation
Belgium	3rd Apr. 1963	27th Nov. 1963	TIAS 5466
Denmark	2nd July 1964	2nd July 1964	TIAS 5612
Germany, F.R. of	29th Nov. 1962	29th Nov. 1962	TIAS 5223
Greece	23rd Apr. 1962	24th Apr. 1962	TIAS 5099
Hong Kong	12th July 1967	12th July 1967	TIAS 6288
Ireland	18th June 1964	18th June 1964	TIAS 5651
Italy	23rd Nov. 1964	23rd Nov. 1964	TIAS 5699
Netherlands	6th Nov. 1963	22nd May 1963	TIAS 5357
Norway	1st Mar. 1963	8th May 1964	TIAS 5576
Portugal	12th Nov. 1964	26th May 1965	TIAS 5740
Spain	16th July 1964	16th July 1964	TIAS 5626
Sweden	6th July 1964	6th July 1964	TIAS 5613
Taiwan	24th Mar. 1967	8th June 1967	TIAS 6303
United Kingdom	19th June 1964	19th June 1964	TIAS 5633
Yugoslavia	23rd Jan. 1967	24th Apr. 1967	TIAS 6826

WHERE TO OBTAIN OECD PUBLICATIONS
OÙ OBTENIR LES PUBLICATIONS DE L'OCDE

Argentina – Argentine
Carlos Hirsch S.R.L.
Galería Güemes, Florida 165, 4° Piso
1333 Buenos Aires Tel. 30.7122, 331.1787 y 331.2391
Telegram: Hirsch-Baires
Telex: 21112 UAPE-AR. Ref. s/2901
Telefax:(1)331-1787

Australia – Australie
D.A. Book (Aust.) Pty. Ltd.
648 Whitehorse Road, P.O.B 163
Mitcham, Victoria 3132 Tel. (03)873.4411
Telex: AA37911 DA BOOK
Telefax: (03)873.5679

Austria – Autriche
OECD Publications and Information Centre
4 Simrockstrasse
5300 Bonn (Germany) Tel. (0228)21.60.45
Telex: 8 86300 Bonn
Telefax: (0228)26.11.04

Gerold & Co.
Graben 31
Wien I Tel. (0222)533.50.14

Belgium – Belgique
Jean De Lannoy
Avenue du Roi 202
B-1060 Bruxelles Tel. (02)538.51.69/538.08.41
Telex: 63220 Telefax: (02) 538.08.41

Canada
Renouf Publishing Company Ltd.
1294 Algoma Road
Ottawa, ON K1B 3W8 Tel. (613)741.4333
Telex: 053-4783 Telefax: (613)741.5439
Stores:
61 Sparks Street
Ottawa, ON K1P 5R1 Tel. (613)238.8985
211 Yonge Street
Toronto, ON M5B 1M4 Tel. (416)363.3171

Federal Publications
165 University Avenue
Toronto, ON M5H 3B9 Tel. (416)581.1552
Telefax: (416)581.1743

Les Publications Fédérales
1185 rue de l'Université
Montréal, PQ H3B 3A7 Tel.(514)954-1633

Les Éditions La Liberté Inc.
3020 Chemin Sainte-Foy
Sainte-Foy, PQ G1X 3V6 Tel. (418)658.3763
Telefax: (418)658.3763

Denmark – Danemark
Munksgaard Export and Subscription Service
35, Nørre Søgade, P.O. Box 2148
DK-1016 København K Tel. (45 33)12.85.70
Telex: 19431 MUNKS DK Telefax: (45 33)12.93.87

Finland – Finlande
Akateeminen Kirjakauppa
Keskuskatu 1, P.O. Box 128
00100 Helsinki Tel. (358 0)12141
Telex: 125080 Telefax: (358 0)121.4441

France
OECD/OCDE
Mail Orders/Commandes par correspondance:
2 rue André-Pascal
75775 Paris Cedex 16 Tel. (1)45.24.82.00
Bookshop/Librairie:
33, rue Octave-Feuillet
75016 Paris Tel. (1)45.24.81.67
(1)45.24.81.81
Telex: 620 160 OCDE
Telefax: (33-1)45.24.85.00

Librairie de l'Université
12a, rue Nazareth
13602 Aix-en-Provence Tel. 42.26.18.08

Germany – Allemagne
OECD Publications and Information Centre
4 Simrockstrasse
5300 Bonn Tel. (0228)21.60.45
Telex: 8 86300 Bonn Telefax: (0228)26.11.04

Greece – Grèce
Librairie Kauffmann
28 rue du Stade
105 64 Athens Tel. 322.21.60
Telex: 218187 LIKA Gr

Hong Kong
Swindon Book Co. Ltd.
13 – 15 Lock Road
Kowloon, Hongkong Tel. 366 80 31
Telex: 50 441 SWIN HX
Telefax: 739 49 75

Iceland – Islande
Mál Mog Menning
Laugavegi 18, Pósthólf 392
121 Reykjavik Tel. 15199/24240

India – Inde
Oxford Book and Stationery Co.
Scindia House
New Delhi 110001 Tel. 331.5896/5308
Telex: 31 61990 AM IN
Telefax: (11)332.5993
17 Park Street
Calcutta 700016 Tel. 240832

Indonesia – Indonésie
Pdii-Lipi
P.O. Box 269/JKSMG/88
Jakarta 12790 Tel. 583467
Telex: 62 875

Ireland – Irlande
TDC Publishers – Library Suppliers
12 North Frederick Street
Dublin 1 Tel. 744835/749677
Telex: 33530 TDCP EI Telefax : 748416

Italy – Italie
Libreria Commissionaria Sansoni
Via Benedetto Fortini, 120/10
Casella Post. 552
50125 Firenze Tel. (055)645415
Telex: 570466 Telefax: (39.55)641257
Via Bartolini 29
20155 Milano Tel. 365083
La diffusione delle pubblicazioni OCSE viene assicurata dalle principali librerie ed anche da:
Editrice e Libreria Herder
Piazza Montecitorio 120
00186 Roma Tel. 679.4628
Telex: NATEL I 621427

Libreria Hoepli
Via Hoepli 5
20121 Milano Tel. 865446
Telex: 31.33.95 Telefax: (39.2)805.2886

Libreria Scientifica
Dott. Lucio de Biasio "Aeiou"
Via Meravigli 16
20123 Milano Tel. 807679
Telefax: 800175

Japan – Japon
OECD Publications and Information Centre
Landic Akasaka Building
2-3-4 Akasaka, Minato-ku
Tokyo 107 Tel. 586.2016
Telefax: (81.3)584.7929

Korea – Corée
Kyobo Book Centre Co. Ltd.
P.O. Box 1658, Kwang Hwa Moon
Seoul Tel. (REP)730.78.91
Telefax: 735.0030

Malaysia/Singapore – Malaisie/Singapour
University of Malaya Co-operative Bookshop Ltd.
P.O. Box 1127, Jalan Pantai Baru 59100
Kuala Lumpur
Malaysia Tel. 756.5000/756.5425
Telefax: 757.3661

Information Publications Pte. Ltd.
Pei-Fu Industrial Building
24 New Industrial Road No. 02-06
Singapore 1953 Tel. 283.1786/283.1798
Telefax: 284.8875

Netherlands – Pays-Bas
SDU Uitgeverij
Christoffel Plantijnstraat 2
Postbus 20014
2500 EA's-Gravenhage Tel. (070 3)78.99.11
Voor bestellingen: Tel. (070 3)78.98.80
Telex: 32486 stdru Telefax: (070 3)47.63.51

New Zealand – Nouvelle-Zélande
Government Printing Office
Customer Services
P.O. Box 12-411
Freepost 10-050
Thorndon, Wellington
Tel. 0800 733-406 Telefax: 04 499-1733

Norway – Norvège
Narvesen Info Center – NIC
Bertrand Narvesens vei 2
P.O. Box 6125 Etterstad
0602 Oslo 6 Tel. (02)57.33.00
Telex: 79668 NIC N Telefax: (02)68.19.01

Pakistan
Mirza Book Agency
65 Shahrah Quaid-E-Azam
Lahore 3 Tel. 66839
Telex: 44886 UBL PK. Attn: MIRZA BK

Portugal
Livraria Portugal
Rua do Carmo 70-74
Apart. 2681
1117 Lisboa Codex Tel. 347.49.82/3/4/5

Singapore/Malaysia – Singapour/Malaisie
See "Malaysia/Singapore"
Voir "Malaisie/Singapour"

Spain – Espagne
Mundi-Prensa Libros S.A.
Castelló 37, Apartado 1223
Madrid 28001 Tel. (91) 431.33.99
Telex: 49370 MPLI Telefax: 575 39 98
Libreria Internacional AEDOS
Consejo de Ciento 391
08009 -Barcelona Tel. (93) 301-86-15
Telefax: (93) 317-01-41

Sweden – Suède
Fritzes Fackboksföretaget
Box 16356, S 103 27 STH
Regeringsgatan 12
DS Stockholm Tel. (08)23.89.00
Telex: 12387 Telefax: (08)20.50.21
Subscription Agency/Abonnements:
Wennergren-Williams AB
Box 30004
104 25 Stockholm Tel. (08)54.12.00
Telex: 19937 Telefax: (08)50.82.86

Switzerland – Suisse
OECD Publications and Information Centre
4 Simrockstrasse
5300 Bonn (Germany) Tel. (0228)21.60.45
Telex: 8 86300 Bonn
Telefax: (0228)26.11.04

Librairie Payot
6 rue Grenus
1211 Genève 11 Tel. (022)731.89.50
Telex: 28356

Maditec S.A.
Ch. des Palettes 4
1020 Renens/Lausanne Tel. (021)635.08.65
Telefax: (021)635.07.80
United Nations Bookshop/Librairie des Nations-Unies
Palais des Nations
1211 Genève 10 Tel. (022)734.60.11 (ext. 48.72)
Telex: 289696 (Attn: Sales)
Telefax: (022)733.98.79

Taiwan – Formose
Good Faith Worldwide Int'l. Co. Ltd.
9th Floor, No. 118, Sec. 2
Chung Hsiao E. Road
Taipei Tel. 391.7396/391.7397
Telefax: (02) 394.9176

Thailand – Thaïlande
Suksit Siam Co. Ltd.
1715 Rama IV Road, Samyan
Bangkok 5 Tel. 251.1630

Turkey – Turquie
Kültur Yayinlari Is-Türk Ltd. Sti.
Atatürk Bulvari No. 191/Kat. 21
Kavaklidere/Ankara Tel. 25.07.60
Dolmabahce Cad. No. 29
Besiktas/Istanbul Tel. 160.71.88
Telex: 43482B

United Kingdom – Royaume-Uni
HMSO
Gen. enquiries Tel. (071) 873 0011
Postal orders only:
P.O. Box 276, London SW8 5DT
Personal Callers HMSO Bookshop
49 High Holborn, London WC1V 6HB
Telex: 297138 Telefax: 071 873 8463
Branches at: Belfast, Birmingham, Bristol, Edinburgh, Manchester

United States – États-Unis
OECD Publications and Information Centre
2001 L Street N.W., Suite 700
Washington, D.C. 20036-4095 Tel. (202)785.6323
Telefax: (202)785.0350

Venezuela
Libreria del Este
Avda F. Miranda 52, Aptdo. 60337
Edificio Galipán
Caracas 106 Tel. 951.1705/951.2307/951.1297
Telegram: Libreste Caracas

Yugoslavia – Yougoslavie
Jugoslovenska Knjiga
Knez Mihajlova 2, P.O. Box 36
Beograd Tel. 621.992
Telex: 12466 jk bgd

Orders and inquiries from countries where Distributors have not yet been appointed should be sent to: OECD Publications Service, 2 rue André-Pascal, 75775 Paris Cedex 16, France.

Les commandes provenant de pays où l'OCDE n'a pas encore désigné de distributeur devraient être adressées à : OCDE, Service des Publications, 2, rue André-Pascal, 75775 Paris Cedex 16, France.

OECD PUBLICATIONS, 2 rue André-Pascal, 75775 PARIS CEDEX 16
PRINTED IN FRANCE
(66 90 07 1) ISBN 92-64-13421-2 - No. 45275 1990

8/90